THE BATTLE FOR SICILY
STEPPING STONE TO VICTORY

This book is dedicated to John,
who should have been a general

Calderdale Council

COMMUNITY SERVICES

LIBRARIES, MUSEUMS AND ARTS

Books should be returned on or before the last date shown below. Any book **not required by another reader** may be renewed.

To renew, give your library membership number.

DATE DUE FOR RETURN		
KING CROSS	TD	
08/08	- 3 NOV 2016	
	- 3 JAN 2018	
29 AUG 2008		
- 6 OCT 2008	27 JUL 2018	
- 1 NOV 2008	27 MAR 2019	
24 NOV 2008	- 8 JUN 2019	
18 DEC 2008	21 DEC 2019	
3 JAN 2009		
24 JAN 2009		
19 NOV 2009		
09 DEC 2010		
28 MAR 2011		
21 FEB 2013		

THE BATTLE FOR SICILY
STEPPING STONE TO VICTORY

Ian Blackwell

Pen & Sword
MILITARY

Published in this format in 2008 by
Pen & Sword Military
An imprint of
Pen & Sword Books Ltd
47 Church Street
Barnsley
South Yorkshire
S70 2AS

ISBN 978 1 84415 759 4

Printed and bound in England
by Biddles Ltd

Pen & Sword Books Ltd incorporates the Imprints of
Pen & Sword Aviation, Pen & Sword Maritime, Pen & Sword Military,
Wharncliffe Local history, Pen & Sword Select, Pen & Sword Military Classics
and Leo Cooper.

For a complete list of Pen & Sword titles please contact
PEN & SWORD BOOKS LIMITED
47 Church Street, Barnsley, South Yorkshire, S70 2AS, England
E-mail: enquiries@pen-and-sword.co.uk
Website: www.pen-and-sword.co.uk

Contents

Picture credits:
Nos 1, 6-10, 13, 21, 22, 30, 31, and 34 are US National Archives. Nos 17, 18, 20, 23, 24 and 29 are Canadian National Archives. Nos 2-5, 11, 12, 14, 15, 16, 19, 25-28, 32 and 33 are Taylor Library images.

INTRODUCTION

Looking back at the events of 1939-45 after an interval of more than sixty years, it is tempting to see the sequence of campaigns and battles as part of some grand design developed by master strategists, particularly when one sits before a map and marks out the paths taken across great tracts of land by the warring armies. Similarly, when reading many histories of these events, especially those written in the years during or shortly after the war when some of the facts were obscured by the need to maintain secrecy, it is possible to gain the impression that everyone involved in the decision-making was in complete agreement and that differences of opinion were unheard of.

That the struggle for North Africa converged on Tunisia, to be followed by the landings in Sicily and then by the push up the Italian peninsula, appears to be a sensible course of action, whereby the Allies traced an obvious route into one of their enemies' heartlands. At the time, however, this route was far from being agreed as being the one to take, and it was less a matter of joining up the dots as the advance progressed across the Mediterranean islands towards victory, than one of debate and compromise as various options were considered. In the Allied camp mutual suspicions were engendered between Britain and America during the planning stages of the Mediterranean campaign, during the North African battles where troops from both nations fought alongside each other before Operation HUSKY, and continued throughout the battles for Sicily. They were to grow and ferment during the remaining years of the Second World War and beyond.

Sicily was a short campaign of only six weeks, which some observers have argued could well have been even shorter had it been better planned and carried out. Such criticism is, of course, made with the benefit of hindsight, which makes exemplary armchair generals of us all. Nevertheless, it is only by taking a critical view of the past and by attempting to draw lessons from those times that we learn what actions are worth repeating and which are to be avoided at all costs.

Extravagant claims have been made for the importance of some battles or campaigns as being the defining event of the Second World War, for example OVERLORD while ignoring those on the Eastern Front. No such claim has been made for Sicily. In the views of some it was a 'filler', something to be getting on with to keep pressure on the enemy while the Allies built up strength in the United Kingdom in preparation for the invasion of North West Europe. As such it kept the Axis from redeploying forces from the Mediterranean to fight the Soviets, who were the major force engaged against the Germans on land at this time, and could therefore be judged as having had some purpose. Once the war in Northern Africa was over, both the Allied and the Axis leaders had to give thought as to where the next stage would be fought out, but Sicily was by no means the obvious way forward.

The Sicilian campaign was conceived, born, aged and died in controversy. Its immediate descendants, the operations in Italy and North West Europe, carried its legacy for both good and bad. Not all of the lessons from Sicily were learned, for some mistakes were repeated, just as some of the factors which led to success were noted and efforts made to repeat them. Perhaps more awareness of the campaign and its failings would be of use to those engaged in coalition warfare even today.

Many early accounts failed to address the issue of inter-Allied cooperation, concentrating on the campaign from the standpoint of formation or regimental histories, without considering the context in which it happened. I hope that I have avoided this pitfall by including a chapter on the background and the debates which were eventually resolved in favour of HUSKY. I believe that this helps explain some of the reasons for the campaign's shortcomings, for it has been argued – with justification – that it was poorly executed and that more might have been achieved had things been done differently.

The story of Sicily does not stop at the level of grand strategy, of course. Regardless of the machinations of the politicians and the chiefs of staff, once the decision was made to invade the island, the men tasked with winning the conflict had to get on with the job, and their part in events is just as much a part of the history, and has to be related in justice to them. Many were to die or to suffer because of the decisions of others.

A colleague of mine once commented that no attempt should be made to write about a battle without having first walked the ground. I could not agree more. Having read innumerable accounts of battles before visiting the actual sites I have always been struck by the way in which the terrain never seems to match the written description. The scale always appears wrong, for a start: the Normandy invasion beaches stretch for over fifty miles, which is a long way to travel when visiting them; whereas Waterloo seems an awfully small area to contain the thousands that fought there. Nothing can take the place of standing on the slopes below Centuripe in Sicily in the heat of early August to drive home the difficulties that the attackers faced – and that is without anyone attempting to kill you, or even trying to scale the hills yourself without sufficient water, in hob-nailed boots, and carrying a back-breaking load. In reading accounts of these events we tend to forget the multitude of other things that assaulted the senses of those who participated in the battles: the noises of bombs and bullets, the screams of *Nebelwerfers* and men; the smells of explosives, of burning fuel, rubber and paint, and of faeces, dead men and animals. What the reader understands from the written description can never live up to the reality. I would not pretend to be capable of giving a description which would go even part of the way towards achieving this, and can only draw the reader's attention to these factors which distracted the commanders from paying full attention to making decisions, and hope that these are remembered when the more clinical accounts are read in this volume. Suffice it to say that the battlefield is not a pretty place.

But visit the sites that feature in this book I have done, and for that I have to thank a number of people. Firstly, the officers of 8 Infantry Brigade, who invited me to research the campaign and to accompany them on a Staff Ride, have to be thanked for their blind faith in my abilities as a very amateur historian. Their request prompted my first visits to Sicily. I have also to thank those officers and soldiers of the British Army who have walked the ground of this and other campaigns with me, and whose observations have expanded my knowledge and understanding. In Sicily, I am indebted to Roberto Piccione, of the *Associazione Impavidus*, who has been of invaluable assistance in guiding me around the island, and to several excellent restaurants! Roberto's enthusiasm for the history of the Sicilian campaign, his generosity and friendship, have greatly assisted me. In Italy, I have once again valued the support of Alessandro Campagna, whose interest in all matters regarding his nation's part in the Second World War has not been confined to mainland Italy alone.

I have also to thank the curators of numerous Regimental Museums in the United Kingdom, who have guided me to relevant sources of information. And, once again, my gratitude is due to the staff of the Prince Consort's Library who have cheerfully produced books for me to retain well past the return date, without whose help I could not have completed this volume.

Finally I have to thank my wife, Bonnie, who despite once forbidding me to write another book, relented and has put up with the fact that I have been huddled over a computer for far too long. Now that the book is finished, I have no doubt that there is a backlog of chores which will be called to my attention.

CHAPTER ONE

Tug of War

THE DECISION TO INVADE SICILY, to those who were not directly involved in it, appeared to be straightforward and uncontroversial. To the world at large at the time, the Allied powers seemed to be acting in complete accord and in tune with each other, deciding strategy without disagreement and moving in unison towards the goal of defeating the enemy by way of a well-thought-through and carefully considered plan. The reality was somewhat different, as was only to be expected by anyone who has ever been involved in trying to bring together groups and individuals representing separate interests – national, political party, single-service, industrial, and so on. It would be naïve to expect that all would see eye-to-eye and that everything would proceed smoothly, and indeed it did not. Far from it. Although there may have been general agreement that the enemy must be defeated, there was often little agreement on the means whereby this aim might be achieved. Different nations, services and individuals endeavoured to pull their fellow-planners around to their preferred courses of action – a tug of war which sometimes tested the strength of alliances.

In the Allied camp differences of opinion on war aims and the means of achieving them, including the setting of priorities and the allocation of resources, both of men and materiel, placed strains on the alliance which, although never likely to prove fatal to the coalition, nevertheless made the decision-making and planning processes tense for those who carried out these functions. Having to argue for diverging options proved both time-consuming and stressful for these men, who had to balance the demands of their own political and military leaders with those of their coalition partners'. Implicit in this process was the need to impose an element of pragmatism on some of the ideas which flowed from those leaders, and here one has Churchill particularly in mind, for his agile brain was apt to throw up schemes which had to be reined back by practicalities and re-moulded into workable courses of action – or even argued into oblivion.

The negotiating process between the proponents of various possible courses of action was not restricted to those operating at the strategic level, of course. Any decision-making procedure considers the identifiable alternative courses of action from which a final selection is made, upon which the plan is then developed. From the global strategic level right down to (and beyond) the decision by a section commander on when to pause for a breather during a march, the options are considered and the relative pros and cons weighed up. Indeed, this process was formalized by the British Army as the 'appreciation' years ago, to provide decision-makers with an aide-memoir to help them arrive at a course of action which was based upon consideration of as many of the relevant factors as possible. Reading historical examples of these thought processes provides a valuable insight into the minds of past commanders.

The decision-making process is also an information- and opinion-gathering exercise. In wartime Britain issues were decided by the War Cabinet which drew upon the advice of those who would have to implement the decisions they made. At the head of the Cabinet was Winston Churchill, who held the dual posts of Prime Minister and Minister of Defence. In this latter role, he represented the interests of the Services, sometimes drawing upon himself the accusation that he ran a virtual dictatorship because this structure allowed him to overrule the Cabinet, the Defence Committee and the Chiefs of Staff. In practice, however, he drew upon a large number of committees for advice. While the process of 'conference and compromise' through the system of committees, sub-committees and their constituent sub-sub-committees, might have been time-consuming, it did generally produce practical plans – even if, at times, it had to pass through periods of confrontation.

The conference and compromise – sometimes after confrontation – procedure was also to be seen in the dealings between the Allied powers. Each nation had its own agenda and interests, which were not always in agreement with those of the other Allies. From the perspective of the Russians, for example, they had been subject to an unrelenting assault from the Germans which they had borne with the minimum of support from Great Britain, despite the efforts of that country to deliver supplies via Archangel. They had fought a war of merciless savagery, incurring massive casualties, with no assistance on the ground; their objective was to get the Western Powers to commit troops to Northwest Europe at the earliest opportunity to relieve some of the pressure on their own front.

The chain of events that led to the Allies landing in Sicily during the night of 9/10 July 1943 highlights these stages in decision-making, which sometimes end with a course of action which some, possibly the majority, of those participating in the process do not anticipate or even welcome. Many of those who were involved in the discussions, who weighed up the advantages and disadvantages of alternative strategies, found themselves argued into a different strategy, often against their wills or their better judgments. Not everyone gave the same emphasis to the various factors that affected a decision – indeed what one individual considered vital was often regarded as irrelevant by another. And even when those at the top echelons of government, of the armed forces, and so on, had come to a compromise and agreed a way forward, all was not yet cast in stone.

A plan was rarely made firm at any level until the individual who would have to implement it had been given the opportunity to express his opinion on its likelihood of success. Even if he were to advise against it, he might well be overruled for reasons of higher consideration, some of which he might well be unaware of. The consultation process wherein the subordinate was asked to consider the plan really amounted to bargaining, as he almost invariably argued the case for greater resources, more time, or some other consideration; whereas the superior would often argue that such 'extras' were unavailable. This is not to say, of course, that there was never any leeway – there would have been little point in going through the procedure if everything was cut and dried. Plans could often be adjusted to cater for the concerns of those tasked with implementing them, and the Sicily campaign throws up examples of this, as will be seen. Montgomery argued for the invasion plan to be changed to concentrate the Allied forces in the south and east of the island, and for the Americans to surrender the road on which 45th (US) Infantry Division was advancing north of Gela, so that the Canadians might support his left flank; Patton was asked by Alexander to consider the latter, and acquiesced – to his later regret. He was not to repeat the mistake. Planning was a two-way traffic, in which practical considerations and experience were fed up the chain of command, and the higher command's intent was fed downwards.

The possibility of invading Sicily had been considered before HUSKY, the plan which eventually turned ideas into reality. In November 1940 the British Chiefs of Staff had raised the possibility of Italy splitting away from Germany because there was dissatisfaction in that country with its role as Hitler's satellite, and because of a growing anti-fascist sentiment. In the event of Italian collapse, the prospect of the Germans entering all or part of that country led British planners to argue for the occupation of Sicily and Sardinia to prevent the enemy controlling the Western Mediterranean. Such an operation would only have been carried out had the Italians raised serious resistance to the Germans, and a landing against opposition was not considered. In January 1941, however, it was clear that the Germans were establishing air bases in both mainland Italy and in Sicily, and the possibility of Italian collapse and resistance receded. The plan for Sicily and Sardinia, INFLUX, was shelved. It is interesting to note, however, that it called for landings in both the Palermo and Catania areas, a plan that was to reappear in the early HUSKY strategy.

Later that year, in October 1941, Sicily was again considered as a target for occupation. This time it was as a result of a suggestion from the American ambassador in Rome that the Italian army was sufficiently hostile to Mussolini that it might overthrow him, declare a separate peace, and appeal for British protection against the Germans. This possibility was attractive: in North Africa, Operation CRUSADER was about to be launched, with good prospects. It was to be followed by ACROBAT, which was designed to capture Tripolitania. In addition, 'Force 110' was assembled in Scotland, comprising somewhat more than two divisions of Marines and other troops, all equipped with the necessary assault craft and shipping with which to carry out a landing in Sicily. Brought together for the purpose of capturing the Canary Islands, a plan which had been twice postponed and was now about to be abandoned, it was immediately available for other tasks. A landing in Sicily would also draw pressure off the Eastern front, where the Russians were struggling to contain the German offensive – an additional bonus which would assist an ally in trouble and answer public opinion in Britain which was demanding that their government did something to help.

The possibility of the Italian army taking the action suggested by the American ambassador was considered by the Defence Committee on 15 October, and planning was set in place for the operation to invade Sicily; by 28 October the operation, codenamed WHIPCORD, had been thoroughly planned, considered, amended – and rejected. Amongst the reasons for this were that the assumptions upon which the plan had been formulated, the preconditions that were considered essential for its success, could not be guaranteed. Indeed, some of them seemed very wide of the mark – it could not be accepted that the morale of the Italian forces in Sicily, in Libya, and especially in the Italian fleet, had collapsed; it could not be accepted that Germany had not reinforced her troops in Sicily or Southern Italy; and Germany had not sent troops into Spain (this last scenario was drawn up as a possible enemy reaction to British success in CRUSADER. As this particular operation failed to achieve its expectations, this assumption was never tested). The Chiefs of Staff, acting upon the recommendations of the Commanders-in-Chief Middle East, recommended that WHIPCORD be abandoned.[1]

It was, however, to be replaced by another strategy for projecting power into the Western Mediterranean – Operation GYMNAST, the landing of troops in French North Africa or Morocco. The planning for this was to provide a basis for TORCH; the pedigree of what was to eventually translate into action was convoluted and lengthy.

Thus far, planning for operations in the Mediterranean was solely a British affair, although the Russians had an interest insofar as activities there might distract the Germans from the Eastern Front. In practice, however, Russia was fighting what was almost a private war and British operational planning was not coordinated with hers except for the provision of supplies via the Arctic convoys. On 7 December 1941 things were to change as America entered the war and began to take a closer interest in its direction.

Until the bombing of Pearl Harbor America's participation in the Second World War had been that of biased neutrality, providing Britain with materiel under the terms of Lend-Lease and acting, in President Roosevelt's phrase, as 'the arsenal of democracy'. The possibility of United States' further involvement in the conflict had not been ignored, however, and during the Summer of 1941 Roosevelt had directed the

Army and Navy to consider options for this under the Victory Program. Here the courses open to them in the event of Russian collapse and of America being drawn into the conflict were outlined. The strategy they drew up was that Germany would be worn down by a campaign of bombing, limited offensives and sabotage, while the Allies would build up forces for an invasion of Europe and the eventual defeat of the enemy on her own territory. Japan, meanwhile, would be contained by a combination of air and naval power, by the Chinese, and by Russia's Siberian forces. Japan was expected to collapse once Germany had been defeated. In short, Germany was to be brought to her knees first; Japan could wait. The manpower bill for this strategy, the Army calculated, was 215 divisions, sixty-one of them armoured, and 239 combat air groups – a total of 8,800,000 men. Five million of these were to be deployed to Europe, for their belief was that 'only land armies can win wars'[2].

This ambitious inventory was more a military wish-list than national policy. American political leaders, like leaders of all nations before and since, were attracted by the less expensive option, in terms of both casualties and cash, of a less direct strategy. Roosevelt was drawn towards Churchill's approach of dealing with Germany by way of peripheral operations. A constant erosion of enemy forces by bombing, commando raids, limited offensives, and by supporting resistance groups, would break down Hitler's Mediterranean allies and lead gradually but inexorably to his fall. While Pearl Harbor was to give support to the American planners' arguments and to force Roosevelt to revise his initial resistance to the Victory Program, it did not completely change his mind. At the ARCADIA conference in Washington in December 1941 and January 1942, Churchill stayed at the White House as guest of Roosevelt, where he lost no opportunity to promote his strategy with the President.

The American war-planning organization was different from the British. The British War Cabinet had Churchill dual-hatted as Prime Minister and Minister of Defence, but he had to be careful to observe constitutional principles and to be wary of taking too many powers onto himself. Notwithstanding these points, Churchill was given overwhelming popular backing because of his strong leadership. In the United States the President was given all executive powers in wartime as Commander-in-Chief of the armed forces. But Roosevelt did not command the same level of support as did Churchill in Britain; as late as the Autumn of 1942, a poll produced a sixty-four per cent vote in favour of removing the right of taking final military decisions from the President. Some of this distrust came from the public view of the way the war should be prosecuted, and for many the 'Germany-first' policy which was becoming apparent, was not popular. There was a considerable body of opinion that felt that, following Pearl Harbor, the principal enemy was Japan and that American efforts should be focused on the Pacific.

Opposition to Germany-first was not confined to popular opinion, ill-informed though that may have been. Within the Joint Chiefs of Staff (JCS), the heads of the American armed forces, there was disagreement, with Admiral Ernest J King, who held posts on the committee as both Chief of Naval Operations and as Commander-in-Chief of the US fleet, being an ardent supporter of 'Pacific-first'. The JCS was nominally headed by its chairman, Admiral William D Leahy, but Roosevelt's insistence on using him as his means of communication to the committee rather than as a proper chairman resulted in General George C Marshall becoming the de facto leader and spokesman. He also became its executive on European matters, with King assuming a similar role for the Pacific.

The US JCS were to work with the British Chiefs of Staff (COS) on Anglo-American strategy, at what were entitled the 'Combined Chiefs of Staff' (CCS) meetings. These were established during the ARCADIA conference and normally sat in Washington, where the British were represented by by the four senior members of the permanent British Joint Staff Mission, headed until late in 1944 by Field Marshal Sir John Dill, the former Chief of the British Imperial General Staff. For conferences attended by the Prime Minister and the President, the Chiefs of Staff themselves were present. The point about the tug-of-war as each group sought to sway others to its viewpoint, was writ large here, and one has only to read the diaries of General Sir Alan Brooke, later Lord Alanbrooke, Chief of the Imperial General Staff, to appreciate the difficulties under which the members of the CCS operated.

In the Spring of 1942 Britain and the United States agreed a distribution of worldwide strategic responsibility. The JCS were to take control of the Pacific war, the British COS the Indian Ocean and the Middle East. Europe, the Atlantic and the Mediterranean were to be the combined responsibility of both staffs. With internal disagreement in the JCS regarding Germany-first, the Americans had to resolve that particular difficulty before they could decide any policy on Europe. During the first half of the year the Japanese were to advance remorselessly across the Pacific. Bataan fell in April, the rest of the Philippines following by early June. Admiral King's men and ships were taking a beating, and he had been putting pressure on Washington for reinforcements, arguing for a virtual Pacific-first policy on the grounds that the United States could not allow the "white man's countries" of Australia and New Zealand to be overrun by Japan "because of the repercussions among the non-white races of the world."[3]

Marshall and his planners had come up with a new strategic shift to stop what they viewed as the dangerous dispersal of Allied forces as implemented by the British policy of peripheral operations. They saw this as running contrary to the military principle of concentration of strength, and it threatened to prolong the war; moreover, it did not achieve the aim of regaining the strategic initiative. The American plan, drawn up by Brigadier General Dwight D Eisenhower and his Operations Division, proposed concentrating all available forces in Great Britain for a cross-Channel invasion of Northern France in late 1942 or early 1943. This would keep the Russians in the war by diverting attention from the Eastern Front and bring the war directly to the Germans.

Marshall won King around with by promising him enough reinforcements for the Pacific to hold Australia and New Zealand, and by the logic of his argument - that only by forcing a quick victory over Germany by a cross-Channel landing in northwest Europe could the pressure on Russia be relieved, thereby ensuring that country's continued participation in the war. Then, and only then, could full attention be given to the Japanese. His personal diplomatic skills played no small part in convincing King. In fact, because of the situation in the Pacific, the bulk of US forces sent overseas during the first half of 1942 went there; only two divisions were despatched to Northern Ireland in support of Germany-first, leaving in June that year[4].

Convincing the Admiral was only the beginning; the Americans now had to bring the British around to their way of thinking. As a prelude, it was necessary to bring Roosevelt on side, a task that was not as difficult as might have been expected, given his earlier support for the British approach. The President had been very attracted to Churchill's arguments for the peripheral strategy, but time had moved on. British defeats in North Africa had forced the postponement of GYMNAST indefinitely, and Marshall was now offering Roosevelt a way of getting American forces into the war in 1942.[5]

Two plans had been drawn up by the Americans. The first of these, ROUNDUP, proposed an Anglo-American invasion of Northwest Europe to take place in the spring of 1943. This was formulated in the hope that the Soviets could hold out until then, with the help of a continued delivery of equipment and with UK-based bombers mounting heavy attacks on Germany. If, on the other hand, it appeared that Russian resistance was in danger of collapsing, then the Allies would invade in 1942 with whatever forces they could muster. This option, codenamed SLEDGEHAMMER, would have to be mounted before the weather deteriorated in September – and it would have to be mounted with an overwhelmingly British force because the Americans would not have arrived in Great Britain in strength by that time. The same, somewhat desperate, plan would be followed in the unlikely event that Germany showed signs of weakness in 1942.

The odds on selling SLEDGEHAMMER to the British were slim. If they had felt that a landing on French soil was a practicable option they would have considered it themselves, and the prospect of committing sizable numbers of troops to such a venture when they were already heavily engaged in North Africa was not attractive. Nevertheless, they welcomed the American willingness to mount a major offensive against Germany in 1943 and agreed to provide more than half the shipping needed to transport US troops across the Atlantic. On the subject of SLEDGEHAMMER, the response was less enthusiastic, although the British were reluctant to appear too dismissive, for fear of pushing the Americans into a Pacific-first decision. The British emphasised that their first priority was holding their position in North Africa, where Rommel had inflicted reverses on the Eighth Army in January and was preparing for a fresh offensive. The autumn cross-Channel proposal was accepted 'in principle' – a phrase that was to endure in Anglo-American consultations, and to cause much trouble[6].

It was not until June 1942 that the first US troops set sail for England on the liner *Queen Elizabeth*. Their crossing coincided with Rommel's attack around the southern flank of the Eighth Army in Libya, and Tobruk fell on 21 June. News of this disaster reached Churchill in Washington, where he had gone to inform the Americans that the British could not agree to SLEDGEHAMMER. General Marshall offered to send assistance to North Africa to support the Eighth Army, consisting of tanks, artillery, and the ground components of three combat air groups. Sending this amount of materiel to North Africa tied up a considerable amount of shipping, which had to be diverted from its task of ferrying American forces to Britain, thereby setting the timetable for ROUNDUP back; by the end of August only some 170,000 US troops were actually in, or en route to, the United Kingdom. The backlog of materiel and supplies was dropping far behind schedule, and the target date of April 1943 for the cross-Channel invasion was beginning to appear impossible.

SLEDGEHAMMER had disappeared into the waste-paper basket of plans that never reached fruition – the prospect of the Germans becoming so weak as to justify an early landing in Europe, when they were about to launch an offensive in the Caucasus and were proving more than difficult to defeat in North Africa, was highly improbable. The British, who would have had to supply the forces for this venture, but without the promised numbers of landing craft from America (the deliveries of these vessels were not arriving as planned) had the veto on the operation, and used it. US planners were being bold, but it was with British, not American lives. The preparations for ROUNDUP were not going to be completed in time for the proposed dates. There seemed no prospect of getting US forces into the ground war before 1944, a factor which disappointed Roosevelt, who was extremely keen to have them involved in the war in 1942.

Churchill had a solution, one that he had been arguing for all along – GYMNAST. He began to lobby Roosevelt again for the Anglo-American landing in French North Africa, a plan which the President had been attracted to earlier. This was, he told Roosevelt, the only option open for 1942, even portraying it as the President's own idea[7].

Marshall was incensed when he discovered the way in which the President was being, as he saw it, manipulated by the British. To counter the move, he agreed with King that they should threaten to adopt Pacific-first as US strategy unless Britain agreed unreservedly to BOLERO, the build-up of American forces in the United Kingdom for the express purpose of a cross-Channel invasion. They presented this complete reversal of strategy to Roosevelt, who was horrified, and who ordered them to London to agree to GYMNAST if the British rejected SLEDGEHAMMER. Marshall and King could see that GYMNAST would delay cross-Channel operations until 1944 at the earliest, and would not benefit the Soviets before then; they feared that such a move would mean giving up on their Russian ally and thereby any possibility of a victory over Germany. To turn their efforts to the Pacific would at least enable the United States to concentrate on an enemy that they might hope to defeat (Midway had just been fought and won), while satisfying the demands of their Far Eastern allies, such as China, which was threatening a separate peace with Japan unless massive American aid was forthcoming. The change of strategy would also satisfy General MacArthur and American public opinion. Nonetheless, they were overruled.

To what extent Marshall and King were bluffing about the Pacific-first threat is uncertain. It did, however, lead Roosevelt to exercise his authority as Commander-in-Chief and to order them to agree to GYMNAST, which was, as will be seen, to lead to the decision to invade Sicily. The tug-of-war between the different players was, at this stage, going the way that the British wanted.

After a vain effort to persuade the British to reconsider an invasion of the Continent in 1942, the Americans reluctantly agreed on July 24 to the North Africa operation, now re-christened TORCH, to be launched before the end of October. The decision was to open a debate on European strategy between the Americans and British that was to continue until the summer of 1944. The tug-of-war would continue through the major international conferences which lasted from Casablanca in January 1943 until Second Quebec in September 1944, during which Churchill was to progressively argue the case for pressing further ahead in the Mediterranean, invading Sicily, then landing in Italy, seizing Rome, then the Pisa-Rimini Line, and then driving on north and northeast. He backed his case with the line of reasoning that the momentum should be maintained against the enemy, that the process of weakening the Germans should continue, that the Allies had sizable forces in the region that should be used to great advantage; all while awaiting the right moment to launch the cross-Channel invasion. Underlying his strategy was the fear that a prematurely-unleashed invasion of Northwest Europe would founder, and that its failure would make winning the war against Germany possible only with a negotiated cease-fire rather than a crushing defeat. In this debate, Churchill had a sympathetic ear from Roosevelt who could see the potential of the Mediterranean approach; the JCS were far from convinced, however.

With Marshall as the spokesman, the JCS made gradual progress as they sought to limit and steer the Mediterranean strategy, directing it towards the west rather than the east, towards Southern France rather than the Balkans, and linking it firmly to their belief in fighting the war by mass and concentration in northwest Europe via a cross-Channel invasion. In arguing their case, they had to convince President Roosevelt, the British, and then the Soviets. The British Chiefs of Staff, for their part, had Churchill, the Americans, and then the Soviets to persuade. The series of decisions reached during the conferences held in 1943 (Casablanca in January, Washington [TRIDENT] in May, First Quebec [QUADRANT] in August, and Cairo-Tehran [SEXTANT-EUREKA] in November and December) resulted in a series of Anglo-American compromises, between the British approach which favoured opportunism and the American which emphasised long-term commitments, and between a war of attrition which gnawed away at the periphery and one which sought to employ mass and concentration in direct confrontation.

The details of the TORCH landings need not concern us in detail here, in an examination that concentrates on the Sicilian campaign. That the Allies had agreed to land forces in Algeria and French Morocco had achieved the aim of getting US ground forces into the war against Germany and Italy, at the earliest practicable date. Britain was no longer standing alone in the west against the Axis. In addition to the Americans, it was hoped that the 120,000 French troops and naval forces stationed in North Africa would enter the war on the Allied side once the Anglo-Americans had taken over, a hope that translated into reality. Whereas the British, acting in isolation, were unlikely to achieve the task of bringing the French onside because of French hostility following the sinking of their fleet in Oran by the Royal Navy to prevent it falling into German hands in 1940, there was no such hindrance to Franco-American relations. More than this, as far as its affect on Sicily was concerned, TORCH placed considerable numbers of Allied troops in the Western Mediterranean. While their presence there could not be said to have made the invasion of Sicily inevitable, especially when there was an ongoing debate about peripheral operations versus direct confrontation, it at least made it possible. The TORCH landings were carried out on 8 November 1942; six weeks before that date, on 28 September, Churchill had written a memo in which he said that, in exploitation of TORCH, action must be taken to draw enemy forces away from the Russian front. To that end, he added, no doubt Sardinia, Sicily and Italy itself had all been considered in this respect. Churchill, at least, was clear about the way in which he saw the war progressing.

In response to this memo, the COS were able to state that the Joint Planning Staff were already preparing two papers. The first of these was an appreciation on the capture of Sicily and/or Sardinia, the second concerned the various offensive operations open to the Allies in the Mediterranean. Combined Operations Headquarters were studying the assault phase for the occupation of the Italian island of Pantelleria, and C-in-C Middle East had just completed an examination of the ways by which Europe might best be invaded from the Mediterranean, and concluded that the best option was to do this through Sicily and/or Sardinia. It was not only Churchill that was thinking along these lines[8].

That the British had clear ideas about the way forward did not, of course, mean that their plans would be translated into action. The Americans, forced into TORCH against the better judgement of the JCS, would take convincing. Before tackling them, however, the North African landings had to be planned and executed.

An Anglo-American agreement dating from the ARCADIA Conference was that Allied forces in each overseas theatre would operate, as far as possible, under a single commander. Accordingly, in June 1942 the newly-promoted Lieutenant General Dwight D. Eisenhower arrived in England to take command of the recently established European Theatre of Operations. After taking advice and opinions from all sides, Roosevelt appointed him Commander in Chief for the TORCH operation. With it becoming readily apparent that America was increasingly taking the leading role in terms of manpower and equipment, it was understandable that this task would be given to the United States. Accompanying the single-commander agreement was one that stated that his deputy should be appointed from the other nationality, and that section and deputy heads would be selected on the same principle. Thus the pattern was set for the command and control of coalition operations for the duration of the war.

The TORCH landings were successful, with US troops landing at Casablanca and Oran. British and American forces landed in Algiers, with the first waves under American command as a sop to French sensibilities and memories of Britain sinking the French fleet. The Allies then moved eastwards towards Tunis, while Montgomery's Eighth Army advanced on the area from the east. Again, the progress of the Tunisian campaign need not concern us here, except insofar as the British were carefully watching the deeds of their newly-arrived American allies. The judgement they made on their performance was to affect the Sicilian campaign, for the Americans did not do particularly well in Tunisia.

As the Allies rushed to build up strength in North Africa (over 250,000 men were ashore by the end of November), the Axis was responding by doing the same thing in Tunisia. An airlift brought over 15,000 men and tons of supplies, and tanks, guns, and equipment were transported to the ports of Tunis and Bizerta. Three fresh German, and two Italian, divisions were sent to reinforce the forces already in North Africa[9].

The TORCH landings had exploited a long coastline that had been sparingly defended; Tunisia, well within the range of Axis air forces based in Sicily, could not be attacked from the sea without risking heavy losses. The route to the two Allied objectives of Tunis and Bizerte was therefore inland, through terrain that was different from that encountered in Algeria. The leading Allied force, the British 78th Infantry Division with supporting US units, none of which was larger than battalion strength, advanced eastwards while naval and air forces attempted to sever the enemy's supply lines from Sicily. Eisenhower intended feeding units forward to build up a two-corps force, but for the immediate future the initial force pushed forwards to feel out the enemy positions. The enemy did the same in the other direction, and the two formations inevitably ran into each other: the opening shots were fired at at Djebel Abiod. For the following week similar encounters were played out as each side moved into position, and then the Allies started their move eastwards in earnest. From the east, following the success at El Alamein, the Eighth Army was pushing towards Tunisia to link up with this thrust and to drive the enemy from the African continent.

On 28 November 78th Division and its supporting American arms began to run into strong Axis defences. Stiffened by the presence of four Mark VI Tiger tanks, the first time that these had been employed against the western Allies, the enemy blunted the advance. By 30 November it had stopped everywhere. Not giving their opponents any opportunity to rest, Axis troops launched a counterattack on 1 December, starting a sequence of Allied losses which amounted to over 1,000 missing (prisoners of war), and seventy-three tanks, 432 other vehicles, and seventy artillery pieces lost[10]. Furious with the way things were going, Eisenhower sent a scathing report on Allied performance to Marshall, stating that in his view Anglo-American operations had thus far managed to violate every accepted tactical principle of warfare and would be condemned in military schools for decades to come.

As December rains turned the land into a quagmire, the Allies lost the race to pinch out the Axis forces before they had reinforced and reorganized themselves; the conflict became a protracted struggle. Rommel's *Afrika Korps* barred the Eighth Army advance on the southern border of Tunisia, while a second powerful Axis force, the *Fifth Panzer Army*, blocked the way to the Tunisian coast.

On 14 February German and Italian forces struck westwards through the mountain passes in the mountains separating coastal Tunisia from the interior, behind which lay important Allied supply dumps and airfields. Each side had over 200 tanks available, but the American armour was spread too thinly to stop the *panzers*, which punched through it in one day.

A US counterattack was ineffective, and the capture of 1,400 of their troops forced them to undertake a major withdrawal. The following day they were again forced to retire, this time to a fresh defensive position on the Kasserine Pass. In four days of defeats the Americans lost 2,546 men missing, 103 tanks, 280 vehicles, eighteen field guns, three antitank guns, and an antiaircraft battery.

The Kasserine Pass was the gateway into Algeria. Rommel increased the strength of his German-Italian army with the addition of two more *panzer* divisions and struck on 19 February; by the following afternoon the Pass was in his hands, and he was poised to seize road junctions which led to the rear of British positions. The series of defeats was ended not by American countermeasures but by Rommel's fear that the British Eighth Army might attack from Libya while his attention was focused westwards; he turned back towards the east to cover the threat[11].

The poor performance of Allied forces in December 1942 and February 1943 forced a reexamination of organization and plans. A major problem which had become apparent was that there was no effective chain of command; Eisenhower had been forced to try to fight the battle while balancing the demands of acting as commander-in-chief, dealing with, amongst other things, the political issues. Sir Alan Brooke, amongst others, had a view of Eisenhower's performance which was less than positive, seeing him as being over-preoccupied with politics (especially with respect to the French) and not paying sufficient attention to the Germans. The fact that before this appointment Eisenhower had never commanded any formation higher than a battalion, and never in combat, did not engender confidence[12].

Eisenhower replaced key personnel and restructured the command structure. Eighteenth Army Group, under General Sir Harold RLG Alexander, was created to take a firmer control of the corps and armies of the three Allied nations – American, British and French. Major General Lloyd Fredendall, commander of US II Corps, who combined avid anti-British and anti-French bias with his habit of trying to command his corps from a well-entrenched bunker positioned far behind the front lines, was replaced by Major General George S Patton. Patton and his deputy, Major General Omar N. Bradley, took a firm grip of the corps and began to turn it into a more professional formation.

With the British Eighth Army now close enough to the Allied southern flank to affect Axis operations, the three national commands in Tunisia narrowed their battlefronts and shifted north. In March, after the British repulsed another German attack, the Allies resumed the offensive. II (US) Corps attacked in coordination with an assault on the German line by Montgomery's troops.

Anglo-American difficulties were not yet over, however. As the Allies increased their pressure on the enemy, an attempt was made by 34th (US)

Infantry Division to open the pass at Fondouk el Aouareb to cut off Axis units retreating north. After a heavy artillery barrage, the division opened its attack on 27 March, but failed to take the pass during three days of repeated efforts. General Alexander then ordered an attack by American, British and French forces after a week's preparation. The Americans crossed the start line on 8 April, but paused to await an air strike that failed to materialize. Five hours later, a British armoured brigade pushed through the American positions without warning, adding to the confusion and forcing a further delay in the attack while matters were sorted out. During the next day, supporting tanks outran the infantry and had to be recalled under enemy fire. The result of these bungled attempts was that the main enemy body was able to escape the trap before the pass was taken on 9 April. The ensuing arguments in the respective headquarters had to be contained by the intervention of Eisenhower and Alexander. It did not bode well for Anglo-American cooperation[13].

The criticism of command styles was not all one-way. While the Fondouk el Aouareb debacle was in progress, General Alexander directed Patton to push an armoured column on to the port of Gabes, possession of which would divide the enemy forces. Patton's task force was dispatched at noon on 30 March, but in three days it achieved little more than losing thirteen tanks. Halting the armour, the mission was given to the infantry. Patton considered Alexander's orders to be not only over-detailed but confusing, as they switched from an infantry-first, to armour-first, and then again infantry-first sequence. Unable to say anything that might disrupt Allied relationships – Patton was prevented by Eisenhower from speaking out – he vented his frustration by writing to General Marshall in Washington[14].

The inter-Allied wrangling did not stop here. Patton and Air Vice Marshal Arthur 'Mary' Coningham – the commander of the Allied Tactical Air Forces in North Africa – clashed somewhat more publicly when Patton criticized what he termed 'the total lack of air cover for our units' which 'allowed German air force to operate almost at will' in a Situation Report. Coningham responded to this comment by sending a signal to all Mediterranean commanders in which he suggested that Patton's statement was an April Fool's joke and that the real problem lay in the lack of battle-worthiness of the II (US) Corps. The exchange nearly created an international incident, which was only defused when Air Chief Marshal Sir Arthur Tedder – Eisenhower's deputy and commander of all Allied air forces in the Mediterranean – ordered Coningham to cancel the signal and to apologise to Patton personally. This he did, and the two protagonists had a frank exchange, after which matters were patched up between them, at least publicly. Eisenhower took the matter so seriously, considering it to reflect badly on his own leadership, that he was only stopped from sending his resignation to Marshall by the intervention of his chief of staff,

Walter Bedell Smith[15].

The inter-Allied tensions were not eased by Montgomery, who sent a signal to Eisenhower on 10 April, the date that the Eighth Army entered Sfax. The signal, which was addressed 'Personal', reported the achievement, and requested that Eisenhower should now send Monty the B-17 Flying Fortress bomber which was the prize in a bet between the British general and Bedell Smith. Perhaps not believing that Monty was serious, Bedell Smith had agreed to give him a Fortress for his personal use if he entered Sfax by 15 April. Now here was Monty demanding that the debt be honoured, as indeed it was – but not without some sucking of teeth, not least by Brooke, who took Monty to task for the matter[15].

The final drive to clear Tunisia began on 19 April. On 7 May British armour entered Tunis, and American infantry entered Bizerta. Six days later the last Axis resistance in Africa ended with the surrender of over 275,000 prisoners of war.

The Americans learned bitter lessons about the shortcomings of their training and leadership during the Tunisian campaign, which had stretched them much further than the earlier operations during TORCH. For them Tunisia had been five months of almost continual setbacks with high casualties. In Algeria and French Morocco they had encountered relatively poorly-equipped French troops who were more concerned with upholding national honour through largely symbolic displays of resistance than with inflicting heavy casualties. In Tunisia they had come up against the battle-hardened German army, more experienced in all-arms tactics, more professional, and in many instances better equipped than they were. The American M3 Medium tank, for example, was hardly a match for German tanks, especially when pitted against the formidable Tiger. Some of these deficiencies could not be put right quickly – replacing tanks, for example, took time, although even here the better Sherman was to replace the Grant as soon as possible – but in other matters such as more realistic training and in getting commanders away from their tendency to micro-manage their subordinates, they were more successful. The short-term legacy of Tunisia, however, was to instill in their British counterparts an air of condescension and mistrust about American abilities on the battlefield, a legacy which was to colour relationships for the future. For their part, the Americans grew to resent the patronizing attitude of some of their allies.

Thus far, the tug-of-war had gone largely the way the British wanted: the Americans were not only committed to Germany first, they were in the Mediterranean. Some of the reason for this was due to British planning and preparation, for the staff work carried by, and on behalf of, the Chiefs of Staff was superior to that carried out by the American Joint Chiefs. The British system called for contingency plans to be drawn up in some detail, so that should the opportunity arise for them to be called into practice most of the work had already been done; an insurance against future events. This system was not followed by the Americans, who regarded – with some justification – it as being wasteful of time and effort; they preferred to wait until a course of action had been authorized before dedicating detailed attention to the plan. But all was not down to staff work. Other circumstances had played their part in getting the United States to deploy forces to the Mediterranean, for example the inability of the Americans to get their men into the European war as swiftly as Roosevelt had wanted. The tug-of-war contest had only started, however. Round one had gone to the British, but the competition had further rounds to be played out.

With the Allies now in control of the North African coastline, attention focused on the next steps. Consideration had been given some time ago to what strategy to pursue once this stage had been reached; it will be remembered that previous plans had been formulated for an invasion of Sicily (INFLUX, 1940, and WHIPCORD, in 1941). Before Eisenhower had departed from London to take command of TORCH, he had been thoroughly briefed on WHIPCORD, and had taken the plans with him for further consideration. Churchill had pushed for, and the COS had provided, papers considering the possibilities for landings on Sicily and Sardinia before the TORCH landings had gone ashore. The next stage of the tug of war was to convince the Americans that their forces should be used for this purpose and not allowed to remain inactive until such time as the cross-Channel invasion became possible.

The planners' attention now turned to the relative advantages and disadvantages of the Sicily-Sardinia options. On 18 September 1942 WHIPCORD had been renamed HUSKY. It was only one of several possibilities for the post-TORCH exploitation that were examined before that operation was launched; Sardinia (BRIMSTONE), the Balkans and the Dodecanese Islands were also considered as potential areas for future development. It was in this context that Churchill had penned his memo of 28 September 1942: post-TORCH action must be taken to draw enemy forces away from the Russian front. HUSKY planning was off to a good start, and by 21 October appreciations carried out by the War Cabinet Office and by those in the Middle East who would have to execute them, were presented to Eisenhower for discussion with the British COS. The Sicilian and Sardinian options were examined in some detail by the Strategic Planning Section to show the arguments for capturing the islands during the early stages of TORCH, which would be the most economical way of cutting the Axis supply routes to North Africa and of opening up the Mediterranean. Eisenhower had given general approval to the plans, and had left part of his staff behind in the United Kingdom to assist in their development when he departed for North Africa.

The impetus was to ensure that if success was quick in North Africa, advantage might be swiftly taken should opportunity arise. This was summed up in the 'assumptions' paragraphs of the paper, which envisaged the plan being put into effect if TORCH proved completely successful; if the whole of French North Africa fell into Allied hands; if the Germans had not penetrated into the southern Caucasus; if the Eighth Army operations had been successful, but that enemy forces facing them were still in the field; and if Turkey was still neutral. The delay in capturing Tunis during the first weeks after the landings meant that the Allies were faced with a winter campaign in North Africa – the early concept of HUSKY as a quick operation to seize territory faded, and the operation became, instead, a British-favoured option amongst a raft of others that were on the table for 1943.

For about two months after the TORCH landings, the planning effort swung between Sicily and Sardinia. The more attention that was given to HUSKY, the more formidable a task it began to appear; the more the initial advantages of BRIMSTONE were examined, the less beneficial they seemed. Capturing Sardinia brought with it the inevitability of also capturing Corsica, which might possibly require a substantial force – or might fall of its own accord once its neighbouring island had been taken.

Churchill had no preference. What mattered to him was the ability to strike at the 'under-belly'. Capture of the North African coastline, when combined with either Sicily or Sardinia, would give the Allies a series of air bases from which to hit at the Axis. But by mid-November 1942 the impetus had gone from the prospect; winter was starting to bite, and the promise of an opportunistic quick advance had been missed. Either or both islands had become longer-term objectives, and with the opportunity to study the problems in depth and at comparative leisure came doubts and arguments.

By 24 November, the British Joint Planning Staff had produced a fresh paper, in which they compared the virtues of HUSKY and BRIMSTONE. Sicily offered the better political prize, but otherwise the relative advantages and disadvantages were finely balanced; both would be formidable undertakings. The JPS believed that the choice should be made on the time factor: whereas it might be possible to capture Sardinia at the end of February 1943, Sicily might not be achievable until July. Therefore, planning for BRIMSTONE should take precedence and should be carried out by Allied Force Headquarters at speed. In fact, the headquarters was too preoccupied with current operations to spend much time on the project, and despite Eisenhower's preference for Sardinia over Sicily, he did not see that the operation could be mounted before March because of the slow build-up of Allied air power in Tunisia. The JPS was therefore tasked with addressing the two plans in more detail. They produced an appreciation and outline plan for BRIMSTONE by early December 1942, a report which comprehensively summarised the relative advantages of each option on 9 January, and a plan for HUSKY the following day. These papers were considered by the COS on 12 January, the day before they left the United Kingdom for the Casablanca conference.

The third of the Anglo-American conferences to be attended by Churchill and Roosevelt continued the development of the strategy, and the framework for executing it, for winning the war. By the time of Casablanca, code-named SYMBOL, the Combined Chiefs of Staff and various other Anglo-American planning boards had been set in place and had already produced an unprecedented degree of inter-Allied cooperation. It was impossible, however, for the war to be seen in the same way by the two countries, and it was at these conferences that the separate perceptions were explored and agreements reached – or not – on the way forward. It has already been explained that there was a strong feeling in some quarters in America that Germany-first was not the route that should be followed, and that, now it had been decided to tread that particular path, going via the Mediterranean was plain wrong.

The Casablanca conference took place in a residential estate at the Anfa Hotel, situated about a mile from the sea. The headquarters ship HMS *Bulolo* was anchored in the harbour and provided telephone lines ashore, to the delegates who were housed in villas surrounding the hotel. Here Churchill and Roosevelt, with the CCS and the various planning staffs, took decisions on a wide range of subjects. These included such matters as the build-up of American forces in Britain as a prelude to the cross-Channel invasion (operation BOLERO), the use of Allied air forces, and amphibious operations in Europe – all of which would have a bearing on future Mediterranean moves. And beyond these issues, decisions were taken on wider issues which provided the wider context within which Sicilian plans had to be considered – operations in the Far East and Pacific, relationships with China and action to be taken in support of that nation against the Japanese, the bombing campaign against Axis oil resources, and so on. All of these issues, and more, affected the future of Mediterranean operations insofar as they placed demands on Allied manpower and shipping, aircraft, and materiel.

During the conference HUSKY was still in its exploratory stages, to be debated and discussed, but not until the end of the meeting was it approved as an operation which would actually be implemented. The discussions revolved around issues that had already been considered by the Anglo-American planning staffs independently, before they convened together in Casablanca. There was, necessarily, a great deal of re-visiting of topics which had been previously been resolved to satisfaction by one nation's staff but not the other's. What was the place of HUSKY in relation to the cross-Channel plans, for example?

High among the difficulties considered were the possible effects of a Mediterranean strategy on naval plans. If the Mediterranean was to be secured, what would be the cost to other operations of having ships tied down on invasions of various islands? What would be the longer term pay-back of being able to send merchant vessels through the Mediterranean and the Suez Canal with fewer escorts because the sea lanes were unthreatened by enemy warships? It was not the numbers of merchant ships that presented the real difficulty, but the numbers of escorts, landing ships and assault craft that were available. Could sufficient vessels of the right type be made available for a series of Mediterranean options, and what would the effect be on BOLERO and cross-Channel? Should the Allies be tying down large amounts of shipping in this theatre when there might – optimistically – be a sudden opportunity to launch a cross-Channel landing to take advantage of a German set-back on the Eastern front? Could the Allies not establish a lodgment in France and draw away German forces from the east, perhaps by landing on the Cherbourg peninsula – that would surely force Hitler to redeploy twenty or thirty divisions!

The Americans felt that the British underestimated the significance of the Pacific, and the drain that it imposed on American resources. To ease this, they wanted the Burma Road opened at the earliest opportunity to allow bombers to operate from China, and action should be instigated in the Aleutians against the Japanese. The British felt that the Americans underestimated the difficulty of mounting a cross-Channel landing against the heavily-defended French coast, and they had the evidence of Dieppe to support their argument. In general terms the Americans were seen as far too optimistic, far too inexperienced; the Americans saw the British as far too conservative, too affected by the reverses that they had suffered in the past against the Germans. The British were wary of the lack of inter-service experience and coordination, and of the lack of training, of the American forces; but they were not yet aware of the speed which the Americans could bring to implementing a course of action once the go-ahead had been given, nor of the capacity for the Americans to learn from the lessons of war.

With these perceptions in the minds of the COS when they met in Casablanca on 13 January 1943, in an all-British conference before the CCS convened, there was an inclination to regard the American contribution to HUSKY to be primarily in terms of shipping and assault craft. This raised concerns because the Americans had placed responsibility for amphibious operations in the hands of the US Navy; and the navy was also responsible for planning for the Pacific theatre. There would obviously be a conflict of interest which the COS would have to work around to bring their allies on side.

The plans for HUSKY that the COS brought with them to Casablanca suffered from indecision. The Joint Planning Staff had ruled the operation out because of the number of escort ships that would be required, but had been ordered to give the problem fresh consideration. One possibility was to mount as much as possible of the operation from North African ports, but the First Sea Lord was adamant that the escort requirement could not be reduced by more than one-third, and that American vessels would have to be relied upon to meet the bill even were North Africa to be used. Churchill's view was that HUSKY should be seen as a rapid exploitation of TORCH, which should be carried out primarily by seasoned (i.e. British) troops moving the short distance from North Africa. Supporting waves could come from elsewhere. In addition, for 1943, some sort of cross-Channel operation should be launched, followed by action in Burma in the autumn. HUSKY should be re-assessed in this framework – but it appeared that Churchill was alone amongst those at the conference in his belief that HUSKY, cross-Channel, and Burma could all be on the cards for 1943.

On 15 January the COS met again, during the morning, to consider the relative merits of HUSKY and BRIMSTONE before going into the afternoon's CCS conference. At this stage they were inclined to accept the Joint Planning Staff's preference for the latter plan, and saw the advantages as follows:

> BRIMSTONE might exclude HUSKY, but could render a Burmese operation possible; HUSKY would rule out Burma, because it would have to be launched at a later date.

> BRIMSTONE, possibly including Corsica, offered a range of possibilities for the follow-up. These might include the south of France or moves eastwards, which would threaten the Axis at vulnerable points.

> More shipping would be required for HUSKY, but air cover would be easier to provide. The shipping losses for HUSKY might therefore be less than for BRIMSTONE.

The uncertainty in the minds of the COS was therefore still unresolved when they met their American counterparts that afternoon. In presenting their thoughts, they identified two alternative policies for the European theatre during 1943. The first was to close down operations in the Mediterranean as soon as the North African coast had been cleared of the enemy, and the through route to Suez was open. Every effort would then be devoted to diverting forces to the United Kingdom for the cross-Channel landing in Northern France.

The second alternative was to maintain activity in the Mediterranean while building up sufficient forces in Britain to make limited cross-Channel operations, and to maximize the bombing offensive against Germany. The Mediterranean offered many possibilities – Sardinia, Corsica, Sicily and Italy, the Dodecanese, and so on; all of these points could be threatened simultaneously because of Allied amphibious capabilities, thereby forcing the enemy to disperse his forces widely to counter these vulnerable locations. If Italy could be taken out of the war, and Turkey brought into it on the Allied side, then the Rumanian oilfields could be attacked and a route to Russia opened via the Black Sea. The reaction of some of the Americans to this restatement of Churchill's First World War Dardanelles strategy may be imagined.

Should the Mediterranean strategy be adopted, continued the British, the main alternatives appeared to be the capture of Sardinia and Corsica, or the capture of Sicily. Sicily was the bigger prize, but also the bigger undertaking – and it could not be carried out until late summer. The implications were taken to be as follows:

If the capture of Sicily were mounted from Great Britain and the United States, it could be launched in early August with the involvement of about 190 escort vessels; mounting the operation from North Africa would save about sixty-five escorts, but would delay matters by a month. This was because amphibious training facilities in the region were very limited, and preparation would take more time.

If the Sardinian option were selected, May could be the target date. However, because of the greater distance from North Africa air cover would be more difficult. Air cover for Sicily could be provided from Malta, and also from the island of Pantelleria if that island were captured as a preparatory measure.

The Sicilian coastline was some 500 miles in length, and was believed to be defended by seven or eight enemy divisions. The coastline of Northern France was much the same, but was defended by fifteen divisions, with almost thirty more in reserve.

Troops required for the Sicilian alternative were estimated to be some nine divisions, with ten to twelve brigade groups engaged in the initial assault. It was doubtful if these could all be provided from the Mediterranean region because of the training time. The assembly and repair of landing craft would also delay matters.

The British had made their case for the Mediterranean, but left the choice of objectives open; the conference adjourned so that the Americans could consider matters with their planning staffs.

A series of questions then emanated from the Joint Chiefs. What more could be done to draw German air and ground forces from the Eastern front? Answer – with only thirteen British and nine American divisions scheduled to be available in the UK by August 1943, there was insufficient strength to present a strong enough threat in Northern France to guarantee a German withdrawal in the east; the forty-four enemy divisions currently in France could hold the Allies quite adequately without reinforcement. Could Allied air power not compensate for this shortfall in ground forces? Answer – not in the only two possible areas in which a landing stood a chance of establishing a foothold without being immediately thrown back into the sea, the Brest and Cherbourg peninsulas. The first was completely beyond fighter range; the second would not only leave ground forces bottled up, but would itself be subjected to overwhelming enemy air strength. Would a continuation of Mediterranean operations rob the Allies of the opportunity to take advantage of a sudden weakening in the German position? Answer – BOLERO must continue; Mediterranean operations would not involve sufficient divisions to make a difference to the possibility of a lightening stroke from Britain, should the opportunity arise. And so the debate waged, with each American point being answered and deflected by the British.

In one area, however, there was a difficulty that had to be resolved. The Commander, Combined Operations (Lord Louis Mountbatten) had submitted a report concerning the availability of landing craft. A period of three months would be required between releasing these vessels from Mediterranean operations until they could be used for the cross-Channel landings. They would have to be recovered from wherever they had been employed, transported to Scotland before being distributed for repair and refurbishment, and then gathered together in the south of England. On the positive side, however, at all times there would be in England sufficient craft to lift four brigade groups with their transport for an opposed assault on the continent.

The final American question was critical, and illustrated their reservations about the whole strategy: was an operation against Sicily to be regarded as a means to an end, or was it an end in itself? The response from the COS was that, at this stage, it was not possible to lay out a detailed plan for winning the war; but if Italy were removed from the equation, then Germany's position would become very serious. HUSKY was a means to the end of confronting Germany with this situation.

The CCS sat again on the morning of 18 January, still unable to come to a decision. BRIMSTONE was, at this stage, the favoured option, but nothing more came from the meeting than an instruction to the CCS planners to re-examine HUSKY in the light of the American and British resources that might be made available for it, and to establish the earliest date by which the operation might be mounted[17].

However, that evening there was a plenary session attended by Churchill, Roosevelt and the CCS. The discussion concerned the production of a document setting out the strategic policy for 1943. The first item on the agenda dealt with the submarine threat in the Atlantic; then followed the point that all efforts should be devoted to drawing German forces away from the Russian front, to be achieved by operations from North Africa to threaten the various areas already identified by the British COS during the first meeting: Sardinia, Sicily, the Dodecanese, and so on.

But now, Sicily was identified as the chosen target whereby this objective was to be achieved. BOLERO should continue, with the intent of mounting the cross-Channel invasion when ready. Matters concerning the Pacific, the Far East, the bombing of Germany, and drawing Turkey into the war completed the discussion.

The swing to adopting HUSKY was brought about, not least, by Marshall supporting Brooke's case for the operation. The morning had not gone well for the British. Brooke recorded that Admiral King appeared to be still wrapped up with the Pacific war to the exclusion of everything else, and when the meeting adjourned for lunch the CIGS was despairing of any progress being made. He met Field Marshal Dill, the head of the British Joint Staff Mission to Washington, after the meal to try to thrash out the line of the general agreement that had been reached, and was discussing the problem when Air Chief Marshal Portal arrived with suggestions of his own about resolving the impasse, suggestions which were much in line with those that Dill was making. These being agreed, Dill met privately with Marshall for further discussions and obtained his agreement before the CCS reconvened. The paper produced the required agreement, being accepted by the Americans with few alterations, and was then brought before Roosevelt and Churchill for the final blessing[18].

HUSKY was now firmly on the cards, with objections by the First Sea Lord being overruled. His concern was the reduced security of the Atlantic convoys that would ensue once escorts were reassigned to the Mediterranean. Four days later, after more argument and discussion, the decision to go ahead was promulgated, and after yet another day's debate the Operational Directives were approved and broad agreement was reached on the date for the landings. The situation had been reversed; whereas it had initially been the British that had been pushing for the operation, now it was the Americans who were trying to push the British into an earlier date than August. They offered to move their North African forces westwards to free up the ports for training British formations for the assault, and the target date was advanced to July; Churchill wanted May.

The Directors of Plans stuck to their date of August, Churchill to May. The British COS compromised on July, but somewhat muddied the waters by asking for a re-examination of BRIMSTONE, and for detailed planning to continue for that option as well. The Joint Planners had come up with the conclusion that capturing Sardinia and Corsica would do very nicely in forcing Italy out of the war, given the time consideration, and the British then appeared at the next CCS meeting, on 22 January, with the tentative proposal that it should be BRIMSTONE rather than HUSKY. The Americans stuck firm with HUSKY, as Brooke had hoped – he feared that they would accuse the British of not knowing their own minds (with some reason) and wish to bring operations in the Mediterranean to a close. Sicily it was, and planning was to proceed accordingly[19].

Despite the dithering between HUSKY and BRIMSTONE, the Casablanca meetings had been a victory for the British. They had secured what they had wanted: that the Germany-first policy be continued, that for the moment the best way of pursuing this policy was through Italy and the Mediterranean, and that the way forward was Sicily. General Eisenhower was summoned to Casablanca and instructed to report, by not later than 1 March, whether any insurmountable difficulty would cause the attack to be delayed later than the July moon, and in that event to confirm that the operation would be launched not later than the August moon. The Command and Planning organization for HUSKY was agreed, and the Directive to General Eisenhower was drafted for CCS approval.

On the final day of SYMBOL, the last plenary session was held, with Churchill arguing for a June date for HUSKY. The timetable was dictated, he was informed yet once again, by the training requirement and the time needed to assemble the necessary landing craft. The agreement was made that July would stand, but that every effort would be made to achieve June. On this note, the conference disbanded.

1 Henriques
2 Office of the Chief of Military History
3 Stoler
4 Office of the Chief of Military History
5 Stoler
6 Office of the Chief of Military History
7 Stoler
8 Henriques
9 CMH Tunisia
10 Ibid
11 Ibid
12 Alanbrooke
13 CMH Tunisia
14 Ibid
15 D'Este, Patton
16 Montgomery, Memoires
17 Henriques
18 Alanbrooke
19 Ibid

CHAPTER TWO

THE OBJECTIVE

S ICILY WAS NOW IDENTIFIED as the target for the next Allied move in the Mediterranean, and it is appropriate here to consider those factors which the planners of HUSKY took into consideration when formulating their detailed plans for the landing and capture of the island.

To begin with a description of the terrain: Sicily, as every schoolboy knows (or should know) lies like a deflated football off the toe of Italy. It is roughly triangular in shape, with the shortest side (on the east of the island) about 120 miles in length, from Cape Peloro in the north to Cape Passero, due south. The other two sides are some 175 miles long, and meet at Cape Boeo, to the west. Distances from Malta and the mainland of Italy are fifty-five and two miles, respectively, which indicates the comparative ease of access to Sicily from their nearest ground bases by Axis as compared to Allied forces. Once ashore, the landscape comprises rocky hills and mountains, cut across by narrow valleys and dry watercourses – which the British, fresh from North Africa, tended to call wadis. Although there are many springs, during the summer months most of the riverbeds are dry. Those that do contain water during the summer months include the Simeto, Dittaino and Gornalunga Rivers, which run across the Catania plain, south of the town of that name, and all of which present obstacles. The plain is also criss-crossed by drainage ditches, again obstacles, and breeding grounds for malarial mosquitoes. Eighth Army were to suffer 11,500 cases of malaria during the campaign[1]. Sandflies are also common, bringing with them the eponymous sandfly fever. To add to the discomfort of military and civilian alike, shade offered by trees is scarce apart from in the northern highlands. In the summer months the temperature during the daylight hours is above 75° Fahrenheit, at times soaring much higher, and not much cooler after sunset. Metal becomes burningly hot to the touch, and armoured vehicles transform themselves into ovens which roast their crews; steel helmets become an even more uncomfortable burden than usual. The ever-present dust coats the skin, and combines with sweat to produce a mucky paste around which swarm legions of flies. One officer commented that Baedeker's Guide advised against visits to Sicily in July and August; for him, the experience was to prove fatal, but that was because of the enemy, not the climate[2].

The mountain slopes and foothills are often terraced, turning them into giant staircases with risers of six feet or more, up which heavily laden footsoldiers had to struggle. Crags and ridges, with both real and false crests, proliferate in the hill- and mountainsides, particularly in the northeastern region, where Mount Etna rises to a height of 10,740 feet. The lower slopes of this feature are covered with orchards and olive groves, before ascending through scrub and bracken and then ash and lava boulders to the summit.

The Sicilian road system in 1943 provided a communications network across the island which centred on the town of Enna. Roads were of three classifications. The best were the state roads, which were all-weather, well-built, and could carry all types of vehicle. These ran mainly along the coast and linked the main cities and towns such as Palermo, Catania, Messina and Syracuse. Second to these, in terms of quality, were the provincial roads, not usually more than nineteen feet wide but usually tarmac-surfaced. The lowest grade of road was the communal, which was generally unsurfaced and narrow, with sharp bends and steep gradients, and unsuitable for heavy vehicles. The roads ran across plains, through hills and mountains, and around the coastline. With frequent bends, particularly in the uplands and along the coast, they sometimes clung to cliff faces where on one side there was a vertical rock feature soaring above, on the other a steep descent into the Mediterranean below. To today's tourist such roads are picturesque and scenic, to soldiers fighting to progress along such routes in the face of a determined enemy, they presented a far different picture. It might only take a few pounds of explosive to drop the carriageway into the sea or to cover it with boulders, and to add to the misery of those trying to move through such an obstacle it took little more than artillery or mortar shells, booby traps or mines, or machinegun fire to ruin one's complete day. To add to the miseries, the roads ran over narrow bridges, which drew traffic into areas easily pinpointed by artillery and covered by machineguns, and which were easily demolished; and through the constricting streets of villages and towns, which were often not wide enough to permit the passage of armour and which provided effective roadblocks. To blow a bridge, or some houses into the street to form a barricade, caused a traffic jam which continued to back up while the obstacle was cleared – and created an attractive target for artillery observers perched in the surrounding hillsides. Off-road travel to by-pass the problem was often impossible on the boulder-strewn slopes latticed by stone terraces or by sheer drops into the valleys or sea below.

The coastline and beaches were of obvious interest to those planning a seaborne invasion. The location and capacities of ports became a particular concern, for through them the Allies expected to have to pour their forces in sufficient number, and at sufficient speed, to contest the enemy formations manning the island, to which reinforcements crossing from mainland Italy, two miles across the Straits of Messina, and from other bases to the north – for example in the south of France – were expected to arrive. The experience of Dieppe had made the Allies wary of attempting to capture a port head-on; the preferred approach was to be to take it from the land after putting troops ashore along the coast. But take ports they had to, for putting the entire mass of men and materiel across beaches was considered to be out of the question. Over three hundred miles of coastline had to be examined before final decisions could be taken on landing areas, with a multitude of factors to be considered. The sea approaches had to provide deep water, give sea-room, be free of natural hazards such as rocks and shoals, and have good anchorages. There should be no currents or heavy swells or surf, and there should be no lee-shore caused by prevailing winds which might drive vessels ashore. The beaches had to be wide and deep enough to give room for men, vehicles and stores; they should be firm enough to bear tracked and wheeled transport and weapons, sloping but not stony; and with sufficient exits inland to allow the passage of the invaders, so that they were unencumbered by cliffs, marshes, lagoons or any other obstacles which might hinder troops or channel them into killing zones. These factors had also come under the consideration of the defenders of Sicily, who had planned their counter-measures accordingly.

About thirty-two main beaches were listed as possible landing sites, of which some twenty-six were to be actually used[3].

The principal ports of Sicily are, and were, Palermo, Catania, Syracuse, and Messina. As we have seen, the earlier plans for the invasion, INFLUX and WHIPCORD, proposed that Palermo and Catania be captured early in the campaign, and that Allied forces be put ashore close to these ports. They were calculated to be able to handle varying tonnages daily, with Messina and Palermo leading. Syracuse, at the bottom of the table, was expected to be able to handle between a quarter and a fifth of the tonnage at Messina. The figures for these ports were calculated using statistics from the North African campaign, and assumed that damage had been inflicted by bombing and demolition. There were, of course, smaller ports dotted along the coastline such as Augusta and Licata, each of which was expected to be able to cope with about half the tonnages of Syracuse.

A glance at the map shows that the biggest ports were to the north, and the largest, Messina, was adjacent to the Italian mainland, where strong enemy anti-aircraft and coastal defences made an initial landing unfeasible. It was also 150 miles from Malta, which placed it out of range of Allied single-seater fighter aircraft. With Messina written out of the possibilities because of its defences, the planners turned to the alternatives. Calculations indicated that after the landings four divisions with associated air forces could be maintained through the combined ports of Catania, Augusta and Syracuse, and two divisions with their air forces through Palermo. Coastal defences made direct assaults on Palermo, Syracuse and Augusta impracticable, but Catania was a possibility if some coastal batteries were neutralized[4].

Seaports were not the only consideration weighing upon the planners' minds, however. While ports were necessary for disembarking land forces, the air forces had priorities of their own. They wished to have use of Axis airfields at the earliest opportunity, so that they might provide both close air support for the ground war, and also so that they might bring Italian and other Mediterranean targets within range of Allied bombers, to prosecute the strategic bombing campaign. The principal Sicilian airfields were grouped around Gerbini, Comiso, Ponte Olivio, Castelvetrano, Milo and Palermo, with more in other locations. These would have to be captured or put out of commission at a very early stage in the invasion to prevent the enemy launching air attacks on Allied shipping, particularly when it was disembarking men and equipment ashore and was relatively immobile: the great mass of shipping required for the operation would provide a very tempting target to the *Luftwaffe* and *Regia Aeronautica*. However, ensuring that the majority of the ports and the airfields were captured at an early date meant that the Allied land forces had to be widely dispersed. They would have to land as closely as possible to these objectives, which were so spread around the island as to contradict the military principle of concentration of force; these considerations might well conflict with army plans and priorities.

So much, then, for the geographical features and locations of the principal sea and air ports. What of the population?

In 1943 Sicily was populated by an independently-minded people, numbering about four million, who regarded themselves as being somewhat apart from the rest of Italy, and not solely because of the physical barrier of the Straits of Messina. The island has been fought over from time immemorial, invaded by one tribe or race after another since pre-historical times. The Greeks settled there in about 757 BC, colonizing the eastern side of Sicily, while the Carthaginians and Phoenicians moved into the western side. The Greek settlement at Syracuse lasted for more than 500 years, but not without strife. The city was besieged by the Athenians in 415 BC and the Greeks were crushed by the Romans during the Second Punic War, events which were reflected upon by General Patton – a keen student of military history – during his time on the island[5].

The aforementioned invaders were not the last. Vandals, Goths, Byzantines, Lombards, Saracens, Normans, Swabians, Angevins, Aragonese, British, Spanish and Bourbons all had periods of power on the island before it became part of a unified Italy following Garibaldi's victory over the Neapolitans near Palermo. Sicily has the unhappy history of being fought over for centuries, a side-product of which may be seen in the defensible hill-top towns which were to feature in the battles of the twentieth century. Ever present, too, are the archaeological remains of by-gone times, which were again to draw comment from Patton.

The people themselves, in Patton's words, were 'the most destitute and God-forgotten' that he had ever seen. The southern Sicilians in particular he considered dirty and lazy in the extreme: too idle, apparently, to remove corpses from their houses. Their living and eating, sanitation and cooking habits, he thought to be primitive and unhygienic. In cities such as Palermo, the locals appeared to be bigger and older[6].

Patton was not alone, certainly amongst the Allies, in his low opinion of the Italians in general and the Sicilians in particular. Wartime propaganda and the recent comparatively poor performance of the Italian army in North Africa had contributed to this opinion, but it was, perhaps, over-simplistic. The Italians were tired of both Mussolini and the war, which had brought them little of what *Il Duce* had promised. During the planning stages of HUSKY, more cautious Allied voices warned that an invasion of the Italian homeland might rekindle a more warlike attitude amongst Italian soldiers and civilians alike.

Italy's ally, Germany, also had reservations about the firmness of Italian resolve, and had thoughts about the way forward should it crumble. Thus, the resident population of Sicily. What of the island's defenders? In January 1943 Allied intelligence listed eight Italian divisions there, of which five were coastal defence and three were field divisions. The former were mostly locally-recruited troops who were tasked with manning the batteries, pillboxes and trenches that lined the coastline of Sicily, which were particularly concentrated around vital ports and areas that were considered vulnerable to landings. The resolve of these troops was questionable, as they might reasonably be expected to tend to their families rather than standing and fighting, although there was always the possibility that they would prove more resolute and prefer to protect their loved ones by fighting it out on the beaches where they were protected by defence works and were better organized and equipped. The three field divisions might be expected to put up a stiffer, mobile resistance.

It was to be anticipated that reinforcements would be able to be sent through Messina and Palermo, which intelligence estimated could handle one and a half divisions per week. By the expected date of HUSKY, it was expected that the Sicilian garrison would have been expanded by five additional field divisions, of which three might be German. In the event, the reinforcements amounted to one extra Italian and two German divisions, bringing the total to eleven. To deal with this force, the Combined Chiefs of Staff proposed to land forces comprising four British and three American infantry divisions, two British infantry brigade groups and two armoured regiments, with a tank battalion; two US armoured combat commands; two British and one American parachute brigades; and three British commando and two US ranger battalions. One British and one American infantry divisions were to be held in reserve. This was the largest force that could be assembled for which ships and landing craft were available, and was considered sufficient for the task which faced it.

Land forces aside, the Axis was expected to be able to put 1,560 aircraft into the skies, apart from transport and coastal machines, from bases in Italy, Sicily, Sardinia and Pantelleria. Of these 810 were German. All of the major Sicilian airfields lay about fifteen miles from the coast, and it was theoretically possible for the enemy to launch about 540 German and 190

Italian aircraft against the landing forces during the first day of the invasion.

At sea the Italian fleet numbered, it was believed, six battleships, seven cruisers and thirty destroyers. In addition, there were about twenty German and forty-eight Italian submarines, and E-boats were to be expected in the coastal waters around Sicily. This was a not inconsiderable force, which could, if its commanders were so minded, put up a stiff fight to protect its homeland. Allied naval officers had to be prepared, therefore, to face this challenge. Although they believed that they had overwhelming command of the sea, it was nonetheless another factor that the Allies had to consider; in fact, the threat from Axis aircraft, particularly those based in the southeast and east of Sicily, appeared greater to the navy than did the enemy warships.

To make best use of Allied airpower, the east coast of Sicily to the south of Syracuse, the south coast, and the western end of the island were within the range of single-engine fighters which would be flying from Malta and Tunisia. The reverse was also true - Allied airfields in these locations could as easily be reached by the enemy based in Sicily. It was therefore imperative that Axis airfields be made inoperable as soon as possible, either by bombing or capture.

The Anglo-American command to mount the invasion of Sicily was formed in accordance with the principle that while an officer from one of the two Allies would assume overall responsibility for a major coalition operation, his deputy would be drawn from the other. Thus Eisenhower was Commander in Chief, while British officers headed the three services involved in the operation: General Alexander was Deputy C-in-C and commander of all land forces, Admiral Sir Andrew Browne Cunningham commander of all naval forces, and Air Chief Marshal Sir Arthur Tedder was C-in-C Mediterranean Air Forces. This strong layer of British officers in key positions had been another result of British negotiating strategy at Casablanca; they had succeeded in getting their system of separate C-in-Cs for each of the three services adopted, which ensured that they retained a great deal of control of Mediterranean operations. Eisenhower retained the overall command, but all of the key appointments reporting immediately to him were British. When a visiting group of US Senators questioned the roles that had been given to the British, 'If Cunningham commands the navy forces, Tedder the air forces, and Alexander the ground forces, what in hell does Eisenhower command?' The answer from the American Secretary of War Henry Stimson was, 'He commands Cunningham, Tedder, and Alexander'[7]. In fact, Eisenhower played a minor role in the planning for HUSKY. As his deputy, Alexander was responsible for this, but he was busy fighting the battle against the enemy in Tunisia. The ground work was done by the planning staff of Force 141, the Anglo-American group of officers who laboured to assemble a workable strategy for the invasion in Room 141 of the Hotel St George in

Algiers – hence the name given to the force preparing for the operation.

For the HUSKY operation Eisenhower failed to display the grasp and control that he was to do the following year, for OVERLORD and the campaign in northwest Europe. The detailed planning for HUSKY was in the hands of Force 141 and the service commanders, who had little time to devote to it because of the ongoing battles in North Africa which demanded their attention, and Eisenhower became relegated to, or chose to become, little more than a chairman who resolved difficulties when his three immediate subordinates failed to agree. And fail to agree they often did, for the individual services carried out their planning with the interests of their own branch of the armed forces foremost.

The core of planning staff who worked away in their hotel room brought with them, naturally, the previous projects for Sicily, INFLUX and WHIPCORD, which proposed landings in both the northwest and southeast of the island; instead of approaching the problem with a blank sheet of paper, the planners had preconceived ideas and solutions ready to hand, which had been drawn up for a different set of circumstances. While these may have helped, they also tended to instill a mindset and to channel thinking; the conclusions of the earlier plans had an authority all of their own which was difficult to ignore.

To add to the difficulties of putting together a comprehensive design for the invasion, planning for it was taking place in several widely dispersed locations: Washington and London were involved because some formations would have to go to Sicily directly from the United States and Great Britain. Because the bulk of forces assigned to the invasion were already in the Mediterranean, planning also took place there: the British were to land in the east of Sicily, and were to be known as the Eastern Task Force (or Force 545); planning therefore took place in British headquarters in Cairo. The Americans formed the Western Task Force (or Force 343) with its headquarters initially in Rabat, in Morocco. In addition to these centres of planning, there were the three service headquarters, all working away on their particular aspects of the task, and communicating with each other by wireless and cable, a factor which raised problems of its own because the efficiency of these means encouraged debate between the various headquarters and prolonged the decision-making process[8].

The post-war paper on the planning of HUSKY[9] records that ten tons of documents were left by those who were tasked with carrying it out. The filing system was 'deplorable', and the greater part of this mass of paper concerned domestic details unrelated to the preparations for the operation itself. In theory, planning started on 23 January 1943, the date on which General Eisenhower was given the Combined Chiefs of Staff Directive. The broad outline of the way in which the CCS saw the operation developing should have provided the executive staff with a skeleton on which to build their ideas; but they had little faith in its feasibility, a feeling that was to grow as they proceeded to work on it.

When the planners began to study the tactical features of the project and the intelligence that had been gathered, they discovered that they could not agree with the conclusions that had been drawn by the staffs in London and Casablanca. In fact, doubts about the general design had probably been expressed before, because the plan had been accepted only with certain reservations. Eisenhower reported that the proposed dispersal of the Allied land forces, to the northwest and southeast, ran contrary to his own suggestion that they be concentrated in the southeast of Sicily to ensure success. For him, the debate was between the option of splitting the force to achieve an early capture of Palermo, a desirable objective for the reasons stated above, of having a major port and control of the airfields in that part of the island; and the alternative of building decisive strength with which to overwhelm the enemy.

General Alexander also had reservations, accepting the plan produced in Algiers as little more than a preliminary, tentative basis for the eventual strategy. He believed that it would need modifying. Again, he recognized the desirability of capturing ports at the earliest opportunity. Messina was out of the question as an immediate objective, but Palermo and Catania were not. The administrative difficulties of the operation demanded that two ports, 120 miles apart, should be captured in defiance of the principle of concentration of force. Moreover, the proposed area in which to concentrate, the southeast, was no more than fifty-five miles away from fighter aircraft cover based on Malta. Underlying the problem, and the cause of it, was the fact that the Allies just did not have the required strength, especially in shipping, to meet both the administrative demands and to concentrate troops to meet the tactical demands. The tug-of-war that was being fought at the highest levels, between the conflicting needs of the Pacific and the European theatres, between a cross-Channel landing and a Mediterranean strategy, had left the HUSKY planners with fewer assets than they would have wished. Rarely do planners have it otherwise.

The Mediterranean tug-of-war was a three-sided affair. On one side was the need for ports, a need driven by the Administrative Appreciation (the study on how best to land and support the invasion forces). The second factor was the requirement to obtain airfields on Sicily at the earliest opportunity. The third was the need to concentrate the land forces in the southeast of the island under the protection of air cover from Malta.

Of these three conflicting issues the first, the Administrative Appreciation which called for the swift seizure of ports so that the cross-beach disembarkation period was as short as possible, later proved to be over-egged. In practice, the need for Palermo as a port through which to pour troops and equipment into Sicily was exaggerated and the Allies managed to do without it until it ultimately fell on the evening of 22 July, thirteen days after Allied airborne forces first landed on the island. Nevertheless, in the absence of evidence to the contrary during the preparation stage, the planners had to take every precaution to ensure that provision was made to capture sufficient port facilities.

With regard to the second issue, the requirement to capture airfields, the air staff were particularly keen to get their hands on the one near Gela. This was one of the most highly developed airfields in Sicily, and its possession would enhance air operations considerably – for both sides. It, and the airfield at Pachino in the southeast, were prime objectives for the airmen, who argued strongly for early capture of the Gela-Catania Plain airfields, without which the entire Sicilian plan would be placed in jeopardy. The naval planners were in agreement, for enemy aircraft launched from these sites had the potential to ride roughshod over the shipping lying off-shore when the landings commenced.

On 11 February Eisenhower nominated the principal subordinate commanders for the land, sea, and air command of the two task forces to be mounted for HUSKY:

WESTERN TASK FORCE

Lieutenant-General George Patton.
Vice-Admiral Henry Hewitt, USN.
Colonel T. J. Hickey, USAAF.

EASTERN TASK FORCE

Lieutenant-General Sir Bernard Montgomery.
Admiral Sir Bertram Ramsay, Deputy Naval Commander Allied Expeditionary Force.
Air Vice-Marshal Broadhurst, Commander Western Desert Air Force.

On 12 May the next of the Anglo-American conferences, TRIDENT, began in Washington. It was a meeting that started with greater optimism than had been displayed at Casablanca, four months earlier, largely because the Allies felt that they had grasped the strategic initiative. This belief was founded on the recent campaigns which had successfully seized the offensive, and not just in the European Theatre where the North African campaign was closing: in the Pacific the Americans had completed the Guadalcanal and Papua campaigns, and on the Eastern Front the Soviets were continuing their counteroffensives after surviving the siege of Stalingrad. The Battle of the Atlantic was turning in favour of the Allies, and the preparations for HUSKY were underway. The dominating question for the conference was 'What next?' and again the debate was between the American desire for long-term planning and the British inclination to defer such plans in favour of opportunism.

At the opening meeting of the conference, Roosevelt declared that the immediate question was how best to make use of the large Allied forces currently in the Mediterranean; while he believed that it was desirable to knock Italy out of the war after HUSKY, he shrank from the idea of landing large armies in Italy, which might lead to a war of attrition which would not assist the Soviets. Perhaps an air offensive, launched from Sicily or from the heel and toe of Italy, would achieve the same aims that

Churchill was seeking – the elimination of Italy from the war, the consequent need for the Germans to divert their own forces to replace Italian troops withdrawn from the Balkans, the removal of the Italian fleet, and the building of a favourable situation to entice Turkey to enter the war on the side of the Allies.

The debate swayed back and forth, and resulted – yet again – in another compromise in which the Americans and British agreed that the final blow against Germany could only be achieved by a cross-Channel invasion, not from the Mediterranean. The opportunities that had arisen in the Mediterranean could not be wasted, however, and the British – as might be expected – were prepared to argue the case for operations here to be continued as the best way to prepare for the final blow. The American response was not to continue resisting Mediterranean operations unless they postponed the cross-Channel landings, for which the target date of 1 May 1944 was now agreed.

For the European aspect of the war, the outlines of a mutually acceptable strategy were beginning to take shape. The Americans could take heart that the British were now committed to a major offensive against Germany which would be launched across the Channel from the United Kingdom, and although the US Joint Chiefs had set restrictions on any future increases in forces in the Mediterranean, they were nonetheless satisfied that operations post-HUSKY against Italy would contribute to, rather than detract from, the cross-Channel operation. They were also hopeful that the 'periphery-picking complex' of the British had been stopped[10].

Both Casablanca and TRIDENT had furthered the continuation of the Mediterranean offensives, but at the expense of limitations imposed to contain them and subordinate them to the long-held American belief that the only way to beat Germany was through northwest Europe. While the Joint Chiefs may have drawn comfort from these decisions, future events were to show that the Mediterranean question was far from being dead and buried. The question that the Americans had been asking about HUSKY – was it an end unto itself or did it lead on to other things? – had not been fully resolved. Consequently, the operation (and indeed much of the ensuing Italian campaign) was carried out almost in a vacuum, with the planners uncertain of where it was to lead.

1 Malony (Official History)
2 Cole
3 Malony
4 Ibid
5 Patton
6 Ibid
7 Quoted in Pack
8 Malony
9 Henriques
10 Matloff

CHAPTER THREE

OPERATIONAL PLANNING

F ROM MID-FEBRUARY 1943 the planning for HUSKY lacked direction. The principal players, Eisenhower, Alexander, Cunningham, Tedder, Montgomery and Patton, were all heavily involved in the Tunisian campaign, and had more on their plates than giving attention to what was planned for several months in the future. The planning, for the moment, was left to a relatively junior and inexperienced group under the leadership of Major General Gairdner, who had to produce something that would be acceptable to their more senior – and more critical – masters.

HUSKY was being planned in five separate locations: Washington, London, Algiers, Malta and Tunis. And in five separate locations, the most elementary question was being debated – where on the island of Sicily should the landings be made? Guidance certainly did not come from the Supreme Commander, for Eisenhower took a detached view of the proceedings. His part in the war effort might later provoke debate amongst historians, who tend to fall into one of two camps, either regarding him as a great strategist or as the capable chairman of a board of military experts, but as far as HUSKY was concerned he played the part of a bystander. His supporting staff were of little better assistance to Gairdner, for Alexander was aloof, and Cunningham and Tedder argumentative.

With little guidance, the planning team had a major task facing them. There was nothing in recent experience to assist them, for mounting amphibious operations on the scale envisaged for HUSKY had never been attempted. The TORCH landings were no blueprint, for the Vichy French were a very different kettle of fish from the Germans and Italians when it came to defending a coastline. The last time an operation came anything near to HUSKY in size was Gallipoli in 1915, and that was an unfortunate precedent. So the planners fell back on the earlier schemes that had been drawn up in the event that Sicily was to be invaded. These, it will be remembered, proposed landings in both the south-eastern and north-western areas of the island. Two distinct assaults, by a British and an American task force respectively, had been the basis of the Joint Planning Staff's plan which had been presented at the Casablanca conference. The northwestern landing, to secure Palermo, would be timetabled for two days after the south-eastern. The plan had also proposed an airborne landing on the toe of Italy to hinder enemy movements to and from Sicily[1].

In March the Force 141 planners recommended a change to this plan, suggesting that the south-east of the island was of such tactical importance that both task forces should land here. The route northwards to Messina appeared easier from this direction, but the area did not have sufficient ports to sustain the ten divisions which were now considered necessary for the operation. This factor was enough for the suggestion to be rejected. It was considered necessary to secure all three ports of Palermo, Catania and Syracuse to do the job. One change to the Casablanca plan was agreed, however, which was that the airborne forces would be used to neutralize the beach defences rather than dropped in Calabria to interfere with Axis movements.

On 13 March this revised plan was presented to Eisenhower, Alexander, Cunningham and Tedder in Algiers, and was approved before the Task Force Commanders, Montgomery and Patton, discussed it in detail. They had been summoned to a meeting on 18 March for that purpose, but on the 15th Montgomery, whose Eighth Army was heavily engaged in attacking the Mareth Line, sent a message to Gairdner stating that the plan as it stood broke every commonsense rule of practical warfare[2]. Furthermore, it was completely theoretical, had absolutely no chance of success, and needed to be rewritten. One has a degree of sympathy for Gairdner and his team as they returned to the drawing board yet again.

At the conference of 18 March Lieutenant General Miles Dempsey, the commander of XIII Corps, represented Montgomery. The news that Monty would not be attending in person led both Alexander and Patton to send deputies in their stead; events in Tunisia took priority. The objections which Dempsey raised to the plan on Montgomery's behalf concerned the requirement to capture the eastern ports of Syracuse, Augusta and Catania at the earliest opportunity after landing. To do this, he believed that he needed at least one additional infantry division. The difficulty was that there were insufficient landing craft available to transport and land it, and the only possible solution appeared to be to sacrifice one of the Western Task Force landings to provide both men and vessels. At this stage in the planning one British infantry division was to be put ashore at Gela, but if this division were to be landed further east to fall in line with Montgomery's wishes, then the airfields around Ponte Olivo, Biscari and Comiso would not be captured at an early stage in the campaign.

Neither Admiral Cunningham nor Air Chief Marshal Tedder would agree to this proposal. With the airfields in enemy hands, the beaches and assembly areas offshore would be extremely vulnerable to air attack. The response time of Allied aircraft flying from North Africa to protect these areas would be longer than the flight time of the enemy. With the conflicting needs of the army and air force unresolved, Alexander was asked to come to a decision. He backed Montgomery's request for the extra division, but not his solution to finding it. Instead, Alexander proposed that the planned American landing at Sciacca and Marinella, on the south-west coast, would be cancelled and that the landings to seize Palermo would be postponed. A factor which apparently brought him around to the view that the port facilities of Palermo might wait, was the introduction of the DUKW, which would enable the two task forces to quickly ferry men and equipment from the ships to concentration points ashore. This amphibious six-wheel drive vehicle was capable of carrying 2$\frac{1}{2}$tons of equipment or twenty-five troops, and was but one of many new designs for landing operations. A variety of landing craft was being produced at high speed by shipyards in the United States and the United Kingdom, designed for a range of cargos and purposes. Amongst them was the Landing Craft Tank (Rocket) [LCT(R)] which was mounted with a thousand 5-inch rocket projectors with which to lay down a bombardment on the shore. These craft were to make their debut during HUSKY[3].

Eisenhower accepted Alexander's suggestions, but had reservations. The American divisions which had been earmarked for the Palermo mission would be kept hanging about indefinitely, and when they did go into action, the enemy airfields at Sciacca and Marinella would still be operational. He therefore ordered that some way be found of getting an extra British division for Eighth Army, hoping that the Combined Chiefs of Staff would come up with the shipping required to transport it.

As the arguments swayed back and forth, it became apparent that the British division could, in fact, be provided from the forces in North Africa; moreover, the shipping problem was not as unsolvable as had been presented. The resulting plan now envisaged British D-Day landings of one division from the Middle East and one from the United Kingdom to land at Avola; a brigade from the Middle East to land at Pachino; one division, from either North Africa of the Middle East at Pozallo; and one from North Africa at Gela.

The American landings at Sciacca and Marinella were cancelled, and the remainder were postponed from D+2 to D+5. Eisenhower approved the plan on 10 April.

Montgomery's reservations had not been fully satisfied, however. He was determined that as many of his veteran divisions would be used as possible, and under the name of 'Eighth Army', not 'Eastern Task Force'. On 17 April Brigadier de Guingand, Monty's Eighth Army Chief of Staff, was appointed Chief of Staff of Force 545 with the rank of Major General. Monty himself was able to leave Tunisia on 23 April to spend a few days with Force 545 concentrating on the Sicilian planning. His first thoughts were not slow in being sent to Alexander, for the very next day he signalled his superior to criticize the fact that, thus far, the planning had been done on the assumption that enemy opposition would be slight and that Sicily would be captured fairly easily. This, he pointed out, ran contrary to the experience the Allies were having in Tunisia, where both

Germans and Italians were fighting desperately; they should be expected to put up a similar performance in Sicily.

With this expectation, Montgomery demanded that the Eighth Army should land and fight with all of its constituent corps and divisions sufficiently close to each other to be mutually supporting. Therefore, he argued, the proposed landings at Gela and Pozallo should be forfeited and the whole of the initial effort should be concentrated at Avola and Pachino. This would secure a lodgement, after which the airfields and ports could be captured from a secure base. This should not be argued about in London and Washington, for that would impose yet more delays which would make a July landing impossible. Meanwhile, planning could not progress properly because everyone involved knew that the current plan could not possibly succeed.

Monty was assertive enough to further inform Alexander that he had ordered the Force 545 planning staff to proceed on the assumption that the revisions he had suggested – that Gela and Pozallo should give way to the concentration he wanted at Avola and Pachino – were to go ahead. Moreover, he reported that Admiral Ramsay was in complete agreement, and demanded that the Air Force should provide the experienced squadrons with which he had worked in North Africa, to give close support to the Eighth Army.

The shopping list that Montgomery stipulated was exhaustive. He had thrown out the plan which he had agreed to earlier, on 5 April, together with the prospect of eliminating the enemy airfields which Tedder was demanding be taken as an immediate imperative. In reforming the plan, he brushed off the fact that it had actually been put together on the assumption that German forces on the island would resist strongly, and that the Italians might be expected to fight hard for their own soil – precisely the opposite of Montgomery's complaint[4].

On 29 April Alexander had a meeting with Cunningham, Tedder, Ramsay, Air Marshal Coningham and Patton, to discuss Montgomery's proposals. General Leese represented Monty, who had returned to Tunisia, sick with tonsillitis. It was not to be expected that Montgomery would get his way without a fuss.

Tedder pointed out that the most strongly defended area of the Sicilian coastline was precisely where the revised plan would put the Eighth Army ashore, largely without air protection. If shipping was to stay in the area, it followed that the airfields must be captured for Allied use; there were thirteen of these which would be left in enemy hands, and the RAF and USAAF could not neutralize them without the assistance of ground forces. Cunningham and Tedder could not accept a plan which left the beaches and offshore assembly areas vulnerable to air attack.

The situation was deadlocked. Eisenhower now stepped in and summoned a meeting for 2 May. This time Montgomery was able to attend, but Alexander and Air Marshal Coningham were prevented from being present because of bad weather, which grounded their aircraft. At this meeting Montgomery produced yet another plan. This time he suggested that the Palermo operation be abandoned, and that the Americans should land at Pozallo and Gela instead. The Eastern Task Force should land as he had proposed earlier, at Avola and Pachino.

On this occasion Montgomery employed every diplomatic technique he could muster to sell his ideas. He started by cornering Bedell Smith in the lavatory of the Ecole Normale, before the conference started, and sold him the plan with the aid of a diagram drawn in the condensation he had breathed onto a mirror[5]. He then went on to preface his presentation to the assembled 'brass' by reading from a prepared script:

> *I know well that I am regarded by many people as being a tiresome person. I think this is very probably true. I try hard not to be tiresome; but I have seen so many mistakes made in this war, and so many disasters happen, that I am desperately anxious to try and see that we have no more; and this often means being very tiresome. If we have a disaster in HUSKY, it would be dreadful.*[6]

He went on to give a clear exposition of his thoughts, carefully presenting the case as a military problem together with the solution he had identified, and avoiding making it an American versus British issue. He made his point.

In a signal to Alexander after the meeting, Montgomery informed him that Eisenhower and Bedell Smith supported this fresh strategy. Additionally, Monty suggested in his signal that the American Corps should be placed under his control, and that the Eighth Army should run the land battle completely. He was nothing if not ambitious, but on this last point he was not to have his way.

Alexander flew in to see Eisenhower the following day. The latest plan was agreed, and it had strength: it concentrated force in the area where it was most needed. It was not universally accepted, however. Both Tedder and Cunningham had reservations about leaving the Gerbini airfields and those in the west of Sicily in Axis hands. Cunningham also felt that the advantage of widely dispersed landings was being given up, and that concentrations of men and shipping made good targets for enemy aircraft; Alexander's concern was that the Palermo port facilities would not be in Allied hands for some time. The restructured strategy also left the Americans playing second fiddle to Montgomery's wishes. This led Cunningham to report back to the First Sea Lord that the leaders of the Western Task Force, Admiral Hewitt and General Patton, were 'very sore about it'. Patton's reply to Alexander, when asked what he thought of the new plan, was terse: 'General, I don't plan – I only obey orders.' Eisenhower also had some lingering doubts about deferring the capture of

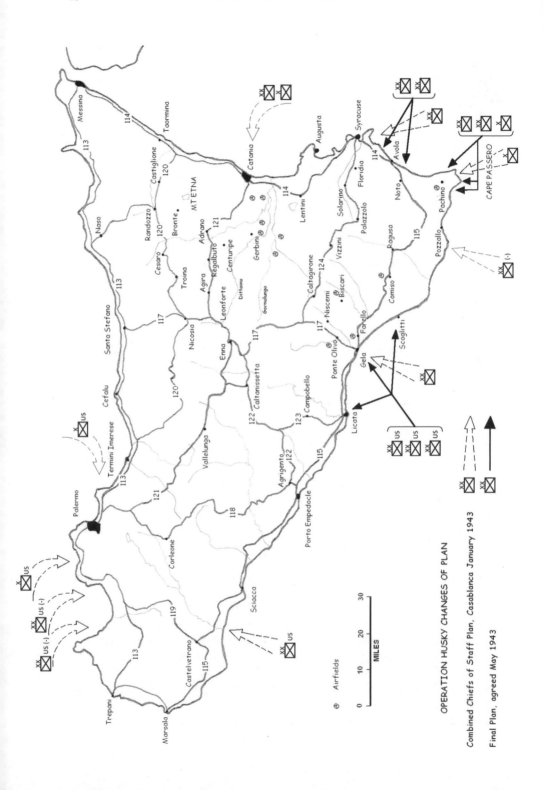

OPERATION HUSKY CHANGES OF PLAN

Combined Chiefs of Staff Plan, Casablanca January 1943

Final Plan, agreed May 1943

Palermo, which he was to dwell upon once the campaign was over, reflecting upon whether or not the Americans might have done better to launch their advance on Messina from the west rather than the indirect route which they were ultimately to take.

It was not only the Americans who were discomfited. Major General Gairdner, who had struggled with Force 141 to produce a workable plan for HUSKY, tendered his resignation on the grounds that his work had been thoroughly discredited. Alexander accepted the resignation, but not without feeling that it was he himself that was at fault for failing to provide Gairdner with the guidance and support that he needed to carry out his task better[7]. Eisenhower might well have felt the same, for his part in the planning process thus far had been notable for his failure to become involved. It was not until late in the day that he was compelled to recognize that the wrangling between the various British commanders was not merely a single-nation problem; it affected the whole Allied situation, and it was he that was ultimately responsible for ensuring that things ran effectively and with the minimum of tension.

Montgomery had resolved the near-paralysis that had seized the HUSKY planners for most of the Spring of 1943. Now preparations could begin in earnest.

Having obtained agreement on where the landings should take place did not, however, mean the end of the debates. On 13 April, the Combined Chiefs of Staff had approved the dates for HUSKY as being within the period 10-14 July, which was when the moon would be at its optimum for the requirements of the air, land and sea forces. Yet the possibility of an earlier date kept being raised, particularly by Churchill, a possibility that the planners had to resist. Eisenhower himself had written to the Combined Chiefs on 7 April warning that the operation had little chance of success if the defenders of Sicily included two or more German divisions, a caveat that drew a withering response from Churchill and from both the British and American Joint Chiefs who saw his warning as defeatist[8].

To add to the arguments, on 5 May Montgomery once again raised the point that 'Only one commander can run the battle in Sicily in the new plan. It seems clear that Eighth Army should command and control the whole operation, with 2nd US Corps included in Eighth Army'. The American view was, not unexpectedly, different. Once Marshall learnt that Force 545 was to become re-titled 'Eighth Army', he decided that on D Day the Western Task Force should take the title of Seventh United States Army, and that Patton should have equal status to Montgomery[9]. Monty was ruffling feathers elsewhere, for his plan to retain most of the Eighth Army for HUSKY did not sit well with General 'Jumbo' Wilson, who had to prepare for possible operations in the Aegean and was unhappy that Montgomery was carefully picking out formations for his own use. Monty was living up to his reputation for being tactless.

At the beginning of May 1943, the various headquarters which were preparing for HUSKY were dispersed as follows:

Allied Force HQ	*Algiers*
HQ Force 141 (later Fifteenth Army Group)	*Algiers*
Force 545 (later Eighth Army)	*Tripoli*
Force 545 Planning HQ (XIII and XXX Corps)	*Cairo*
Force 343 (later Seventh [US] Army) HQ	*Rabat (later Mostaganem, Algeria)*
Naval HQ Western Task Force	*Algiers*
Naval HQ Eastern Task Force	*Cairo*
CENT and DIME Naval Commanders	*Oran*
JOSS Commander	*Bizerta*
Air Commander-in-Chief (ACM Tedder)	*Algiers*
HQ NW African Tactical Air Forces (Maj Gen Spaatz)	*Constantine*
HQ NW African Strategical Air Forces (Maj Gen Doolittle)	*Constantine*
HQ NW African Coastal Air Forces (AVM Lloyd)	*Constantine*
Air Forces operating from Middle East (ACM Douglas)	*Cairo*
Air Forces operating from Malta (AVM Park)	*Malta*

Despite this scattering of planners around the Mediterranean, and the others in London and Washington, with all of the difficulties that the distances and communications problems involved, Force 141 was able to issue an Operation Instruction, the second, on 21 May 1943. This gave the preparatory measures to be taken for the operation, and outlined the assault areas. Details were given of which formations were to land on what beaches (given by alphabetical letter rather than name, for security reasons), and when. Their embarkation areas and methods of transport to Sicily were also listed, for example as 'Ship to Shore' (by ships to the beach areas, and then transferred to landing craft for the assault) or 'Shore to Shore' (troops sailed the whole distance from embarkation to landing beaches in the same craft. Only 3rd [US] and 51st [Highland] Divisions travelled this way). It was, at least, something for the army, corps and divisional planners to be getting on with.

The forces allocated to the assault were as follows:

Force 545 (or Task Force East – Eighth Army)
XIII Corps, comprising 5th and 50th Infantry Divisions, which were to land on Beaches ACID North and ACID South respectively.
XXX Corps, comprising 51st and 1st Canadian Infantry Divisions, and 231 Infantry Brigade, which were to land on Beaches BARK South, BARK West and BARK East respectively.
1st Airborne Division and 78th Infantry Division (less those airborne

troops which were to participate in the initial assaults) were in reserve, with 46th Infantry Division earmarked as reinforcing division for follow-up if required.

Force 343 (or Task Force West – later Seventh [US] Army)
3rd (US) Infantry Division, to land on JOSS Beach.
II (US) Corps, comprising 1st (US) and 45th (US) Infantry Divisions, to land on Beaches DIME and CENT respectively.
2nd (US) Armoured Division, less Combat Command A, but with one Regimental Combat Team from 1st Division, was to act as floating reserve.
82nd (US) Airborne Division less those airborne troops which were to participate in the initial assaults was in reserve.
9th (US) Infantry Division was the reinforcing division, not to be committed without authority from Force 141.

Amongst the preparations for Operation HUSKY, considerations of intelligence and counter-intelligence were inevitably at the fore. Among the less conventional schemes – British and American respectively, and both of which were to become the subject of popular films – were Operation MINCEMEAT and the involvement of the Mafia. The first of these was a plan to mislead the enemy about the true target for the Allied forces once the war for North Africa had been won, and played upon German uncertainties about the future moves of Anglo-American forces.

For the Germans, the difficulty lay in identifying the most likely course of action that the Allies might take. They had determined to keep the enemy as far away from Germany as possible, to the extent that they would fight to maintain control of Italy even if that country should collapse[10]. But precisely where the Anglo-Americans would strike was very uncertain. Hitler considered that Sardinia was most at risk, whereas Mussolini and Kesselring felt that it was Sicily. *OKW*, the German High Command, had concerns about Allied intentions in the Aegean and the Peloponnese, and expected that attacks here would coincide with, or shortly follow, operations in the western Mediterranean. While the Balkans might appear to be an unlikely choice for future Allied operations because of the unfavourable terrain, *OKW* considered that the strategic targets of minerals and Rumanian oilfields would be attractive. Allied deception plans worked to build on these worries.

MINCEMEAT[11], or 'The Man Who Never Was', was the deliberate planting of misinformation which indicated that the Allies intended to invade Sardinia, rather than Sicily. Such a plan was not only at one stage actively considered, it was feasible. As such, it was sufficiently credible as a strategy to tempt Axis intelligence into believing it. The problem was to find an effective and convincing way to present this information to the enemy, and this task was addressed by a branch of MI5 known as the XX

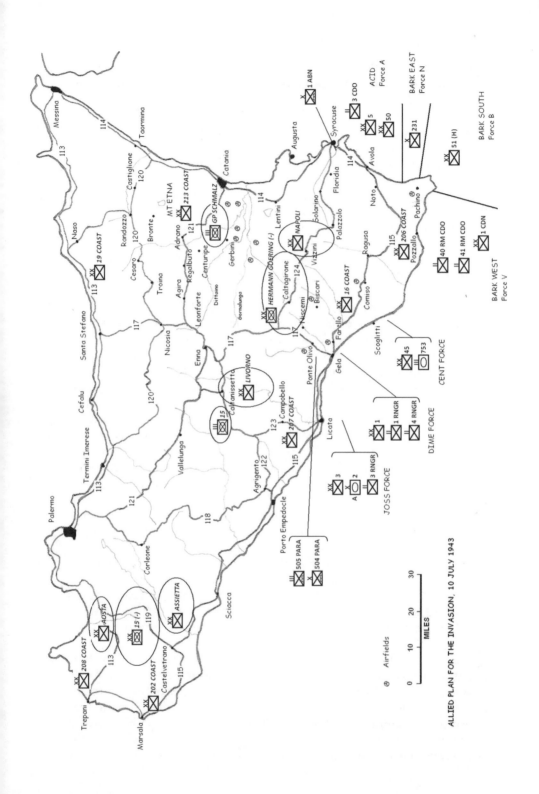

ALLIED PLAN FOR THE INVASION, 10 JULY 1943

(for double-cross) Committee, responsible for – amongst other things – deception. Two of the officers on this committee, Lieutenant Commander Ewen Montagu, RNVR, and Flight Lieutenant Charles Cholmondeley, RAF, conceived the idea of planting false information on the body of what would appear to be a Royal Marine major who had died when the aircraft in which he was travelling crashed into the Atlantic off the coast of Spain. 'Major William Martin', the *nom de guerre* of a man who had recently died of pneumonia in Great Britain, was equipped with a detailed false identity which included love letters and a photograph from his fiancée, suitably tattered to give the impression of having been carried about in a wallet. To add further veracity, there was a letter from Martin's bank manager, drawing attention to the parlous state of his bank balance, overdue bills, theatre tickets, and other items which painted a picture of a young officer in wartime. All of this was to add dressing to what was contained in the sealed briefcase handcuffed to his wrist. Here was to be found a letter from Lieutenant General Sir Archibald Nye, Vice Chief of the Imperial General Staff, to General Alexander, discussing an Allied invasion of Greece. As part of the deception plan for this strategy, the Allies would pretend to be preparing to invade Sicily – in other words, they wanted the Germans to believe that the preparations for HUSKY were a feint to cover the 'real' Greek operation. Letters were also included from Mountbatten, describing Martin as an expert in amphibious operations.

Martin's body was packed into a container of dry ice and loaded onto HMS *Seraph*, a submarine which carried him to the Spanish coast, off the town of Huelva, northwest of Cadiz. Here he was put into the sea to drift ashore with the tide, along with a capsized rubber raft. Huelva had been chosen because an *Abwehr* agent was known to be active in the region; and very useful he proved to be in furthering the deception. As MI5 had anticipated, within hours of Martin's body being washed ashore, the Spanish authorities presented it to British consular officials, but without the briefcase. The bait appeared to have been taken, but to ensure that it really had been swallowed, the British Naval Attaché built upon a series of urgent signals from London concerning the briefcase and its contents – which MI5 expected to be intercepted – by demanding its immediate return. It duly was, some two weeks after Martin's body had been washed ashore. Sent to London, tests soon confirmed that the case had been opened: the *Abwehr* agent had unwittingly carried out his part in the deceit.

To complete the sham, Martin was reported as missing in *The Times*, together with the crew and passengers of an aircraft that actually had been lost near the location and on the date that the plot had stipulated.

After the war, captured German documents revealed how successful MINCEMEAT had been. On 11 May Grand Admiral Dönitz and Hitler met and decided that Sardinia would be held with all available forces; an invasion of Sicily was considered less likely. Dated two days later, a German report stated that the Allies would apparently attack Sardinia, while landings on Sicily would be threatened as a feint.

MINCEMEAT's success has to be linked to another plan, codenamed BARCLAY, which indicated to the Germans that the Allies intended to launch a campaign in the Balkans once North Africa had been secured. This would be staged via Crete and the Peloponnese, and carried out by an entirely fictitious Twelfth Army Group which was supposedly eleven divisions strong. Following this operation, the Americans would land in Sardinia, Corsica, and the south of France. There were additional deception plans under an assortment of codenames ('CASCADE', portraying false Allied formations; 'ANIMALS', raids and reconnaissance carried out in the Balkans; and so on) which supported this fabrication. Dummy landing craft and aircraft were deployed, troops destined for Sicily were trained for Greece with appropriate maps, and Greek currency obtained for their use, and so on.

While the Italian *Comando Supremo* (High Command) did not fall for this deception, and remained convinced that the Allies' targets were Sicily or Sardinia, the Germans were more susceptible, and moved 1 *Panzer Division* from southern France to the Peloponnese. The Axis forces defending Sicily were not weakened to meet the supposed threat in the Balkans, but those that could be called upon to reinforce the island were.

Deception was only one aspect of the preparation for HUSKY. Gathering intelligence was an essential prerequisite of the operation, and this was not as straightforward as it was in other countries which the Allies were planning to invade. In France and northwest Europe the support of at least part of the population could be counted upon; here there was an understandable antipathy to the occupying German forces, and in many cases an active resistance which gnawed away at the enemy's strength and tied down troops in security duties when they might have been usefully occupied on the front line. Sicily was part of Italy, which was a hostile power, and no matter what individual Italians thought about the progress of the war and their support, or lack of it, for Mussolini, they were unlikely to provide practical assistance to an invader. It was true that there was a long-standing dislike of the German army amongst many Italian officers, and that the population was weary of the war. Morale was low, but the Allies could not yet expect active support in overthrowing Italy.

In a closed society such as was Sicily in 1943, strangers would have been immediately obvious, thus making it hazardous, if not impossible, to infiltrate agents onto the island. ULTRA, the decoding of German Enigma-generated messages, and signal intelligence – SIGINT – (the rather more mundane interception and analysis of other signals) gave some useful information, but even here this was less than might otherwise be the case because the Italians did not use Enigma, but relied heavily on book ciphers which proved to be less vulnerable to the code-breakers. ULTRA gave the Allies some insight into the strength and dispositions of German forces in Sicily, but information on the Italians had mainly to be gained through reading the letters from the island to Italian prisoners of war[12].

The US government reportedly approached this problem by enlisting the aid of a Mafia leader, 'Lucky' Luciano, who was serving a thirty-year sentence for compulsory prostitution in America. The story has attracted considerable attention, with some writers seeking to debunk it while others have given it their support. The tale, according to the supporters, is that Luciano was offered a deal whereby he would be paroled after the war on condition that he used his Mafia connections, both in America and Italy, to counter possible Axis infiltration of United States' waterfronts and counter their sabotage and espionage attempts, which could have fed information to the U-boats waiting in the Atlantic. That US Navy intelligence came to such an arrangement with Luciano was borne out by a post-war inquiry. More controversial, however, was the part (if any) that Luciano played in assisting Allied operations in Sicily and Italy.

The more imaginative stories include one that tells of signals being given to Sicilian Mafia leaders that the invasion had been given Luciano's blessing and that support should be given to American ground troops. In this version, an aircraft dropped a golden flag emblazoned with a black letter 'L' (for Luciano) on the town of Villalba as the Americans approached, whereupon the local Mafiosi arranged for resistance to melt away. The United States' successes in Sicily were supposedly greatly attributable to Mafia assistance, in return for which the organization was permitted to take control of the island after the hostilities had ceased. But whereas it is incontestable that Luciano was deported from America to Sicily in 1946 (despite his objections, on the ground that as an American citizen he could not be deported from his own country), and there is some evidence that he had been permitted to continue his criminal activities while in jail, it is also clear that much of the reason for the lack of enthusiasm displayed by many Italian troops had more to do with war-weariness and lack of commitment to Mussolini than it had to Mafia influence. Where the Italian-American community, Mafia members included, contributed to Allied intelligence about Sicily, it was more to do with passing on details of ports and harbours and the geographical background of the landscape. The Villalba incident proved to be no more than local legend; on the date that it reportedly occurred, US forces had already passed the town.

Of undisputed value to the planners was the work carried out by small groups of courageous men known as the Combined Operations Pilotage Parties. Officers and men from the Royal Navy and the Army (with a preponderance of Royal Engineers) made detailed reconnaissance of the beaches from submarine – as fast vessel-launched folboats – collapsible canoes – determining the location and strength of enemy defences, the slopes and nature of the beaches, hazards, and a multitude of other information essential to the planners who were selecting the best places to put the Allied forces ashore. By March, eleven of the thirty-one men involved in these operations had been lost; apart from the casualty rate, there was a fear that some may have been captured and that the enemy had discovered the nature and purpose of their work.

Operations preceding HUSKY

In planning for HUSKY, Force 141 had also to consider operations in areas other than Sicily itself, the success or failure of which might have an impact on the main event. Sicily had two outlying islands with Axis garrisons, which Allied commanders felt should be captured in preparation for HUSKY, despite the possibility that to do so would send a clear message to the enemy about future plans. Pantelleria lies 150 miles northwest of Malta, and was portrayed by the Italian propaganda machine as that nation's own Gibraltar. It was presumed to be the home of squadrons of Stuka bombers and fleets of E-boats, both protected in bomb-proof shelters and waiting for the opportunity to spring out at Allied shipping; but intelligence was unable to test this assumption, so a worse-case scenario was adopted. Despite the fear that an operation against Pantelleria might give the game away, Eisenhower himself made the decision that the island should be reduced. The task was given to the air forces, with the codename of Operation CORKSCREW.

In an offensive which started on 8 May, and continued intermittently until the island fell, the bombers pounded Pantelleria. The attack reached its crescendo during the period 6-11 June, when 5,324 tons of bombs were dropped in 3,712 bomber and fighter-bomber sorties. The main target area was no larger than eight square miles. Naval bombardments added to the defenders' misery, and when a landing party from the Coldstream Guards set foot on Pantelleria as the leading unit of 3 Infantry Brigade, the island's Italian commander promptly surrendered the 4,600 Italian and seventy-eight German troops of the garrison. Without supplies of water, which had been polluted by the bombing, he announced that he was unable to continue the resistance[13].

The second island to be captured before the launch of HUSKY was Lampedusa, to which the bombers and naval forces now turned their attention. It held out for twenty-four hours before surrendering to the crew of a Fleet Air Arm air-sea rescue Swordfish which had been forced to make an emergency landing on the island's airstrip. The only British casualty for CORKSCREW was a soldier bitten by a mule[14].

The fall of Pantelleria and Lampedusa was immediately hailed by the air forces as justification of their case for more resources to be devoted to the strategic bombing campaign against Germany. The air commander for the operation was Major General Spaatz, who – like the RAF's Air Marshal Harris – was a proponent of strategic bombing and who argued that air power alone could reduce an enemy to the point of surrender within six months. Even Eisenhower was beginning to ask whether such a strategy could be employed for HUSKY. The less supportive story that was produced by an Operational Research Team which examined the evidence and discovered that only sixteen of the 130 guns on the island had been destroyed or damaged by the bombers, that the underground hangers were untouched, and that the garrison had suffered less than 200 casualties with only thirty-five men killed, was brushed aside. In fact, CORKSCREW was an example of massive overkill.

Naval Planning

Operation HUSKY was the biggest landing of the Second World War. It was bigger than Normandy and any of the amphibious operations in the Pacific[15]. Some 3,200 ships and major landing craft, not to mention other vessels, were involved in the transport of 66,000 Americans, some from the United States, and 115,000 British troops from the Middle East, Tunisia and the United Kingdom, for the initial assault. About 400 tanks, 1,800 artillery pieces and 14,000 vehicles of various types and descriptions were to go with them, and follow-up troops and equipment would have to be carried as the operation progressed. That it was mounted at such comparatively short notice (the HUSKY planning only started in earnest five months before D-Day, whereas the Normandy landings had been on the drawing board for some fifteen months before 6 June 1944, and cross-Channel operations for considerably longer), with shipping converging on Sicily from ports in the Middle East, Tunisia, Algiers, Scotland, and the United States, all to arrive at their destinations at the same time, called for a degree of precision in the planning that leaves one wondering why railway timetabling today is evidently so much of a problem.

The HUSKY Naval Orders were issued by Admiral Cunningham on 20 May 1943. They had taken twenty typists seven days to produce the originals, from which 800 copies were then duplicated.

The Eastern Task Force, under Admiral Bertrand Ramsey, was responsible for the Eighth Army landings. Three Assault Groups - A, B and V – and a Support Force – K – were assembled, with the following tasks:

Force A (Rear Admiral Troubridge) was to transport XIII Corps from Middle Eastern ports to ACID North and ACID South Beaches between Cape Murro di Porco and Avola.

Force B (Rear Admiral McGrigor) was to carry 51st (Highland) Division from Tunisia to BARK South Beach at the south-eastern end of the Pachino peninsula, and 231 Infantry Brigade on the final stage of its journey to BARK East near Mazameni.

Force V (Rear Admiral Vian) was to bring 1st Canadian Division from the Clyde in Scotland directly to the western side of the Pachino peninsula.

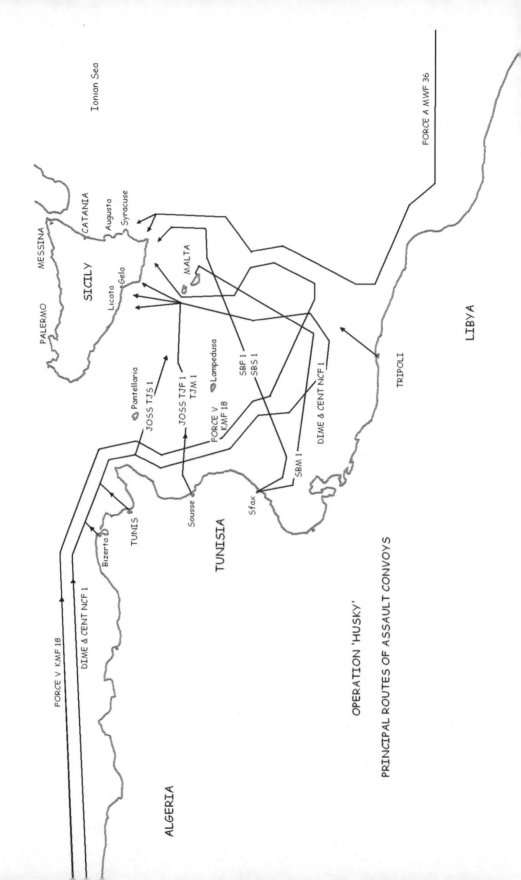

OPERATION 'HUSKY'

PRINCIPAL ROUTES OF ASSAULT CONVOYS

Force K (Rear Admiral Harcourt) was tasked with providing additional escorts to the assault convoys during the final approach to Sicily, and then – with extra support from monitors and gunboats – to provide bombardment groups for the Eighth Army beaches. Once this task was complete, Force K would protect the northern flank of the Task Force, taking over from Force Q (two cruisers and two destroyers) which had been detached from the main convoys. Force K consisted of four cruisers and six destroyers.

The Western Task Force, under Vice Admiral H Kent Hewitt USN, was responsible for the American beaches. It was split into three Assault Groups, named after the beaches on which Patton's Seventh Army was to land, and a Control Force.

CENT Force (Rear Admiral Kirk) was to carry 45th (US) Infantry Division from New York to Scoglitti, with a brief stop in Oran.

JOSS Force (Rear Admiral Connolly) was to transport 3th (US) Infantry Division and a Regimental Combat Team from 2nd (US) Armored Division from Tunisia to Licata.

DIME Force (Rear Admiral Hall) was to carry 1st (US) Infantry Division and the rest of 2nd (US) Armored Division from Algiers to the Gulf of Gaeta.

In addition to the above Forces, there was a main covering force (Force H), under the command of Vice Admiral Sir Algernon Wills, which included the British battleships HMS *Nelson*, *Warspite*, and *Valiant*, and the aircraft carriers *Formidable* and *Indomitable*. There were eight Fleet Air Arm squadrons of Seafire, Albacore and Martlet aircraft aboard the two carriers, a hundred in total. Apart from these, there were another two battleships (HMS *Howe* and HMS *King George V*, in Force Z, which was to provide cover for the eastbound convoys and to cause a distraction to the west of Sicily), fifteen British and American cruisers, seventy-one destroyers, twenty-three submarines, 319 major and 715 minor landing craft, and a host of other naval and merchant shipping. Thirty-one Belgian, Dutch, Greek, Norwegian and Polish ships were also present.

All of the foregoing makes the operation appear straightforward, if enormous. This is misleading. Each of the aforementioned Forces included both fast and slow convoys, depending upon the speed of the ships. With codes such as NCF and NCS, for North African ports to the CENT Beaches, fast and slow convoys respectively, the shipping had to depart their ports at dates staggered so as to ensure that they all arrived off their assigned Sicilian beaches at the same time. The first convoy left from America as early as 28 May 1943, en route for the North African assembly ports. NCS 1 left Oran on 4 July, sailing at eight knots, NCF 1 left Algiers two days later, sailing at thirteen knots. NCF 2 sailed, again from Algiers, three days afterwards (9 July). They were followed by NCS 2, NCS 3, and NCS 4, the follow-up convoys.

For the JOSS Beaches, convoy TJF 1 (Tunisia-JOSS-Fast) set out from

Bizerta on 5 July for Sousse, and from there on 9 July. With 106 Landing Craft Infantry, it steamed at 12½ knots. TJS left Tunis with 116 LCTs on 8 July.

From the United Kingdom convoys coded KMF 18 and 19, and KMS 18 and 19 ('K' for the United Kingdom) sailed from the Clyde, bringing 1st Canadian Division to BARK West. From the Middle East, MWF 36 and MWS 36 sailed from Port Said and Alexandria on the 5th and 3rd of July respectively.

This list is far from being exhaustive, but should give a flavour of the scope of the operation and of the complexity of the planning needed to bring it about. It was a tremendous piece of work.

The convoys were fortunate in their passages to the landing beaches. U-boats were active in both the Atlantic and the Mediterranean, but only succeeded in sinking the *City of Venice* and the *Saint Essylt*, from convoy KMS 18B (one of the Canadian convoys) off the coast of North Africa during the night of 4/5 June. The following day, the *Devis* was also sunk. Fifty-five Canadians were lost, together with 562 vehicles. Their absence during the days to come would present problems, especially for the Divisional Headquarters which had lost most of its transport. Convoy MWS 36 from Alexandria lost the *Shahjehan* off Derna. She, too, was loaded with transport. To give some balance to the score, escort ships for KMF 18, the fast Canadian convoy, sank a U-boat on 6 July.

Aboard the convoys, conditions for the troops were far from comfortable. Strict secrecy was enforced, and until the ships were on the final leg of their journeys only the most senior of the officers knew where they were headed. Although the troops were familiar with the photographs and models of the beaches, and the jobs they were to carry out once they went ashore, they did not know where these beaches were. To add to the overcrowding and monotony of the meals, the ships were 'dry', and offered no alcoholic refreshment to those that desired it.

The routine included physical training, despised at the time but valued later, and study of pamphlets on Sicily, which explained what to expect from the delights of the island and its inhabitants. Details of the geography, history, government, religion, industry, and so on were included, as were instructions on relationships between the soldiers and the civilian population. Amongst other details, town mayors and chiefs of police were to be impounded, and wine distilleries guarded. No hope of a drink there, then. Final briefings and weapon training helped fill the time.

The Air Element

The overriding aim of the Allied air forces was the destruction of enemy air power. To carry out this policy, there was a complicated command system, under the leadership of Air Chief Marshal Arthur Tedder. The senior American officer reporting to him was Major General Spaatz, who commanded the North-West African Air Force (NAAF), which included the North-West African Strategic Air Force (NASAF), of seventy-three squadrons, and the North-West African Tactical Air Force (NATAF), with a further forty-three squadrons. The latter came under Air Marshal Coningham and included the XII US Air Support Command, which was to provide direct air support for the Western Task Force. NAAF also included the North-West African Coastal Air Force (NACAF), with thirty squadrons, and the Malta Air Command, which was to provide fighter protection for all of the assault forces within fifty miles of Sicily, with its twenty-six squadrons. The Eastern Task Force was supported by the Western Desert Air Force (WDAF), which was based in the Tripoli area until airfields became available in Sicily. Further east was the Middle East Air Command (MEAC), which had a coastal force of sixteen squadrons for convoy protection, and an Air Defence Force of eighteen squadrons for fighter protection[16].

This apparently haphazard configuration of air resources gave Tedder the flexibility he required for forthcoming operations. Under his control he had strategic, tactical and coastal aircraft, but the system suffered insofar as the individual headquarters for each of these elements were widely dispersed across the southern Mediterranean. This was largely because the war in Tunisia did not come to an end until May.

The air plan had three phases. The first of these was to open as soon as the Tunisian campaign was over, and was to consist of a systematic bombing campaign of Axis airfields and Italian industry, with care being taken to spread the attacks so that no indication was given of a particular interest in Sicily. RAF bombers from the United Kingdom would mount missions against Italy and Germany, while those from the Middle East would attack targets on the Dodecanese and Aegean Islands. Strategic bombing missions would continue against airfields in Sicily, Sardinia and southern Italy until 3 July.

The second phase aimed to destroy enemy fighters and communications on Sicily and Sardinia during the week preceding the invasion, but coastal defences would remain untouched so as to maintain surprise.

The final phase was an all-out attack on enemy airfields, to be coordinated with the land force operations. D + 1 was considered to be the most dangerous for shipping approaching or lying off the beaches, because by that time it would be clear to the enemy where the main Allied thrusts were. Fighter aircraft would then have to be diverted from their offensive roles to concentrate on defending the fleet from enemy bombers. In broad terms, the North West Coastal Air Force would provide protection for ships from North African ports, while the Middle East Air Command would perform the same function for shipping from the Middle East. Day and night fighter cover would be provided off the landing beaches by aircraft based on Malta and Pantellaria, until such time as Sicilian airfields had been captured and taken into use[17].

The Land Forces

Planning was also carried out at divisional and lower formation levels, as the broad outlines of the scheme came down to the respective commanders. The plans became more specific and focused as the staff at these levels teased out the problems of ensuring that their men and equipments were landed in the right place and the right time to carry out the missions assigned to them. Like their counterparts in Force 141, they had to analyse intelligence and a complex mass of information in order to make sense of things and to produce workable solutions. Among the concerns were information, often incomplete, about new equipment that was being shipped to them for use in the invasion, but which had yet to be fully trialled and proved. Amongst this equipment were several types of landing ships and craft, which were essential for the operation.

As an example, the staff of 3rd (US) Infantry Division produced a plan which proved sound in practice, but which during its preparation was felt by many of the officers concerned to be unsatisfactory during its development. They had to struggle without the presence of an air liaison officer on the 'Joint Planning Board' which was established by the naval and military commanders of JOSS Force, Rear Admiral Connolly and Major General Truscott.

Intelligence was considered to be slow in coming, and scanty. While the British liaison officer with the division felt that it was mostly fairly accurate, his opinion was not shared by other officers in the Allied force assembling for HUSKY[18]. Obtaining accurate information about the island before the invasion was not one of the success stories. It was hard to understand, wrote this officer after the operation, why, when Corporal Hodgson from 2nd SAS Regiment who had been willingly assisted by the local Sicilian population to evade capture when he had become separated from his party, the Allies had not taken advantage of local sympathies to parachute reconnaissance groups onto the island.

Nor were the Allied air forces of great assistance. They were absorbed in their own planning, which had more to do with preparing a strategic bombing campaign than with providing aerial reconnaissance photographs for the ground and naval forces.

With information given in the second Operation Instruction the lower formation commanders could commence their detailed planning. As an example of the minutiae of detail, 231 Brigade's order of battle for D Day and D+3 included two Nomad Pigeon Lofts, manned by three men and equipped with two vehicles[19]. The number of pigeons is not recorded, but all of them, together with all the other brigade units and their manpower, weapons and equipment, had to be allocated space on the transport vessels, which were to move them Ship-to-Shore in the Middle East. Here arose another problem, for the planners did not necessarily know the numbers of personnel that could be accommodated on the various ships allocated to them. General Truscott's 3rd (US) Division had been given craft which none of his staff had seen before, including Landing Craft, Infantry, and the new Landing Ship Tank Mark II. As commander of JOSS Force, his division had been reinforced with many extra units, including Combat Command A of 2nd (US) Armored Division and additional artillery, and amounted to some 56,000 men and their equipment[20]. Although Truscott had personal experience of amphibious operations – he had been responsible for the training of US Rangers at the first British Commando School at Achnacarry, had served with British Combined Operations Headquarters and had been an observer at Dieppe – his staff, and those of the other divisions, had little more than the TORCH landings to go by, and HUSKY was a far different affair. The only existing doctrinal literature to assist them were British Combined Operations pamphlets[21].

Without Assault Scales or Light Scales of mechanical transport and equipment in existence to guide his headquarters in their planning, Truscott's staff had to create their own from scratch. Without these, the Order of Battle of the division and its associated units could not be put together, but there was little use in drawing up an Order of Battle before the Outline Plan was finalized. And the plan could not be determined without beach intelligence, which was thinner than required. It appeared that the shipping allocated to JOSS Force could only carry half the total assault force on D Day (although JOSS Force had a more generous amount assigned to it that the other American divisions because of its vital role in protecting the left flank of the invasion), but even this estimate could not be agreed until the draft Order of Battle had been produced. The task facing the headquarters seemed insoluble. Not helping their problem was the fact that the headquarters was initially situated in a forest of cork trees near Jemapps, which was more suited to jungle warfare training than to the Sicilian terrain, until the beginning of June (after they had produced the Full Outline Plan), when it moved to Bizerta to be with the naval headquarters. JOSS Force Headquarters was over 600 miles away from the Western Task Force Headquarters, a two and a half day journey, and all intelligence and other planning material had to make a thousand mile trip before it reached the users. This delay to effective communications meant that decisions had to be made even faster than might be expected if the tight deadlines for production of plans were to be met.

While Lieutenant Colonel Robert Henriques, the British JOSS team liaison officer from Combined Operations Headquarters, noted that naval-military relationships and cooperation were excellent, the same could not be said for relationships with the third service, the air force, which did not provide a representative at the JOSS Force headquarters throughout the whole planning process. Henriques[22] commented that the naval personnel could not have been more helpful, taking the view that their role was to assist the ground troops in whatever way they could, and they rarely turned down a request. This positive attitude was to pay dividends – the army came to realize that when the navy said that something simply could not be done, they meant it, and the judgement was accepted without further discussion.

The absence of an air force representative was particularly felt because of the paucity of air reconnaissance photographs of the proposed landing beaches; the airmen were too busy, apparently, using the aircraft equipped for this role in planning air force missions. The photographs that were available to the JOSS Force planners by the date on which the Outline Plans had to be firm, were small-scale and incomplete. Interpretations supplied by the Fifteenth Army Group were often substantially different from those made by the interpreter attached to JOSS Force, an able and experienced British officer seconded from the Eighth Army, whose reading of the evidence was invariably proved to be correct. The problem was resolved by General Truscott, who made private arrangements with 'influential friends' in the Air Corps to obtain the required photographs. Within a day of his request, 36-inch coverage of the fifteen mile stretch of coast of interest to JOSS Force was provided by RAF sorties flown from Malta at the request of the US Air Corps[23].

The isolationist attitude of the air forces was to continue: the air element of HUSKY was not communicated to the ground and naval forces, who did not know what 'softening' action had been taken against coastal targets as they set sail for the actual landings. American commentators ascribed this to the RAF's tradition of independence from the other two services, unlike the American concept of the air arm as having a support function as well as its own mission. With the British holding the appointment of C-in-C Air, the RAF position that air strength should not be parceled out to individual landings or sectors but kept under a single command to ensure the greatest flexibility, pertained; this was of small consolation to their earth-bound colleagues, however[24].

3rd Division, with Combat Command A of 2nd (US) Armored Division, was fortunate in its commander, whose background in combined operations was outlined above, but also in that these two formations had participated in TORCH, landing on a defended coastline against a foe who had elected to resist, and that they were based in North Africa. Other formations destined for HUSKY were less experienced, particularly those which were embarked from outside the Mediterranean – 45th (US) Infantry Division from the United States, and 1 Canadian Infantry Division from the United Kingdom. For these divisions, the loading sequence onto the transports for Sicily, which should ideally have been done so that they could be landed in the correct sequence for their committal to the battle for the beaches, had to be carried out ignorance of the final plans.

Training for the operation had also to be carried out, albeit incompletely while the plans were being finalized. For 3rd (US) Infantry Division, this was in part the desire of Truscott to ensure that all ranks were fully fit and capable of fighting effectively; he ensured that everyone, including clerks, cooks and drivers, was able to speed march at a rate twice that accepted as the norm for American infantry. It became known as the 'Truscott trot', and required everyone to be able to march at the rate of five miles per hour for the first hour, four miles per hour for the next two hours, and then three and one-half mph for the remainder of the thirty-mile march. By the time they landed in Sicily, 3rd Division was capable of rapidly moving on foot and fighting a battle at the end of the march, a quality that was to stand them, and their commanders, in good stead. As a finale to the training the division undertook a dress-rehearsal, Operation COPYBOOK, which was so realistic that most of those participating in it believed that HUSKY had actually started – until they found themselves back on North African beaches[25].

Amphibious training had also to be carried out, and for some of the British this was done in the Bay of Callo in Algeria, where the 5th Battalion of the Black Watch exercised with the Royal Naval Volunteer Reserve, officers from which organization were afterwards entertained, together with those from other battalions of 51st (Highland) Division, the American forces, and the Free French, to a fork supper enlivened by the Second-in-Command's ability to distil Algerian wine and use the resulting alcohol as the base for a fruit cup, which proved particularly popular with the American guests, and ensured that they did not easily forget a night with the Black Watch. The exercise was repeated later for a visiting group of dignitaries which included the Secretary of State for War, Sir James Grigg, and the Secretary of State for Air, Sir Archibald Sinclair, escorted by the Commander in Chief Middle East, General Sir Harold Alexander. The battalion was later moved eastwards round the tip of Tunisia to the Port of Sousse, some of them aboard an LCI commanded by Lt Cuffe, RNVR, who was better known to the theatre- and cinema-going public under his stage name of Alec Guinness. He was also to land some of 7th Battalion of the Black Watch on the Sicilian beaches during the assault[26].

50th Division had a greater distance to travel before it could rehearse for HUSKY. The division was returned to Egypt from Enfidaville in Tunisia to Sidi Bishr, near Alexandria, a distance of 1,300 miles. This was done by road, with short halts in Sfax and Tripoli, after which parties of officers went ahead to attend courses at the Combined Operations School, Kabrit. A four-day leave was enjoyed, in either Cairo or Alexandria, by the men of 151 Infantry Brigade (the Durham Light Infantry Brigade) before they, too, assembled at Kabrit for amphibious training. This was followed by a full scale invasion exercise in the Gulf of Akaba on the Red Sea, with the remainder of 5th and 50th Divisions, and an airborne brigade[27].

For those troops who had to journey from the United States and Britain, the major part of the training had to be undertaken before they set sail. 45th (US) Infantry Division trained in the Chesapeake Bay, and had a brief refresher once they arrived in the Mediterranean, at Arzew near Algiers. 1st Canadian Division had been well trained in the United

Kingdom, but its final rehearsal was cancelled as soon as it had begun because of bad weather. For some of the Commandos, exercises were carried out in great detail. A dummy battery was built at Suez, at precisely the right distance from the sea and reproducing as many of the Sicilian features as possible. Every man had committed to memory the number of paces from the beach to the assembly point, the compass bearings for each leg of the advance, and the details of how the objective was to be attacked.[28]

Without knowing the precise target, the land forces had probably done as much as they could to prepare for HUSKY.

1 Henriques.
2 Malony.
3 Morison.
4 Malony.
5 Montgomery – Memoirs.
6 Montgomery – Memoirs.
7 Malony.
8 D'Este – Bitter Victory.
9 Malony.
10 Malony.
11 Montagu.
12 D'Este – Bitter Victory.
13 D'Este – Bitter Victory.
14 Ambrose – The Supreme Commander, quoted in D'Este, Bitter Victory.
15 Morison.
16 Malony.
17 Malony.
18 Combined Operations HQ Bulletin No Y/1.
19 Henriques.
20 Taggert.
21 Henriques.
22 Henriques.
23 Combined Operations HQ Bulletin No Y/1.
24 Morison, Henriques and other sources make the same point.
25 Henriques
26 McGrigor
27 Barues
28 Durnford-Slater

CHAPTER FOUR

THE AXIS DECISIONS

W HILE THE ALLIES WERE CONSIDERING the strategy they would pursue after the North African campaign, the Axis powers had also to take decisions. The fall of their armies in Tunisia and the worsening situation on the Eastern Front put them on the defensive; they had lost the initiative – hopefully, for them, temporarily – and had to structure their strategy accordingly. In May the Germans had lost some 100,000 men in Africa, and apart from this blow to their strength the losses had contributed to a decline in the morale of their Italian allies. Italy had not been prepared, or equipped, for global warfare and had been led into it by the aspirations of Mussolini. Now they had lost their best divisions in Africa, Greece and Russia. Criticism was rising against Mussolini, especially in the army and among supporters of the monarchy.

This deterioration in Italian determination to continue the war had not passed unnoticed, naturally, in Germany. In May 1943 Hitler began to take steps to deal with any situation that might arise: the *Oberkommando der Wehrmacht* started to draft plans to take over the defence of Italy and the Balkans should the Italians falter, or worse, should they come to a separate ceasefire agreement with the Allies. They believed that the Allies were about to make further advances in the Mediterranean, and that the Italians could no longer be relied upon to play a worthwhile part in defending either Italy or the Balkans. To counter the Allies in these two locations the Germans had few resources close to hand. Those German forces currently in Italy were little more than a few thousand soldiers who had been destined for North Africa, but who were now without a role.

There were alternative courses of action which the Germans could take. Italy could be left unsupported, and thereby possibly – even probably – would fall to the Allies. This option would save Germany tying down troops there, which might be usefully employed elsewhere, for example against Russia. Or the Germans could elect to defend Italy at some geographical point that would protect the Po valley and the industrial and agricultural resources that would be of benefit to the Fatherland. To evacuate the whole of Italy, leaving it to the enemy, would allow the Allies to progress to Germany's southern borders, which would give them the ability to mount bombing raids on the homeland from that direction as well as from the United Kingdom. The Allies could also use northern Italy as a base from which to mount an invasion of southern France, and so strike at Germany by that route; not as direct, certainly, as mounting a cross-Channel landing, but as effective in the long term. There were other considerations if this course of action were to be selected: the Balkans and Hungary might regard a German willingness to surrender Italy as an indication that they might follow the Italian lead and opt for a separate ceasefire, and the strategy might be just the thing to bring Turkey off the fence and into the war on the Allied side. Hitler's instinct was to move into Italy and defend the whole territory.

Rommel was tasked with drawing up plans to carry out this strategy. He was to form a headquarters in Munich, and was provisionally allocated eight *panzer* or *panzer grenadier* divisions from the Eastern Front and France, and two parachute divisions to carry out the plan. A great deal of secrecy was observed, so much so that even Field Marshal Kesselring, C-in-C South, the German theatre commander, was not informed until planning was under way.

In June, the situation in Italy evidently seemed less threatening to Hitler, for he decided to use the panzer divisions in the east that had been earmarked for Rommel, to mount a limited offensive against the Russians. Without them, Rommel declared that the possibility of defending the whole of Italy was now out of the question, and the attention turned to developing plans for a limited alternative, holding a line north of Rome.

Meanwhile Kesselring was continuing his plans on the assumption that the Italians would hold firm. Working in agreement with Mussolini and the *Comando Supremo*, German forces had been built up independently of the Rommel plans, and two divisions had been sent to Sicily by the time of the Allied invasion there. A further *panzer grenadier* division was being formed in Sardinia, and two *panzer grenadier* divisions and a *panzer* division were transferred from France to central and southern Italy. In theory, these divisions were under the command of the *Comando Supremo*; in practice, they answered to Kesselring[1].

Kesselring may have been an optimist, and strongly pro-Italian, but he was not a fool. He recognized that the Italian navy and the Axis air forces were unlikely to be able to prevent Allied landings on Pantellaria, Sicily, or Sardinia; they were inactive or of diminishing strength. As far as land forces were concerned, the defence works on the islands and the mainland of Italy were mostly – in Kesselring's estimation – 'eyewash'. Plans had been made but not implemented. The coastal divisions manning these fortifications were of low standard, and 'with such troops in these defences it was hopeless to offer resistance'. Those on Corsica and Sardinia were the best, those on Sicily and the Calabrian coast left much to be desired.

Kesselring's analysis of the threat was as follows: the Allies had accumulated forces in Tunisia which indicated that they would pursue a Mediterranean policy – the question was where they would strike (he, of course, had no knowledge of the debate at Casablanca about whether there were to be any more Allied advances in this region). Sicily was one option, which led directly to the Italian mainland; this could be carried out in conjunction with a diversionary attack on Calabria. If, however, the Allied objective was a swift move to capture Rome, they would probably choose to attack Sardina and Corsica as a preliminary operation. The effect on Axis forces in Sicily and southern Italy, should Sardinia and Corsica fall, should not be underestimated. However, if these two islands were the objective, the Allies would have to worry about the threat to their flank from Sicily. Allied occupation of Corsica would provide them with an 'aircraft carrier' to support further moves against the south of France[2].

The Allies might, however, be considering a thrust in the eastern Mediterranean. They could reach the Balkans by pushing across the Italian mainland, but this would involve a landing on Italian soil, possibly via one of the islands such as Sicily. Although the Allies had little to fear at sea, Axis air forces on Crete, in the Peloponnese, around Athens and Salonika, could be reinforced and would present a defence in depth which would be difficult for the Allies to counter. Should the Allies succeed in getting a foothold in the Balkans and be able to mount an offensive in the rear of the Eastern Front to effect a link-up with the Russians, it would be both a military and political achievement with far-reaching repercussions.

Kesselring narrowed down these possibilities by considering previous Allied experience. The TORCH landings he thought to be no more than a peacetime exercise – there were no coastal defences to speak of, and the Allies' amphibious capabilities had neither been tested nor practised against opposition. They would probably only embark upon a course of action in which the odds for success were overwhelming, and their reliance on overpowering air-power meant that they would limit their operations to areas within fighter range of fixed bases, because they did not have sufficient carriers to provide enough cover beyond this distance. These calculations ruled out the south of France, northern Italy or the Balkans, at least as a direct strike without crossing the Italian mainland first. The distances involved pointed to Sicily as the most likely target, but by-passing the island and going for Sardinia and Corsica as a prelude to a strike on Rome could not be completely ruled out. An attack on Calabria was also possible.

The threat to the Balkans was still at the front of many minds in Germany, however, and this fact meant that Kesselring's attempts to organize the defence of Italy had competition. As late as 17 July Hitler told Admiral Dönitz that the next Allied move – after Sicily – would be expected there: 'it is as important to reinforce the Balkans as it is to hold Italy.'

As for dealing with the threat of Allied landings, the Axis forces, like the Allies, had little experience of organizing and fighting from shore defences – apart, of course, from Dieppe. They, too, had little to learn from TORCH. The Allies would be vulnerable during the sea crossing, from naval and air forces, including U-Boats and bombers, and the static coastal fortifications had to be built up, particularly in the areas Kesselring considered vulnerable. He had German construction engineers and troops sent to instruct the Italians in the latest techniques, and building material was assembled. Fresh German divisions were made up from those troops already in Italy and sent to Sicily: *15th Panzer Grenadier Division* and the *Hermann Göring Panzer Division*, the former taking its title from a division that had been lost in Tunisia, the latter from elements of the division which had not been sent to North Africa before the German collapse. Italian divisions were provided with weapons and equipment to boost their capabilities, and supply dumps were prepositioned so that Allied strikes against communications would have limited effect.

The Germans expected that the fall of Tunis would quickly be followed by landings in one of the anticipated locations; each day of delay served to give them breathing space in which to build up their defences, but these would never be sufficient to give confidence. In Sicily, for example, Kesselring was of the opinion that the Allies could not carry out a *coup de main* – a swift surprise operation that would secure them the island – but they could not be prevented from establishing a landing with a large-scale set-piece planned invasion.

With General Guzzoni, the Commander-in-Chief of the Italian *Sixth Army*, and the unit commanders based on the island, Kesselring worked out plans to defend Sicily. He left after the conference reassured by the bullish attitude displayed by General Conrath of the *Hermann Göring Panzer Division*, who showed a confidence and aggressiveness that appeared to be absent in some of the Italian officers.

On Sicily, by the time of the invasion, General Fridolin von Senger und Etterlin was the senior ranking German officer. Officially, he was subordinate on the island to Guzzoni, but he had been withdrawn from his position of the commander of *17th Panzer Division* on the Eastern Front by Hitler to take up this appointment as liaison officer. Hitler, together with Field Marshal Keitel and General Warlimont, had briefed von Senger on 22 June. They had made clear their scepticism about the firmness of the Italians and the problems of holding Sicily with only two German divisions, and it was readily apparent that they expected the defection of Italy in the not-too-distant future[3].

Three days later von Senger was in Rome, where he received a different picture from the optimistic Kesselring. von Senger found the Field Marshal over-impressed by the ease with which the Dieppe landing had been repulsed; furthermore, he had not grasped the fact (in von Senger's opinion) that the North African landings, while not likely to provide a blueprint for future similar operations because they had not been opposed, demonstrated that the war had entered a new phase in which the Allies had the advantages of surprise and superior mobility.

Kesselring had, however – again in von Senger's view – a more realistic approach towards working with the Italians. Regardless of what they might do if and when the Allies landed in Sicily, the Germans had little option but to work with, rather than against, them. The Italians had supremacy of command on the island, in line with the agreement between the German and Italian governments that the defence of the mainland and the offshore islands was to be under the sole command of the Italians. While von Senger may have had reservations about Kesselring's sunny view of conditions, he was reassured about his own role in Sicily.

Von Senger was less impressed, however, with the position taken by the *Luftwaffe*. Field Marshal von Richthofen, C-in-C of *Luftflotte 2*, was persuaded that the Allies' next objective would be Sardinia, and he had concentrated most of the air strength there rather than Sicily. His opinion was supported by Marshal Badoglio who held that Sardinia would have been the operationally more correct choice. It appeared that the German Air Force, like those of the Allies, preferred to fight its own war rather than work in coordination with the other services[4].

The defenders of Sicily, the Italian *Sixth Army*, comprised five immobile coastal divisions and two brigades which were deployed in the inadequate defences, mostly concentrated around the principal ports. A large number of the soldiers in these divisions were Sicilian, living close to their families, and many of them were elderly men. In addition, Guzzoni had four mobile Italian divisions. The Italian *XVI Corps* was in the east, with two divisions, the *4th Livorno* and the *54th Napoli*; and in the west was *XII Corps* with the other two, the *26th Assietta* and the *28th Aosta*. Equipment was mostly antiquated, and horse-drawn transport was common. The Italians had *Mobile Groups* able to deploy as required, but equipped with obsolescent tanks, and *Tactical Groups* which were usually based on *Bersaglieri* or *Blackshirt Militia Companies*. Additionally, of course, there were the two German divisions, each of which Guzzoni considered to have half of the fighting power of an Allied division; the Italian mobile divisions he thought to be only a quarter of the strength of an Allied division.

In addition to these formations, von Senger had been informed in Germany that at his disposal were about 30,000 men from the *Luftwaffe* ground organization, and from supply units and administrative depots. These he was supposed to organize into 'alarm' units, but without transport they would be of limited use. The anti-aircraft units would be employed as the mainstay of fixed defence locations, and von Senger appointed their *Luftwaffe* commanders as 'battle commanders' for their districts, with the 'alarm' units of the army subordinated to them. In practice, therefore, the 30,000 men provided static forces, with very limited capability when it came to being deployed against an invader.

Communications were another problem which beset von Senger. He had no reliable radio nor land-line link between the *Sixth Army* Headquarters in Enna and Kesselring in Rome apart from the *Luftwaffe's* telephone line, which ran along the coast and by cable across the Straits of Messina. His links to the divisions were land-line and one radio station, far from ideal when the divisions were expected to be mobile. To command these formations effectively, he needed a corps headquarters, instead of which he had one staff officer and no signals unit of his own.

The disposition of German troops on Sicily was agreed between Guzzoni and Kesselring. Once again, relations between allies resulted in compromise, for both realized that the defence of Italy was in the hands of both nations, Italy and Germany. Neither was powerful enough to achieve it independently. Having to rely on each other forced them into arrangements that neither was entirely happy with, and the positioning of the Sicilian formations was one such example. Guzzoni believed that the two German divisions, on which he relied heavily, should be kept on the eastern side of Sicily as a mobile reserve, which would support the weaker *Livorno* and *Napoli* divisions.

The Italians would fight a delaying action against the invaders while the Germans were held ready to counterattack when and where the most favourable opportunity arose. This concept ran contrary to the German doctrine that the Allies should be hit at the moment of their greatest weakness, when their forces were still in their landing craft.

The argument against this strategy was that, if located close to the coast, the German divisions would be vulnerable to the overwhelming firepower of the fleet, a threat which they were not equipped to counter because of the weaknesses in the Axis naval and air strengths.

The second objection to Guzzoni's preference was that the Germans would be held in concentration areas well inland, in the district of Caltanissetta. Here the narrow mountain roads would make it difficult to deploy, and without effective fighter cover they would be subject to Allied air strikes, meaning that any movement would have to be restricted to the hours of darkness. The choice was a difficult one to make. The alternatives were a static, coastal-based defence which would probably be wiped out by the naval and air bombardment; or the retention of a reserve, which would be too weak to defeat an invader which was well-established ashore.

The same difficult choice would face the Germans in Normandy, the following year: commit the strength to the beaches (which might well turn out to be the wrong ones) and risk being annihilated there; or to keep it back ready to deploy as situations dictated, but risk having it destroyed by Allied airpower as it moved forward[5].

Kesselring's compromise was to station one German division in the west and the other in the east of Sicily, to act as strong mobile reserves and to cover the possibilities of landings on either side of the island. *15th*

Panzer Grenadier Division was to go to the Salemi district, the *Hermann Göring* to near Caltagirone. His reasons for this move were that he wanted to prevent the divisions from being cut off from Messina should the Allies land in overwhelming strength in the southeast. By separating them, each could act as reserve for the other, and that the *Hermann Göring*, more powerful in armour, would be better suited to the ground in the east. Guzzoni, von Senger, and General Roth, the commander of *15th Panzer Grenadier Division*, felt that the decision to move this division was wrong, and von Senger reported that Kesselring himself was unhappy about it. Von Senger's reservations included his belief that *15th Panzer*, having been on Sicily for a longer time than the *Hermann Göring* was more familiar with the southeast of the island.

It was also the stronger of the two divisions, having three infantry regiments, each of three battalions, whereas the *Hermann Göring* had only three battalions of infantry in total. The latter formation did, however, have an armoured regiment, with ninety-nine serviceable tanks (including thirteen Tigers) and assault guns, compared to the sixty-odd PZKW III and IV tanks in *15th Panzer Grenadier*.

On the debit side, some of the *Hermann Göring* officers were not of high quality. The infantry regimental commander was removed from his post by General Conrath, the divisional commander, and the armoured regiment commander was sacked on the orders of von Senger immediately after the fighting had started. The division was overrated, particularly by the Italians, possibly because of the parachute cachet.

On 10 July the composition of the *Sixth Army* was broadly as follows:

XII Corps, commanded by General Mario Arisio:
Aosta Division
Assietta Division
202, 207, and 208 Coastal Divisions
Three Mobile Groups
Four Tactical Groups
Two-thirds of *15th Panzer Grenadier Division*

XVI Corps, commanded by General Carlo Rossi:
Napoli Division
Livorno Division
206 and 213 Coastal Divisions
18th and 19th Coastal Brigades
Five Mobile Groups
Four Tactical Groups
Hermann Göring Panzer Division
One-third of *15th Panzer Grenadier Division*

In addition, there were the 'Alarm Units' formed from the German Army and *Luftwaffe*.

1 Mavrogordato
2 Kesselring
3 Von Senger
4 Ibid
5 Ibid

CHAPTER FIVE

THE AIRBORNE LANDINGS

The first part of the Allied air attack was completed by 1 July, and for the following nine days the Air Forces' attention turned to the forthcoming battlefield. Bombers attacked the Sicilian airfields, especially those around Gerbini, where the *Luftwaffe* had concentrated its fighters. After assaults by heavy, medium and light Allied bombers – American by day and Wellingtons of 205 Group RAF by night – seven of the Gerbini landing grounds, together with those at Comiso, Bocca di Falco and Castelvetrano, were out of action. Despite enemy resistance, for example on 5 July when a hundred or so German fighters engaged the American Flying Fortresses, the missions achieved their objectives, for when D Day came the *Luftwaffe* was incapable of operating effectively enough to make a serious impact on the landings. During this nine-day period, the attacks on communications were reduced; but seventy five Wellington sorties were flown against Palermo and twenty six against Catania[1].

This preparatory phase ended on 9 July, and during the afternoon of that day the convoys began to arrive in their assembly areas south of Malta. Some 2,000 vessels of all descriptions converged under an air umbrella from the Northwest African Coastal Air Force reinforced by Beaufighter squadrons, and by fighters controlled by Air Headquarters, Air Defences Eastern Mediterranean. Nearly 3,000 sorties were flown by these aircraft in two days, which prevented the enemy from doing more than dropping a few bombs on Bizerta harbour during the night of 6 July.

During the night of 9 July, the largest concentration of air power ever assembled in the Mediterranean commenced operations in support of the landings. From Malta Mosquitos flew on intruder patrols over enemy air bases in Sicily and southern Italy. More Mosquitos and Beaufighters flew patrols over the landing beaches, some being controlled by Ground Controlled Interception stations based on ships of the assault armada. Sicily was partitioned by night bombers, with Wellingtons flying sorties against Caltagirone airfield and communications targets at Catania and Syracuse; Mitchell bombers flew against Biscari airfield and also against communications; Liberators against the Avola-Noto area; Bostons and Baltimores against Milo and Sciacca airfields, and communications around Niscemi.

On D Day itself Fortresses bombed the Gerbini airfields, and Mitchells attacked the airfields at Sciacca and Milo, the marshalling yards at Catania and communications around Palazzolo. Liberators flew sorties against the

Italian landing ground at Vibo Valentia in Italy. Fighter-bombers were in action supporting the landings: American Mustangs dive-bombed targets including communications and defensive positions at Caltanissetta, Agrigento, Vallelunga. Their biggest strike, with 111 of the 152 sorties that they flew that day, was in the Barrafranca area. Lightnings bombed communications around Grammichele[2].

From ten minutes after first light, the beaches had fighter cover. Five Malta-based Spitfire squadrons were allocated to each of the Avola, Pachino peninsula and Scoglitti areas. American Spitfires based on Gozo covered Gela, and Licata had a group of American Kittihawks, flown from Pantelleria. As a reserve, five additional Spitfire squadrons were standing by on Malta. On D Day Allied fighters flew 1,092 sorties over the beaches and the shipping anchored offshore. Other sorties were flown to protect the bombers, on offensive sweeps over Sicily, and to provide cover for shipping in the open sea.

The air cover, comprehensive as it might appear, was not sufficient to stop every enemy attack. With the Allies spread across great areas of coastline and sea, the screen of defensive measures was too thin. Axis aircraft managed to sink the hospital ship *Talamba* off the British beaches, and two ships off the American beaches. At Licata and Gela, they broke through to attack ground troops; here, the anti-aircraft gunners were particularly nervous and persistently fired on Allied aircraft, a distraction the pilots did not need when they were supposed to be watching for the enemy. Elsewhere, American fighters made one interception of the enemy, and the Malta-based Spitfires reported meeting fifty-seven enemy aircraft. No 229 Squadron claimed three Italian Mc 200s[3]. It would appear that only about one hundred Axis planes were in action during the day. Whatever criticism of the Allied Air Forces during the days before the landings, in failing to provide photographic reconnaissance and being rather uncommunicative with the other services, they kept the landing areas mostly clear of the *Luftwaffe* and the *Regia Aeronautica*.

Everything was set for the landings, but as the convoys began to sail northwards the wind rose and the sea became rough. This did not augur well for the operation, which called for this vast number of ships to assemble and discharge their cargos onto the beaches in the hours of darkness, but it was too late to call a halt to events. The fleet sailed onwards as the weather worsened.

The invasion convoys were not the only Allied shipping moving across the Mediterranean that night. To contribute to enemy uncertainty and confusion, the Royal Navy was active in the Ionian Sea to give further credence to the 'Major Martin' deception of a landing in the Peloponnese. And off Cape Granitola PT 213, an American torpedo-boat, with a group of ten air-sea rescue launches were tasked with providing the enemy with evidence that the landings in western Sicily were still scheduled – just in case they had got wind of the earlier invasion plans. In the event the latter deception, which was to be carried out by the 'Beach Jumpers' (the nickname given to a small flotilla whose role was 'To assist and support the operating forces in the conduct of Tactical Cover and Deception in Naval Warfare') was ineffective. The group was the brainchild of Lieutenant Douglas Fairbanks Junior, who had served with Mountbatten in England. Its intent was to give the illusion of a landing force assembling off the coast, by sending false radio messages, making visible signals including rockets, and broadcasting – by means of gramophone records – the sound of anchor chains rattling and landing craft being lowered into the water. The bad weather caused the mission to be delayed until the following night, 10-11 July, but it failed to impress the enemy[4].

Above the convoys heading towards Sicily the aircraft towing the gliders of 1 Airlanding Brigade were assembling for their part in the plan. If the rising winds were of concern to the sailors, they were no less so to the airmen and their passengers, for airborne operations are extremely vulnerable to such conditions. Observing them passing overhead from his vantage point on Cape Delimara, the southeastern point of Malta, was General Alexander, who had established a Fifteenth Army Group Tactical Headquarters on the island for the invasion.

The 1 Airlanding Brigade, of the British 1st Airborne Division, was to land in gliders near Syracuse. Its mission was to seize Ponte Grande, the bridge over the River Anapo and the canal which ran parallel to it, and to capture part of the city, including the railway station and some factory buildings which lay to the south of the city's seaplane base. The bridge had to be captured intact, to allow the seaborne forces which were to come ashore to the south quick access to the city and its vital port facilities.

The 2,075 men of the Brigade flew in 147 gliders, British-built Horsas (carrying thirty men) and the American Waco (known as the Hadrian to the British, and carrying fourteen). Most of the tug aircraft were American-piloted Dakotas from the Northwest Africa Troop Carrier Command, but the remainder were twenty-eight Albemarles and seven Halifaxes of No 38 Wing, RAF[5]. The Troop Carrier Command had also to deliver parachutists of 82nd (US) Airborne Division to their drop zones near Gela and Licata.

Taking off from six airfields near Kairouan, the gliders were escorted by a squadron of cannon-equipped Hurricanes, whose role was to fire on enemy searchlights, and specially-equipped aircraft were to attempt to confuse the radar stations en route to the Landing Zones. Wellingtons were to provide a diversion by attacking Syracuse, Catania, Caltagirone and Caltanissetta, and were also to drop a number of dummy parachutists to add to the enemy's confusion.

The glider-borne troops of the 1st Battalion The Border Regiment, and 2nd Battalion The South Staffordshire Regiment, together with 9th Field

Company Royal Engineers, had set out with six jeep-towed, 6-pounder anti-tank guns. They were accompanied by Gunner officers and Naval telegraphists who were to provide forward observation for the guns on the cruiser HMS *Newfoundland* and the monitor HMS *Eribus*, which had been assigned to the brigade as support for the operation.

As the aircraft flew over the convoys near Cape Passero, some anti-aircraft gunners on merchant vessels opened fire on them, mistaking them for the enemy. This incident, together with the gusting winds and the difficulties of estimating distances by moonlight, particularly when approaching a coastline, caused several of the pilots to release their gliders early. Of the gliders which had left Tunisia, sixty-nine landed in the sea, resulting in 252 of their passengers being drowned. About fifty-nine gliders landed at various points along the coast between Cape Passero and Cape Murro di Porco, two were shot down by ground fire and ten were forced to turn back to Tunisia. Only twelve descended onto their appointed Landing Zones. One was within 300 yards of the Ponte Grande bridge.

The disaster was nearly the death of the mission. Many gliders released over the sea were unable to maintain their airspeed and to reach the comparative safety of land. Some had to ditch because they were unable to gain sufficient height to clear the cliffs of Cape Murro di Porco; others failed to get closer than three or four miles to land. Injured or trapped inside the sinking gliders, many men drowned without hope of rescue. Not for nothing were the gliders dubbed 'flying coffins' by the men of the Airlanding Brigade.

Off the Sicilian coast, and in the harbour south of Syracuse, gliders littered the water with survivors clutching their wings. The more fortunate of them were rescued by naval vessels, but many were less lucky. Ashore, the gliders that had made it to land had encountered the stone-walled, boulder-strewn fields, and most of their passengers found themselves in unfamiliar territory, in some cases many miles from their expected destinations.

There were examples of black humour recorded during this tragedy. One glider landed intact, whereupon the men disembarked and prepared to move off towards their objective, only to find that they were, in fact, on the main airstrip on Malta, and blocking the runway – much to the annoyance of the ground crew who were trying to launch fighter aircraft. Another instance concerned the survivors of a glider who found themselves in the sea alongside an anchored cruiser. They climbed up the anchor chain but found the decks deserted, until a startled sailor suddenly appeared, intending to throw a bucket of slops over the side. He shouted to his shipmates for help, a cry which produced reinforcements who started to beat the unfortunate soldiers into a pulp before they were able to convince the Navy that they were, in fact, British troops[6].

Near the Ponte Grande bridge, Lieutenant Louis Withers and twenty-six men of the South Staffordshire Regiment had landed in the correct place. Unable to find the Landing Zone until an Italian searchlight illuminated it, the pilot put his Horsa down accurately. Withers soon realized that his group was alone and that he had to take on the task with the limited resources at hand, and proceeded to get on with things. He was joined by a Royal Engineer officer who managed to remove the demolition charges fixed to the bridge while Withers swam the canal and attacked the pillbox which defended its northern end. The defenders, from *121st Coastal Infantry Regiment*, carried out a running battle with the Staffords for several hours. The sounds of battle drew other troops to the area: by dawn, there were some eighty-seven men defending the bridge from the Border and Staffordshire Regiments, the Royal Engineers, and the Glider Pilot Regiment, all of whom had gradually assembled at their objective[7]. Among them was one American, one of a number of US officers who had volunteered to join the mission as glider pilots.

At about 0800 hours an Italian officer, evidently unaware that the bridge was in British hands, arrived in a staff car and demanded that the barrier be raised. His car was immediately riddled by small arms fire and the prisoners were shut up in the pillbox on the bridge – where they were killed shortly afterwards by fire from an Italian force sent to recapture the bridge. The first to arrive were two companies of sailors, and then at about 1130 hours a battalion of *75th Infantry Regiment*. With four armoured cars and mortars, and supported by a field gun located 300 yards away, Italian troops tried for seven hours to dislodge the British. At about 1530 hours the survivors, now down to fifteen men and out of ammunition, threw their weapons into the river and surrendered. They were not long in captivity, however, for as they were being marched off towards Syracuse they were rescued by a patrol from the 2nd Battalion, The Northamptonshire Regiment. The Italians had regained the Ponte Grande for no more than thirty minutes when they lost it again, this time to the 5th Battalion of the Royal Scots Fusiliers, the advance guard of 5th Division which had landed to the south[8].

The remainder of the Air Landing Brigade, though widely scattered, created much alarm and despondency among the Italians. The enemy reported airborne landings – which were both British and American – all over the southeast of the island: Priolo was 'infested' by them; they were seen on Cape Passero, at Ragusa, Comiso, Caltagirone and Castelvetrano; and there were 'thousands' at Gela. Small groups of glider-borne troops succeeded in seizing a radio station on Cape Murro di Porco – but only after its occupants had been able to send news of their arrival – and Colonel OL Jones, the Deputy Commander of the Airlanding Brigade, led a group from the Brigade Headquarters – including the Padre – which overwhelmed the garrison of a coastal battery at Caderini Point in

Syracuse harbour and blew up its weapons and an ammunition dump. Jones later decided to capture a nearby villa, out of which emerged an attractive American girl whose Italian husband was hiding in the cellar. She invited him to lunch and suggested that he bring a friend, which he duly did, riding to the rendezvous on a fire engine of 1900-vintage, which had been commandeered to tow a 6-pounder anti-tank gun. With sentries posted, Jones and Colonel Chatterton lunched with the American on spaghetti, washed down with Chianti, while the sounds of battle gradually lessened in the distance. There appeared to be occasions when dealing with the enemy could wait for the finer things in life[9].

The 82nd (US) Airborne Division which was to drop in the Gela-Licata area had a similar experience of having its aircraft scattered because of the combination of friendly and enemy anti-aircraft fire, wind and navigational problems. The paratroops were widely dispersed over an area of some fifty square miles and as a result were unable to seize their objective – the high ground overlooking Gela. The 505th Parachute Infantry Regimental Combat Team, reinforced with an extra battalion and artillery and engineers, was given the task of landing north and east of Gela during the night of D-1 to D Day to disrupt communications and any move of enemy reinforcements. Once 1st (US) Infantry Division had landed, the paratroops would come under its command and would then assist in capturing the landing field at Ponte Olivo[10].

The designated Drop Zone for the Regimental Headquarters and 1st and 2nd Battalions, together with two artillery batteries from 456th Parachute Artillery Battalion, was just north of a road junction seven miles east of Gela. The 3rd Parachute Infantry Battalion and the 3rd Battery of artillery would drop south of the same junction and occupy the high ground overlooking it. The 3rd Battalion of 504th Parachute Infantry Regiment would drop south of Nisceme and establish road blocks on the road that ran south from that town. Commanding the operation was Colonel James M Gavin. The Divisional Commander, Major General Matthew Ridgway, was to travel to Sicily aboard the *Monrovia*, the Seventh Army command vessel, with a party of his headquarters officers, and disembark at Gela on D Day.

Between 2010 and 2116 hours on 9 July, D-1, the parachutists took off from ten airfields near Kairouan in a fleet of 226 C-47 (Dakota) aircraft[11]. The route took them to Malta and thence to the Sicilian coast east of Gela, with an expected flight time of three hours and twenty minutes. Although the wind diminished as the evening progressed, it was still sufficiently gusty to make many men airsick, as well as scattering the aircraft. As night fell after 2130 hours, the darkness and the absence of communications between the aircraft, together with the low flying required for tactical purposes, made keeping formation even more difficult. Tracer fire from below – again from Allied merchant ships – added to the problem, and some pilots missed the navigational aids on Malta altogether. The aircraft approached Sicily from all directions. As pilots searched for the DZs, parachutists stood and hooked up to their static lines ready to jump. For some, there was then an interminable wait of thirty to fifty minutes before they leapt from their aircraft, buffeted and thrown about as the pilots attempted to avoid flak and to find their correct positions.

With their formations broken, most of the pilots missed the DZs and the paratroops were dropped all over the coastal strip from the area of Gela to Syracuse. Only twenty-six aircraft dropped their loads, an equivalent of three companies, on or near their objective. Eight aircraft failed to return to their bases, but the parachutists managed to jump before the planes crashed. Three aircraft turned back without dropping their loads; all of the men concerned were cleared of responsibility for their failure to jump, and participated in the second lift, which flew during the evening of D+1[12].

The only subunit of the 505th Combat Team which landed on its assigned DZ was Company I, and even here one aircraft-load was missing. The company carried out its tasks of taking out a blockhouse and several pillboxes, and took a great many prisoners.

Most men found themselves alone or near only a few of their comrades, and generally they set out to find others. While the majority only succeeded in assembling themselves in groups of platoon strength or less, almost the whole of 2nd Battalion had formed together within twelve hours of landing. Colonel Gavin was dropped some ten miles south of Vittoria, thirty miles from his correct position, and did not rejoin his command until the following day. Others were dropped as much as sixty miles off course. These groups, penny-packets spread all over the countryside though they might have been, began to attack whatever targets made themselves available. They attacked enemy patrols and positions as they encountered them, laid ambushes, cut telegraph wires, and tore up railway track.

An example of such actions was that fought by two aircraft loads of B Company, 307th Airborne Engineer Battalion, which landed fifteen miles northeast of their DZ. They were joined by one stick from A Company of the 505th, and spent the night searching for the DZ and cutting telephone lines. Just before dawn they dug in near a crossroads. A German motorcycle combination with three passengers arrived there at 0530 hours, and the Germans were shot and killed. A second motorcycle drove up fifteen minutes later, and the event was repeated. The parachutists then moved off to the DZ and made contact with G Company. That afternoon infantry from 45th (US) Division arrived, and the paratroops attached themselves to this unit for the next two days[13].

Another paratrooper recorded that his aircraft ran into anti-aircraft fire as it crossed the coast, which forced the pilot to dive and bank. The paratroops had got to their feet to hook up, and had just been given the order to jump, when the plane was hit. Although the men were thrown about, they managed to exit, and landed near two pillboxes which were burning from the bombing raid which preceded the drop. The paratroops began to assemble in an orchard, when artillery rounds began to land amongst them. The enemy fire soon stopped, and the group, having left one man who had suffered a broken leg wrapped in a parachute hidden in a patch of vines, set out to find its DZ. As they approached a bridge they ran into Germans who fired upon them, causing the group to disperse. Eventually he and one other linked up with men from 1st (US) Division.

A bloodless victory was achieved by 1st Lieutenant Thomas, who was being given a meal by friendly civilians after he and several men had landed. They were surprised and taken prisoner by German soldiers, who had three disabled tanks and one severely wounded man nearby, who was in need of medical attention. Thomas negotiated his party's release, pointing out the inevitability of an Allied victory and giving a promise that the wounded German would receive the best of American medical treatment. The remainder of the Germans agreed to this suggestion, put their tanks out of commission and retired[14].

1 Malony.
2 Malony.
3 Ibid.
4 Morison.
5 Malony.
6 The Border Magazine, Sept 1954, quoted in D'Este – Bitter Victory.
7 Malony.
8 Ibid.
9 D'Este – Bitter Victory.
10 US Army – 82 AB Division Report.
11 Ibid.
12 Ibid.
13 Ibid.
14 Ibid.

CHAPTER SIX

THE LANDINGS FROM THE SEA

THE NAVY'S TASK OF LANDING the Army units at the right place and at the right time was not an easy one. It was made considerably more difficult by the weather that had blown up before the landings were to have taken place. As outlined earlier, the invasion convoys were converging on Sicily from several directions and at varying speeds. The weather conspired to throw the plans and calculations awry, and Task Force commanders had to adjust their orders accordingly.

Although fair on the morning of 9 July, the wind rose slightly by midday. The convoys of the Eastern Task Force were in their correct assembly stations south of Malta, where during the afternoon and evening the wind increased steadily from the northwest to Force 6. By 1800 hours a nasty sea was running, which tossed the ships about and caused a great deal of discomfort to the embarked troops, crammed below decks. A lance corporal of the Black Watch was reported to have died from seasickness, his internal organs ruptured by continuous vomiting.

With the weather so unfavourable, many of the smaller craft were delayed in reaching their landing beaches. Despite the fact that the wind and the sea began to settle down after midnight, the journey to Sicily was an unpleasant one; although the Landing Ships Infantry (LSI) of the Western Task Force arrived at their release positions on time (at 0300 hours on 10 July) the seas were still sufficiently high to make matters uncomfortable when the Landing Craft Assault (LCA) were lowered and when the Landing Craft Infantry (Large) [LCI (L)] came alongside to take on board their passengers. Embarking in these vessels in such conditions was a hazardous business.

Not all ships made it to their destinations on schedule. The Landing Craft Tank (LCT) convoy intended for BARK East turned up at BARK South, six hours late; the one intended for ACID arrived in the correct place, but two hours late. Amended plans enabled the LCT convoy for BARK West to be in position only thirty minutes late, after it had been given a shorter route. Because of the delays, the only LCT to land before daylight were those on BARK South.

The submarines which had been assigned to mark the approaches to the beaches were generally in the right positions, although some of the smaller craft which marked the inshore navigational points, such as the folboats, were swept off their bearings by the seas. One benefit of the weather conditions was that the Italian coastal defenders appeared to have decided that a landing under such conditions was out of the question. No enemy fire was brought to bear on the Allied shipping of the Eastern Task Force as it assembled, and when the Italians became aware of what was happening at first light, what little resistance they raised was quickly subdued by naval gunfire.

As far as the assembly of convoys was concerned the operation went, in Admiral Cunningham's words, 'like a well-oiled clock'. On the beaches, however, things went less smoothly – but the troops got ashore. The delay in landing was particularly true on the American beaches, which were more exposed. Time lost because of the swell was, however, quickly made up because of the weakness of the defence.

The northernmost landings were made just south of Syracuse by the 1st Special Raiding Squadron of 2nd Special Air Service Regiment. Its task was to capture and destroy a coastal battery on Cape Murro di Porco, the headland that jutted into the sea below Porto Grande, the larger of Syracuse's two harbours. The gun batteries on this headland protected the harbour entrance, and the easternmost one, the *Lamba Doria Battery*, also overlooked the Bay of Ognina to the south, where 5th Division was to land. The *Emmanuele Russo Battery* lay further north, covering the harbour, on the far side of the headland from the ACID Beaches. Armed with 152mm naval guns, the batteries posed a serious threat. Removing them posed more than the difficulty of dealing with their crews and other defence works – they stood above sheer cliffs.

The Raiding Squadron, commanded by Major 'Paddy' Mayne, sailed in two ships: HMS *Dunera* and HMS *Ulster Monarch*, both equipped with LCAs. The *Ulster Monarch* was a vessel familiar to Mayne, as before the war it had been a ferry on the Liverpool-Belfast route. Mayne, a founder-member of the SAS, was to become a legendary figure, winning no less than four Distinguished Service Orders during the course of the war, the last of which was substituted for the Victoria Cross for which he had been recommended[1].

After transferring to the LCAs in a sea that was still far from calm after the gale, which had now subsided, the squadron made for the foot of the cliffs at a quarter-past-three in the morning. En route they paused to pick up Brigadier Hicks, the commander of the Airlanding Brigade, who was clinging to the wing of his glider, having ditched in the water. There was no sound from the shore as they approached, and no sign of enemy activity. Crossing the short beach to the foot of the cliffs, they commenced the climb with the assistance of scaling ladders, coming across another airborne officer on a ledge as they ascended. Having cut through the wire on the cliff-top, the squadron set off for its objectives. By now the Italians had become aware of what was happening and began to respond, firing at their assailants from all around the gun site.

One troop headed straight for the battery, with the other two intending to attack it from the flank and from the rear, but one of these had landed in the wrong place and – in the darkness and confusion – began to fire on their own men. It was not long, however, before the mistake was realised, and the gun crews were coaxed out of the underground bunkers beneath the gun positions and made prisoner, and the guns made ready for demolition.

Behind the guns lay their command post and some barrack buildings, which were subjected to a mortar bombardment before the SAS troopers went in with the bayonet to clear the place out. In the underground bunkers they discovered, not only Italian soldiers, but families sheltering from the aerial bombardment which had preceded the landing earlier in the evening. There were also a number of British troops from the Airlanding Brigade who had been taken prisoner.

By 0500 hours the battery had been captured and destroyed, and the order given to fire the success signal to the ships offshore: three green rockets. Gathering the squadron together at a farm, Mayne decided to move north-westwards and attack a second battery. As they worked their way towards it, by now in daylight, they accumulated groups of prisoners, too many to handle. This problem they solved by ordering them into a field with instructions to await the arrival of the main landing force. The resistance put up by the enemy, mostly coastal defence soldiers conscripted locally, lacked determination; many of them being more concerned with the safety of their families than risking their lives in a cause which they had little enthusiasm for.

By the end of the day, 10 July, Mayne's squadron had captured not only its primary objective, the *Lamba Doria Battery*, but had also taken three additional batteries, taken 450 prisoners as well as killing 200 to 300 Italians. For this day's work and that on the following day, Mayne was awarded a bar to his DSO.

Number 3 Commando

Three Commando units took part in HUSKY. They were Number 3 Commando, formed from army personnel, and Numbers 40 and 41 Royal Marine Commandos.

No 3 Commando, which had suffered heavy losses at Dieppe, had been brought up to strength and after a period of training at Weymouth had moved to Alexandria where it came directly under the orders of General Dempsey, Commander of XIII Corps. From him they learned of their role in HUSKY which was to land several miles south of Syracuse and capture a coastal battery some three miles inland near the little village of Cassibili. This would assist the main body of the Corps to land in the Avola area without too much opposition. They built a replica of the objective in their training area near Suez and rehearsed the operation no less than twelve times.

About midnight on 9 July No 3 Commando climbed into the eight landing craft carried by their ship, a converted cross-channel steamer named *Prince Albert*, in preparation for their run to the shore. Each landing craft had been equipped with a Vickers K machinegun in the bow, to deal with any opposition from the beach defenders. They were lowered into the water on schedule, at 0115 hours, and set off, guided by a submarine-launched folboat flashing the pre-arranged signal. It was not long before the commanding officer, Lieutenant Colonel Durnford-Slater, who was well-briefed from maps and photographs of the coastline, realized that the current must have taken the canoe from its proper location and they were off course. Having obtained the correct bearing from the crew of a nearby destroyer, Durnford-Slater and his half of the unit were put ashore at precisely the right place. There was a short burst of enemy opposition when a machinegun situated in a pillbox opened up as the landing craft made their run-in, but the bow-mounted machineguns silenced it very quickly.

Passing through defence works of wire and pillboxes, which were manned by Italians of shaky determination, the commandos formed up inland ready to move off against their objective, the gun battery. As Durnford-Slater was talking to his batman, a tracer round passed between their noses – they were under fire again, but again not for long. They set off, led by two scouts across the open fields divided by the omnipresent stone walls, each of which was four or five feet high. Climbing over them, particularly for the men who were carrying the three-inch mortars, was time-consuming.

Unhappy with the speed of the advance, Durnford-Slater used a torch to flash back to the following men, trying to hurry them along so that he might reach the objective by the planned time. Passing by a farmhouse, the commandos disturbed a farmer who appeared with a shotgun, which he fired at them. He was swiftly dealt with, not without regret from at least one of the commandos, who felt that the Italian had shown spirit.

Shortly after this incident, the battery was heard firing, and Durnford-Slater sent ten men to harass it with a two-inch mortar and rifle fire while the three-inch mortar and four Bren guns were put into position. Under fire from two directions, the battery was assaulted to the sound of a bugle-call. Blowing their way through the surrounding wire with Bangalore torpedoes, the commandos dashed into the battery and took it at the point of the bayonet. On this occasion the defence was firmer than it had been on the beach, but to no avail; the guns and their ammunition magazine were blown up, five minutes before General Dempsey's schedule. No 3 Commando suffered no casualties during the whole operation.

The commandos then settled down to breakfast of eggs from a nearby farm. As they were finishing their meal, they heard firing from another battery, two miles away. As they prepared to set out to deal with it, it came under a heavy bombardment from the naval vessels off-shore. They wisely decided to leave it alone, and instead moved into Cassibili. Here two ex-bandsmen discovered a trumpet and a bass drum, with which they proceeded to entertain their comrades – and to surprise the piper of the Seaforth Highlanders who was with the leading troops advancing from the beach, who had rather expected to be the first Allied unit into the village.

The other half of the unit under Major Peter Young had been less fortunate. They had spent several frustrating hours at sea while the leader of their flotilla of landing craft searched for the correct beach. He found it eventually, but it was daylight by then and they landed unopposed. They met the rest of the Commando soon after landing, and had the consolation prize of being sent off to deal with some Italians who were holding out in a fort nearby[2].

5th Division

In 5th Division's area the first flight of 17 Infantry Brigade landed well south of its beach, 'George' Sector of Beach 44. It was nearly on schedule, but the following waves of landing craft, although arriving at the correct site, were up to an hour late. Beach 44 was secured by five in the morning, and the 6th Battalion of the Seaforth Highlanders went on to Cassibili – where No 3 Commando awaited their arrival – to be followed by the Northamptons. The Royal Scots Fusiliers turned northwards towards Syracuse, re-taking the Ponte Grande as described in the previous chapter. The city was in the Brigade's hands that evening.

15 Brigade had less good fortune during the landings. It was nearly an hour late, and came ashore some distance from its designated beaches, 45 and 46. They also came under fire from Italian guns, which were neutralized by the destroyer HMS *Eskimo*. Nevertheless, by 1000 hours the brigade was established in the Cassibili area, while behind them the beaches were being organized for the build-up[3].

50th Division

50th Division had set out on 5 July, and sailed westwards along the coast of North Africa. Its slower-moving MT convoy had already departed from Alexandria, with the intention of arriving at the landing beaches at the same time as the troop transports. The intention was that the essential guns and vehicles would be ashore within four hours of the assault waves landing. On 6 July one of the MT ships was torpedoed and sank, taking with it some badly needed vehicles. As the wind freshened on 9 July the troop convoy caught up with, and then passed, the MT convoy. Some of the vessels, particularly two troop-ships of pre-war vintage and the LCTs and LCIs, had difficulty in maintaining their speed during the voyage, and the divisional commanders and the Senior Naval Officer Landing held discussions on the possibility of delaying the landing[iv]. At sunset, however, their concerns were somewhat allayed as the wind dropped. At 2000 hours, as darkness was about to fall, the summit of Etna could be made out; and just before midnight the ships stopped at their release positions.

As the division progressed towards Sicily daily training had been carried out to ensure that every man could find his way to his landing craft station without confusion in the hours of darkness. They now moved silently from their mess decks to their LCAs and embarked, to be lowered into the sea at 0100 hours. A second wave followed fifteen minutes later. After a period of confusion as the craft sorted themselves out in the swell and formed up into their landing formations, they set off for the shore.

The water was extremely choppy, and not a few men experienced seasickness during the last leg of their voyage to Sicily. From the decks of the transports, the bombing of Syracuse was clearly visible, but there was no sign of the enemy on the beaches ahead.

The sector where 50th Division was to land in Sicily was not ideal for the purpose. Much of the coastline consisted of cliffs about twenty to twenty-five feet high; these were scalable in places, but it was difficult to tell from air photographs exactly which places could or could not be climbed. In the sea there were a good number of rocks which were a danger to navigation, particularly opposite the cliffs. In the centre of the sector and about a thousand yards inland lay Avola, a town of nearly twenty-two thousand inhabitants, and about one and a half miles north of it was the only beach over which vehicles could be landed with certainty.

There the water off shore was deep, the beach consisted of fairly hard sand, and though no exits for wheeled vehicles existed, it was known that there would be no difficulty in making them by bulldozing a passage through the low sand-bank bordering the beach, and making gaps in the stone walls which covered the whole of the cultivated area. This beach, marked as No 47 on the special charts which were prepared for the operation, was given the code name of 'Jig Green'. Its left-hand limits were clearly marked by two concrete pillars and a circular concrete platform in the sea, the locality being known as the Lido d'Avola.

Opposite the town was a second landing place, possible for infantry only, which was given the code name 'Jig Amber'. Immediately to the south was the Marina d'Avola, which consisted of a very small anchorage and pier used by local fishing boats, but it was well fortified, and considered unsuitable for the discharge of vehicles.

The enemy defences consisted of a succession of pillboxes and entrenched localities along the coast, averaging fifty yards apart. Likely exits from the shore had been wired. There were few mines, though before landing this fact was not known. Once the troops got ashore they would have to operate in a coastal plain intensively cultivated with vineyards, olive groves and citrus orchards. In addition to the stone walls which bordered every field and road, the ground was crossed by many dry water courses and some ditches, many of which were tank obstacles. From the coast the ground rose slowly for about one to two thousand yards and thereafter more sharply. At three thousand yards from the coast, hills rose steeply. The summits, which were about a thousand feet above sea level, lay some seven thousand yards from the coast. The hills were rocky, or covered with grass or low scrub. One good lateral road ran through Avola roughly parallel to the coast, leading to the north to the village of Cassibili just outside the Divisional sector, and to the south to the town of Noto, on the edge of the area which the Division was initially going to occupy. Another good road ran inland from Avola to Palazzolo Acreide, ascending the hills in a succession of hairpin bends, and roads connected Avola with the Lido and the Marina. In the 50th Divisional sector there were no coast-defence or field guns in action, but just outside it field guns manned by Italians were in action in a coastal defence role.

The beaches were to be assaulted by 151 Brigade in the dark, H Hour being laid down by the Army as 0245 hours, two hours before first light. The operation was to take place in three phases. The first task was to secure the two landing places and mop up all of the enemy on the coast. This task was to be carried out by the 9th Durham Light Infantry, who would land on 'Jig Green', and by the 6th Durham Light Infantry, who would land on 'Jig Amber'. In the second phase the two battalions were to secure a beachhead so that any enemy forces which were inland would be prevented from bringing effective small-arms fire to bear on the beaches. The limits of the beachhead were defined by the inter-divisional boundary, which ran inland about three thousand yards north of Avola, to the railway, which ran parallel to the coast from one to two thousand yards inland, and then to the River Mammeledi, which flowed into the sea about a mile south of Avola.

To carry out these two tasks the first two battalions ashore were to turn south and work their way through the beachhead position, mopping up any defences, before establishing themselves along the line of the beach road. They would then advance onto the high ground where they would deny the enemy the use of any place from which they could observe the beaches or the Divisional maintenance area. With the necessity of seizing each and every height overlooking the aforementioned sites, it was estimated that the perimeter that the brigade would have to hold would be some 19,000 yards long, which was considered excessive for a force twice that size. Nevertheless the situation was unavoidable, although because of the openness of the ground it was possible to control most of it from a comparatively few dominant points. The areas between these locations could be covered by the machineguns.

The third of the brigade's battalions, 8th DLI, was in reserve. It was to come ashore at 'Jig Green' and push on to the most important heights just after dawn broke.

The Durhams' landings were not smooth. The waves were steep and the wind was still strong, making the sequence of lowering the landing craft, assembling them into their attack formation, and then steering for the beach, difficult. To add to the problem, the launches which should have carried the naval guides to their posts for bringing the flotillas ashore had not arrived and less suitable craft had to be substituted. The rough seas added to the discomfort of the troops, many of whom were already seasick, and flooded the boats. Baling became necessary, but sometimes too late to prevent radio sets from being 'drowned' and rendered useless. Binoculars became fogged up, and navigation became even more of a problem. When the beaches were reached, men were put ashore in an haphazard manner, with units being intermingled and uncertain of their precise locations. If there was a saving grace, it was that enemy opposition was equally disordered and largely symbolic: a few bursts were fired before the Italians made off.

It was not known to what extent the enemy would attempt to hold the town of Avola, but it was appreciated that it might be necessary to secure the beachhead and covering positions before the town had fallen.

The role of the follow-up brigade group, the 69th, was not laid down in the operation order. It was to land on orders from Divisional Headquarters, and brigadiers were informed in the operation instruction that it was the Divisional Commander's intention that it should take over the left sector of the covering position. Some units of 151 Brigade were, however, to remain in that sector so that 69 Brigade could, if desired, be withdrawn to move further north to relieve units of 5th Division. 69 Brigade was also to organize a mobile column to be ready to deal with any enemy batteries in action south of and outside the covering position.

168 Infantry Brigade was to land on D+3.

231 Brigade

231 Brigade, which had been in Malta throughout the siege, was ordered to land at the village of Marsamemi on the Pachino peninsula, about two miles northeast of Pachino town. Comparatively full information had been received from Intelligence, which in addition to describing the ground and local industries, gave details of the enemy troops in the area. It stated that there were a few Italian troops in the area but was vague about German forces.

The journey from Port Said to Sicily was uneventful, without interference from aircraft, submarines or surface vessels. For most of the journey the weather was good but the storm on 9 July affected 231st Brigade no less than the other formations. The landing craft left for the beaches at 0245 hours, moving off into the dark night which was only made lighter by the air raid in progress on Syracuse. Many of the crews of the landing craft found it difficult to locate the correct beaches, many of the soldiers were soaked to the skin by spray and more than a few were sick.

On the brigade's beaches the Italian coastal troops were in strongly fortified positions which at first they defended with vigour. Several enemy strongpoints were quickly put out of action by determined attacks, but there was an element of the inevitable confusion as the landing progressed in the darkness – No 17 Platoon of the Hampshires, instead of landing on the left flank of the Brigade, found themselves well to the north of the beaches. They had to pass through the Dorsets' positions before joining up with the rest of their company.

The Dorsets had a rockier sector in which to land but met less resistance. One company had the task of clearing the village of Masamemi and securing a path for the rest of the battalion. The Devons were the reserve battalion for the landing and had the task of passing through the beachhead and securing a wooded ridge beyond. This they did, capturing large numbers of Italian soldiers in the process.

By midday, the Brigade had captured most of its objectives but the Dorsets, who had been delayed, were soon subjected to a spirited counterattack by Italians in French M35 tanks. This attack had been anticipated and the Italians were met by Sherman tanks and 17-pounder anti-tank guns which succeeded in beating them off. As this battle took place in a wood, few people who were not directly involved in the action knew about it at the time; such is often the case in battle .

By 1600 hours the Brigade had carried out its allotted tasks, assaulted the beaches, captured the defensive positions and repulsed a counter-attack. It only remained for a swift-moving column to be sent off to the north to make contact with the left flank of 151 Brigade which had landed in the area of Avola.

51st (Highland) Division

The Highland Division started its journey from Sousse to Malta on 5 July, arriving the following day. The troops were disembarked and accommodated in transit camps, where Montgomery visited them on the 7th. He found their morale to be very high, but doubtless some men found their spirits dampened by the sea crossing and the sickness which accompanied it. Nevertheless, at 0245 hours on 10 July the leading units landed on the beaches of Sicily. Their path was eased by rockets and naval gunfire, which convinced the Italians manning the coastal batteries to call it a day.

The Divisional Commander, General Wimberley, had decided that the apparently excellent beach in Portopalo Bay was too likely to have struck the enemy as a likely landing ground. To avoid the possibility that the beach had been heavily mined, he put 154 Brigade ashore on both sides of it, where the ground was more difficult but probably safer[5].

Apart from a few men of the 7th Battalion of the Argyll & Sutherland Highlanders who were wounded by a grenade[6], the landing of 154 Brigade passed without incident, and the battalion pressed through the town of Pachino to a ridge line five miles to its northwest. The other assault battalion, 7th Black Watch, suffered a delay because only one of its companies was put ashore in the correct place. It took until 0615 hours before the battalion moved off to take its objectives on the high ground overlooking the beaches, a task which was accomplished within forty-five minutes, but at a cost of one officer and ten men who fell foul of anti-personnel mines.

1st Battalion, The Gordon Highlanders had as its objectives Cape Passero Island, the village of Portopalo, a tuna factory and a lighthouse, before capturing a 200-foot high ridge which commanded the approaches to Pachino. Once the defenders of the tuna factory had been cleared out, the ridge was in British hands by 0900 hours. Advance patrols were in Pachino by early afternoon, making contact with 5th Black Watch.

Delayed by the seas, LCTs arrived two hours late and started to beach at 0400 hours. Two hours later the first artillery and tanks (B Battery 11th [HAC] Regiment RHA, and 50 RTR) were in action; and early in the afternoon the LCIs carrying units of the Division's other two brigades, 153 and 152, began putting men ashore. By nightfall the 51st (Highland) Division was moving inland.

1st Canadian Division

The Canadians left Scotland in convoys between 19 June and 1 July, depending upon the speed of the ships, en route for Sicily. The task was to land on the west side of the Pachino Peninsula, capture the Pachino airfield and contact other formations of XXX Corps in the vicinity of Pachino town.

2 Brigade was due to land with the Seaforth Highlanders of Canada on the left and the Princess Patricia's Light Infantry on the right. The assault craft carrying the Seaforth went off course and landed its men to the right of the Patricia's. As the craft approached the shore promptly at 0245 hours they came under desultory small arms fire which ceased as the assaulting troops reached the beaches. Once ashore, the troops easily cut through or blew up the few wire obstacles in their path, quickly disposing of a few machinegun posts manned by a handful of bewildered Italian soldiers.

1 Brigade, on the right of the Divisional front, was also due to attack at 0245 hours but was delayed in leaving its transport ships. It was 0320 hours before the first wave of the Hastings and Prince Edward Regiment headed for the shore and 0400 hours before the Royal Canadian Regiment followed suit. LCTs each carrying seven DUKWs were used by 1st Brigade. The assault companies of both regiments were landed in approximately the right places but a reserve company of the Hastings was put ashore five thousand yards too far to the west.

Despite the late arrival of 1 Brigade, the division had captured all its first objectives by 0645 hours. Little resistance was encountered and the Pachino airfield was found to be ploughed up but deserted. There were a few minor skirmishes against isolated pockets of resistance but only on the Division's left flank was any serious resistance encountered. There, late in the afternoon, a *Blackshirt* unit held up the Commandos by mortar and anti-tank fire. A mortar detachment of the Sasketoon Light Infantry engaged the target, allowing the Commandos to close in and capture horse-drawn guns and large quantities of ammunition[7].

During the night of D Day the Division completed the second phase of the operations. 2 Brigade had moved some four miles towards Ispica, and 3 Brigade on the right made a similar advance.

The first day had been highly satisfactory. Canadian losses were seven other ranks killed, three officers and twenty-two other ranks wounded. The enemy had lost about one hundred killed and wounded and by 1900 hours some 650 prisoners had been captured.

Forty-eight minutes after midnight the Canadian Headquarters ship, HMS *Hilary*, dropped anchor about seven miles off the Sicilian coast. Rumours aboard ship reported that the convoy had been detected by enemy radar. Although the wind had dropped, the sea was still running with sufficient swell to make the task of transferring from the transports into landing craft a difficult one, and tense soldiers felt that the noise of the anchor chains rattling as they were lowered announced their arrival to the Italians, already awakened by the bombing which had been going on for the last hour and a half, softening up the defences. At 0110 hours the first flight of LCAs carrying Commandos were lowered into the water and a little less than half an hour later the assault troops from 2 Canadian Infantry Brigade were on their way towards SUGAR Beach, the western of the two Canadian landing areas. As they approached the shore the monitor HMS *Roberts* bombarded the airfield at Pachino and its defences with its two 15-inch guns.

The run-in to shore was lit up by enemy flares and tracer bullets, and occasional explosions could be seen on the beach. As the LCAs dropped their ramps some men found themselves deposited in six feet of water and had to abandon their weapons and webbing in order to swim ashore. The men of the Princess Patricia's Canadian Light Infantry and the Seaforth Highlanders of Canada were the assault troops, expecting to land on the right and left, respectively, but their craft became mixed up as naval officers lost their bearings. The Seaforth came ashore on the right, at 0245 hours, and the two battalions moved across the beach to find little opposition other than fire from a solitary mortar and a scattering of hand grenades, which failed to affect their advance. Blowing gaps in the wire with Bangelore torpedoes, the Canadians passed through and mopped up the few machinegun posts awaiting them, clearing the way for the second wave which came ashore shortly afterwards. Just before four in the morning the Brigade Headquarters, still afloat, received success signals from the two battalions.

No's 40 and 41 Royal Marine Commandos of 1 Special Service Brigade had been training in Scotland for their task which was to land near Pozzallo and put out of action some coastal defence batteries thus enabling 1 Canadian Division to land without too much interference.

No 41 (RM) Commando was ashore first but at 0300 hours was half an hour behind schedule owing to the heavy swell. Some of the coxswains of the landing craft were worried by the sand bars which lay 300 yards off the coast so about three quarters of the Commando had a very wet landing in which many mortar bombs and wireless sets were rendered useless. Once the men were ashore, however, they quickly formed up and moved off towards their objectives. Dawn was breaking as they closed with the enemy and fought a brisk action with a series of machinegun posts. There were a few casualties including two officers, and at half-past five the Brigade reported that all defences east of Punta Mura had been captured; a little over an hour later, contact was made with the Seaforths, who had turned west and made their way through the sandhills and moved parallel to the shore to the town of Pantano Longarini, picking up 'a sorry looking group of Italian soldiers' who had surrendered after firing a few shots[8].

No 40 (RM) Commando was landed too far to the east in two feet of water.

By 0500 hours the initial defences had been overrun and it was found that No 41 Commando had captured the objectives allocated to No 40 Commando as well as their own. The dawn also revealed that the 'Coast defence guns' were, in fact, only machinegun posts.

1 Canadian Infantry Brigade was to attack on the right, on ROGER Beach. It had more trouble in getting clear of the transports than 2 Brigade, because a last-minute change of information about the beaches, which reported a false beach off ROGER, had caused the Divisional Commander to order that three LCTs were to be used to land a company of the Hastings and Prince Edward Island Regiment and two from the Royal Canadians. These LCTs failed to arrive at the assembly point as the fleet anchored for the landing, so the three companies were ordered ashore in LCAs instead. Not unexpectedly, this change of plan led to a delay, which at one stage caused Rear Admiral Vian to signal his Senior Naval Landing Officer for ROGER, 'Will your assault ever start?' Twenty minutes later, General Simonds signaled to the Commander of 1 Brigade, 'You must get your assaults away in either LCTs or LCAs.' By 0316 hours the two assault companies from the Hastings had got away in LCAs, but the Royal Canadian Regiment companies had yet to follow because of the choppiness of the sea. And now the missing LCTs arrived, so the troops went original plan, but not without incident, for bringing them alongside the transport *Marnix* was difficult in the seas. Each of the two LCTs that were employed for this already had seven DUKWs aboard, and these were used to drive the troops up the beach as the LCTs grounded.

Enemy shells had landed amongst the RCR as they neared the shore, but naval gunfire soon put a stop to this hazard, which came from a coastal defence battery inland, behind the town of Mauili. The infantry came ashore unopposed at 0530 hours, followed by a second wave half an hour later, and after a few minutes to reorganize, the battalion moved off towards its first objective, Maucini.

The Hastings and Prince Edwards' came ashore with two companies to the east of ROGER Red and Amber Beaches, where they should have landed. Having blown their way through the wire and disposed of a few snipers they were on their way. Five thousand yards too far to the west, A Company and Battalion Headquarters came under machinegun fire, but pushed through the wire and, with some commandos, captured an enemy machinegun position and took about twenty Italian and German prisoners. A degree of confusion reigned – having signaled that ROGER Red Beach was safe for vehicles, the Hastings had to retract two hours later to report that they had got it wrong, and were in fact on SUGAR Beach. The fog of war was no stranger to those participating in Operation HUSKY, and would reemerge time and time again.

At 0645 hours Divisional Headquarters was able to report to XXX Corps that the first objectives had been captured. The reserve battalions now started to come ashore. They had been sitting offshore in the swell, aboard their LCIs, and were no doubt glad – as were the great majority of soldiers who had endured the storms of the previous few hours – to get ashore, enemy or no enemy.

The infantry landed, again not without incident, for amongst other events the LCI which carried the 48th Highlanders of Canada first grounded on a sandbar off ROGER Green Beach, and then on a reef during the second attempt. Some strong swimmers managed to get a line ashore, but this then fouled two LCMs which had broken down. Eventually the troops were transferred to DUKWs and LCAs which took them across the deep water to the beach where they landed with the pipes playing.

The two assault brigade headquarters landed at 1800 hours and 3 Brigade, the follow-up, was warned to be ready to come ashore three hours later. The first tanks of the 12th Canadian Tank Regiment disembarked into six feet of water at nine o'clock, and the sappers and pioneers with bulldozers and other equipment began preparing beach exits, blasting a passage through the sandbar.

Once established ashore 1 Canadian Infantry Brigade lost no time in pushing on with its task of capturing Pachino Airfield. The RCR advanced through the town of Maucini and took the battery beyond it, which appeared to be deserted. Voices were heard coming from a dugout, which drew a shot from one of the Canadians. This resulted in the entire garrison, consisting of a captain, two lieutenants and thirty-five soldiers, emerging to surrender. It took no longer than twenty minutes, and no casualties, for the battery to be captured.

The airfield was reached shortly afterwards, and found to be ploughed up. The Canadians met some tanks from 51st Highland Division at a corner of the airfield, which were moving west through Pachino, and after a brief skirmish to clear some enemy troops from the airfield barracks, the place was secured. Groups of enemy soldiers in the surrounding area were mopped up, with nearly 200 being taken prisoner. The resistance was nothing if not half-hearted, and well-equipped and well located defensive positions were swiftly yielded. Amongst these was one which contained three medium machineguns and two 75mm field guns. Another battery had four 6-inch howitzers, four medium and several light machineguns. 130 men of its garrison surrendered after a brief fight when five Canadian privates succeeded in getting inside the perimeter and putting two of the machineguns out of action. Total Canadian casualties for the action were two killed and two wounded.

Further west, 2 Canadian Infantry Brigade was proceeding with even less difficulty. Moving steadily inland they, too, took Italian prisoners, and in doing so released two American paratroopers who had been captured earlier[9].

Late in the afternoon the Special Service Brigade, to the left of 1 Canadian Infantry Brigade, came under heavy fire from enemy mortars and anti-tank guns. With only automatic weapons and rifles, the commandos had difficulty in closing to effective range. Fortunately a mortar detachment from the 2 Brigade Support Group was found nearby, which obliged by laying down 160 4-inch mortar rounds onto the target. Under this covering fire, the commandos closed with the enemy, who abandoned their anti-tank guns and quantities of ammunition, amongst a heap of dead horses and dead and wounded Italians.

Seventh (US) Army

45th (US) Infantry Division landed some forty miles to the west of the Canadian beaches. Like all of the Seventh Army landing areas, they were more exposed to the weather than were the British beaches, with the exception of the Canadians'. Lying to the west of Cape Correnti, they were not sheltered from the wind, and the landing craft and escorting vessels were affected more by the high seas than were those of their British counterparts to the east. There was also more opposition from the defenders of these beaches than the Eighth Army encountered, from both ground and air forces.

The CENT Force had two stretches of beach on which to land, about seven miles apart. They were selected because of their proximity to the airfields at Biscari and Comiso, respectively. The village of Scoglitti lay about midway between the two beaches, both of which turned out to be ill-chosen. That to the west, closest to Biscari, was known to the Allied planners as 'Wood's Hole', or Red, Green and Yellow Beaches. It lay 6,500 to 8,000 yards away from the coastal highway, with a thousand yards of sand dunes and no firm beach exits along the shore. The second, 'Bailey's Beach' was 2,500 yards from the nearest road and backed, again, by sand dunesx. The vessels intended for CENT Beaches were guided to their destinations by the submarine HMS *Seraph*, which had already

1. Churchill and Roosevelt at Casablanca.

2. Eisenhower and Alexander, the Commander-in-Chief and his Deputy.

3. Field Marshal Albert Kesselring.

4. Pantellaria. The damage wrought by bombing was to raise the question of how effective the same strategy might be against Sicily.

5. 1 Airlanding Brigade in North Africa before the D Day operation to capture the Ponte Grande, south of Syracuse.

6. US Airborne dead. The casualties were not all inflicted by the enemy.

7. Gela Beach. The high seas from the previous day's storms made beaching landing craft difficult.

8. DUKW on CENT Force Beach, near Scoglitti. The introduction of these amphibious vehicles allowed the Allies to come ashore without port facilities.

9. The Liberty ship *Robert Rowan* off Gela. Hit by German bombers, the ammunition ship caught fire and exploded spectacularly. All of the crew were evacuated beforehand, but the column of smoke acted as a marker for future German attacks.

10. Patton comes ashore at Gela on D+1, immaculate in tie and polished boots, and with his ivory-handled revolvers.

11. Italian troops surrendering. A great number of Italians had had enough of the war and were only too pleased to see their part in it come to an end.

12. Sherman passing Sicilian horse and cart. The dust was an ever-present discomfort of the campaign, coating men and machines alike.

13. US paratroops in Vittoria. The 2/505th on 12 July, making best use of whatever form of transport is available.

14. Primosole Bridge. The fighting for control of this river crossing was among the fiercest on the island, and the failure to seize it swiftly was to prolong the campaign.

15. July 12. German paratroops make a text-book drop on Sicily to reinforce the defenders.

16. German paratroops collecting weapons containers before moving south to Primosole.

17. 25 pounder in front of Etna. The mountain dominated the east of Sicily, and Axis observation posts on its slopes were able to plot the moves of the Eighth Army on the Catania Plain.

18. Bren carrier on a Sicilian road.

19. General der Panzertruppen Hans Hube.

20. Princess Patricia's Canadian Light Infantry in action near Valguarnera. Enemy vehicles burn below.

21. Montgomery and Patton at Palermo airfield. A belated realisation that the US Seventh and the British Eighth Armies had to act in concert led to meetings between the two generals – the first since well before D Day took place on 25 July, followed by this one three days later.

22. US M3A1 Scout vehicle and Sicilian greeting. The population generally welcomed the invasion forces, and many regarded them as liberators.

23. Allied jeeps on the way to Agira pass wrecked German Kübelwagen.

24. Agira was taken by the Canadians on 28 July.

25. German paratroops on the march to the north and a new defence line.

26. British infantry clearing buildings in a Sicilian town.

27. Having taken Centuripe, men of the Inniskillings look towards their next objectives in the valleys below: the crossings of the Rivers Salsa and Simeto.

28. German paratroops retreating to a new position.

29. Canadian tanks moving through Regalbuto. The narrow streets and debris from destroyed houses hindered the advance throughout Sicily.

30. Patton with Lt Col Lyle Bernard, whose 2/30th Infantry group made the 'end runs' at Sant' Agata and Brolo.

31. US Engineers at Cape Calava, repairing the road which the retreating enemy forces had blown into the sea below.

32. Ernst-Guenther Baade. The architect of the evacuation of German forces from Sicily.

33. German paratroops leaving Sicily.

34. Generals Eisenhower and Montgomery at Messina, looking towards the Italian mainland. Montgomery's plan for crossing the Straits was carefully structured – and missed the opportunity to strike quickly.

contributed to HUSKY by setting 'Major Martin' afloat off Spain to deceive the enemy about Allied intentions.

Rear Admiral Kirk, the CENT naval commander, delayed the landings off Scoglitti for an hour to allow the seas to settle a little, and to permit those vessels which had been struggling to maintain the pace to rejoin the fleet. Sand banks and rocks presented further hazards, and the landing of 45th Division was scattered and uncoordinated. At 0334 hours, shortly before H Hour, Italian shells from coastal batteries landed amongst the assembled craft, forcing them to veer to the right; the USS *Philadelphia* returned the fire, contributing to the barrage from the Allied warships, amongst which was the Royal Navy monitor, HMS *Abercrombie*. Ten minutes later, the first seasick troops from 179th Regimental Combat Team came ashore on CENT Yellow and Green Beaches, followed by the 157th Combat Team on the right, on Yellow 2 and Green 2. Several landing craft broached, and thirty-eight men were drowned in the surf, where waves rose as high as ten feet. Some had disembarked in deep water and sank to the seabed under the weight of the weapons, ammunition and equipment they carried. The 180th Combat Team, on the left, faced even greater difficulties, and was disembarked between Gela and three miles west of its allocated beach, Red. Problems in lowering and assembling the assault boats into their flotillas led to even more scattered landings. Amongst those who were landed in the wrong places were the shore party, which led to delays in getting the beach organized and troops moving inland. A major contributory factor to the disorganization was the fact that one hour before sailing from the United States, at least half of the well-trained landing craft ensigns and coxswains had been replaced by men straight from basic training; there had been no time to train them before the landings[11].

Resistance to the landing was patchy. Apart from the coastal batteries which fired onto the landing craft, the enemy launched an air attack on the armada at 0430 hours. A squadron of torpedo-bombers from Sardinia and thirteen high-altitude bombers from Perugia made the attack, but failed to inflict much damage – most of the bombs were near-misses – and the aircraft were driven off by anti-aircraft fire and a squadron of Spitfires from Malta. The beach defences were quickly overrun and the defenders killed or captured; the stiffest resistance was against the 180th on the west.

Among the crews of the landing craft bringing the 180th ashore was Seaman 1st Class Francis Carpenter, who had visited the area before the war. He was asked to scout ahead of the troops to clarify some features that had been uncertain from the aerial photographs, which appeared to be a road and an olive grove. Having ascertained that the former was the assumed road, he returned to signal his finding. On the way, he showed an Indian GI some disturbed ground which he thought might indicate the presence of landmines. The GI ignored him, and was promptly blown to pieces; Carpenter was thrown 'some distance' by the blast, but continued with his mission. Having completed it, he found himself in charge of a frightened Italian peasant family, complete with babies and a donkey, and two Italian soldiers who had seen fit to surrender to him. He escorted them to the peasants' cottage and calmed their nerves by singing 'La donna e mobile' and drinking wine until the commander of the 1st Battalion of the 180th arrived[12].

By 0600 hours, most of the 1st Battalion was ashore, about 3,000 men in all. Apart from one platoon that landed in the wrong place, the remainder was ready to push inland to Biscari. Before them were demoralized Italian coastal troops, who were generally only too willing to surrender: a spotter aircraft from USS *Philadelphia* passed low over a group of them, the pilot indicating that they should move down to the ground forces on the beach and give themselves up. As they did so, the group grew in number until there were more than a hundred of them[13].

A first-aid post was established on the sand which began to tend to American and Italian casualties. Amongst the former were men who had suffered bayonet wounds from their own and their comrades' weapons as their landing craft were thrown about in the rough seas. Some 200 Italian and a few German prisoners were held in a makeshift POW cage. A burial party was organized from the bandsmen of the 157th, which established a temporary graveyard three miles inland. Behind the front line, the administrative elements were carrying out their solemn tasks.

At 0625 hours Admiral Kirk started to move the transports closer to the shore, to about five thousand yards distance from it, despite the waters not having been swept for mines; fortunately intelligence was correct, and none had been laid here. The unloading was disordered – with so many LCVPs broached, the services of the remaining vessels were at a premium and ships were 'borrowing' them to disembark their own passengers and equipment. To add to the confusion, some Italian batteries were tempted into activity by the approach of the transports, and had to be silenced by the fire support ships.

The soft sand of Bailey's Beach proved too difficult for the heavy equipment which was being landed there, and it had no less than three false beaches offshore on which landing craft with deeper draughts grounded. These factors led King to close this landing area just after noon, and another beach, Blue 2, was opened as a substitute. Wood's Hole was no better, with only one beach exit being usable. Along the shoreline about 200 landing craft lay abandoned, knocked out by enemy fire, stranded on rocks or mechanically disabled. Salvage parties were overwhelmed by the magnitude of their task, and bottlenecks were building up; to clear the stranded vessels out of the way, LCMs were diverted from their tasks of bringing men and equipment ashore to drag them out to sea. Without their cargo-carrying LCMs, the transports were further delayed in putting their charges ashore[14].

On the beaches the shore party, made up of Army Engineers, was not performing well. The Divisional Commander and naval officers were united in their scorn for these men, who included rejects from combat units. They were largely untrained and insubordinate, and some preferred to spend their time rifling through the barracks bags and personal effects of the men fighting further inland[15]. All in all, the scene on the beach itself was less than rosy.

The Divisional Commander, Major General Troy C Middleton, and his staff came ashore on Green Beach at 0830 hours and established their headquarters as the troops pushed inland. Scoglitti was captured by the 1st Battalion, 179th RCT at 1400; the 1st Battalion of the 157th took San Cruce and Camerina at 1445 hours, and the 2nd Battalion was in Dunna Fugata at 1715 hours. The 180th, disorganized by its scattered landing, was not assembled until late in the afternoon, when it moved inland to the area of Highway 115[16].

On DIME Beach, which was silhouetted by fires in Gela, 1st (US) Infantry Division had an easier landing, and the assault waves arrived on time at their appointed sites. Rear Admiral Hall, the naval commander for these landings, had driven his cruisers and transports hard to get to the assembly areas on time; so hard that they passed the minesweepers that should have ensured that the waters were cleared before they arrived. Like those off the CENT beaches, however, the enemy had not laid mines, so no Allied ships came to grief. Despite the Admiral's speed the transports were about half-an-hour behind schedule and the LCIs and LSTs arrived two or three hours late.

The plan for Gela was comparatively straightforward. With cliffs on the coast between Manfria and Cape Soprano topped with gun batteries, the only landing place was at Gela itself. 1st Division was to come ashore on a stretch of shore about a mile east of the mouth of the Gela River, from where it could quickly take the Ponte Olivo airfield about six miles inland. At Gela, a steel pier jutted into the sea, connected to the town by a winding road. The 1st and 4th Ranger Battalions were to land on either side of the pier on Red and Green Beaches to distract the enemy from the main assault.

Having waited in their landing craft (which included fourteen British LCAs) for half an hour until their control craft joined them, the Rangers made for the pier. As they approached it, the Italians detonated explosives under the central portion, blowing a gap in the structure. A three-foot surf also caused difficulties, and some craft broached. The majority succeeded in putting their passengers ashore, but the Rangers found themselves in a minefield. One company lost almost a complete platoon, partly because it came under crossfire from two pillboxes. A wounded first sergeant led the remainder of the company to capture the pillboxes, while three other companies fought their way into Gela[17].

The Rangers were followed ashore by infantry and a motorized chemical battalion equipped with 4.2-inch mortars. One LCI put its load ashore on Green Beach at a spot where there were few mines – for the very good reason that the Italian civilians who had been tasked with laying them had lost two of their number and the remainder had quit.

While naval gunfire reduced all but one of the coastal batteries (it remained operational until the afternoon) the main landings came ashore on Yellow, Blue, Red 2 and Green 2 Beaches to the east of the river mouth. The men had been on firm land for twenty minutes before the enemy responded. The beaches were heavily mined against vehicles and a number of DUKWs, bulldozers and trucks were blown up. LCI-220 grounded at 0500 hours and lost her stern anchor and the use of her port propeller from a near miss, but kept her guns in action until she was pulled off during the afternoon[18]. Apart from these setbacks, the landings went well until daybreak, when the enemy began to step up their response.

At 0430 hours, the beaches and shipping came under air attack, and at 0500 hours the destroyer USS *Maddox*, which was on anti-submarine patrol south of Gela, was sunk by a Ju-88 with heavy loss of life. It had the unfortunate distinction of being the fastest-sinking US warship to be lost during the war, one of the bombs having hit the ammunition magazine. The USS *Sentinel*, a minesweeper, was fatally damaged a few minutes later and sank shortly after dawn[19].

By 0800 hours the town of Gela had been captured by the Rangers and the Division was on its way inland. The *33rd Regiment* of the Italian *Livorno Division* with the panzer regiment of the German *Hermann Göring Division* was ordered forward from the areas of Caltanissetta and Caltagirone in response to the landings. Towards the end of the morning the Rangers near Gela reported enemy tanks approaching across the plain. They were the Italian *Gruppo Mobile 'E'*, of *XVI Corps*, moving from the direction of Ponte Olivo, and consisting of thirty-two French ten-ton Renault 35s, sixteen three-ton baby tanks and some 1914-18 Fiats. Led by Captain Giuseppe Granieri, the black-painted tanks drove into Gela. The Americans were without anti-tank guns, apart from bazookas; nor were any Allied aircraft available to attack the tanks. In desperation the Americans used bazookas, grenades and small arms at close range, and eventually the tanks withdrew harassed by field artillery with the assistance of naval gunfire from HMS *Abercrombie* and the cruiser USS *Boise* and the destroyers USS *Jeffers* and *Shubrick*.

To the west of Gela a battalion of the *33rd Regiment* was driven off by Rangers, and after 1400 hours a German attack by most of the *Hermann Göring Panzer Regiment*, with two infantry battalions and Tiger tanks of *Panzer Abteilung 215*, which converged on the town from the north and northwest met the 1st and 2nd Battalions of the 16th Infantry, supported by diverse groups of paratroopers. Again with naval gunfire support, the Germans were driven off and withdrew northwards. To assist on DIME, Vice Admiral Hewitt – the commander of the Western Naval Task Force –

ordered HMS *Abercrombie* to move from CENT. Her first mission was to fire on Niscemi, about eight miles inland, which was known to have an Italian observation post and strongpoint. Captain Falkner was so keen to help that he shifted ballast to give the monitor's 15-inch guns extra elevation, a tactic which evidently paid off, for when Niscemi was occupied the following day it was found that the enemy headquarters had been destroyed[20].

The furthest west of the beaches, JOSS, was the objective of General Truscott's 3rd Infantry Division, supported by Combat Command A of 2nd Armored Division. The convoy carrying the formations moved in three echelons, leaving Bizerta on 6 and 7 July and assembling south of Gozo on the 9th. When the weather worsened, the slower vessels were ordered to cut corners to reduce the sailing time to ensure that they reached the assembly area off Sicily on time.

The headquarters ship, the USS *Biscayne*, dropped anchor in the transport area at 0135 hours on D Day. Nothing having been heard from the other ships, it was assumed that they had all reached their positions on time; radio silence had been imposed, with the exception of emergency messages, which included informing headquarters of delays which might affect the operation. At 0200 hours gunfire could be heard from the direction of Gela, which had evidently also been heard by the defenders ashore. Searchlights located on the heights above Licata and the ridge to the west began to sweep Yellow and Blue Beaches and the sea offshore, illuminating the vessels lying there ready to disgorge their troops. The *Biscayne* was highlighted by four searchlights from the shore, which were strong enough to permit those aboard to read. Rear Admiral Conolly, believing that the ship had been seen, gave the order to prepare to open fire, but delayed the decision until Truscott had been consulted. He counselled waiting until the enemy fired, and the moment passed – after about ten minutes in which the ship sat in the glare of the lights, they were switched off, the *Biscayne* evidently not having been seen[21]. The landing operation proceeded as planned.

By 0340 hours reports began to arrive that the flotillas of landing craft were all present and that the landings were underway, and an hour later Truscott was informed that the first wave of troops was ashore on Blue, Yellow and Red Beaches. No word came from Green Beach, and the pilots of two Cub aircraft which were posed on an improvised flight deck on LST *386* were warned to stand by to fly a spotting mission to ascertain what was happening there. Through a misunderstanding, the aircraft were launched and on their way by daybreak. Shortly afterwards, one reported back that American troops were seen climbing the cliffs to the rear of Green Beach. The Cubs continued to provide updates on their progress and to spot enemy artillery locations for the next two hours.

On Red Beach, 1st Battalion of 7th Infantry, the assault battalion, came ashore at 0400 hours. It had tactical surprise and managed to cross the beach to the cliff behind it before the enemy responded with machinegun fire from both flanks. The GIs climbed the cliff through gullies and within an hour all resistance in the immediate beach area had been overcome. The battalion then pushed inland for about a mile to an assembly area. The other two battalions from the regiment followed about forty minutes later, but enemy artillery fire and soft sand delayed matters, particularly in clearing vehicles off the beach through the exits up the steep dry stream beds which were the only way up the cliffs.

Enemy artillery fire continued to fall on Red Beach for some time, and a 47mm gun which was on the left flank hit two LCTs. Smoke was laid to cover the disembarking troops and the Italian guns were eventually dealt with by the Navy. At 0630 hours the first Field and Armored Artillery guns came ashore, established positions inland, and began to provide support to the infantry; they were followed by a company of tanks at 0900 hours.

On Green Beach the 3rd Ranger Battalion was landed by British-manned LCAs from the *Princess Astrid* and the *Princess Charlotte*.[22] They began to arrive on the beach at 0300 hours, achieving complete surprise, and the Rangers were across the beach and through a wide belt of wire before being discovered. The enemy brought machinegun fire on them, a two-edged sword because they gave away their positions which allowed the Rangers to deal with them quickly, thus giving a clear run for the following troops, the 2nd Battalion of 15th Infantry Regimental Combat Team.

The infantry pushed eastwards through the Monte Sole hill pass towards Licata, and at 0735 hours the American flag, brought specifically for the purpose, was raised over Castel Sant' Angelo, on the high ground west of the city. Four hours later, following a naval bombardment, Licata was in American hands.

Yellow Beach was the objective of 3rd Battalion of the 15th Infantry, which landed at 0345 hours, H+1. As the landing craft beached the enemy opened fire with machineguns and small arms, but the resistance was swiftly overcome, and the infantry seized the spurs above the beach and pushed along Highway 123, arriving in Licata at 1130 hours, about the same time as the 1st Battalion arrived there from the north and 2nd Battalion from the west.

The 2nd Battalion of the 30th Infantry Regiment was the assault unit on Blue Beach, landing there at 0330 hours. Again, tactical surprise was achieved but the troops were fired upon by rifles and machine guns from pillboxes along the beach, and then artillery opened up from a strongpoint on the east of the beach. Prearranged naval gunfire soon neutralized the enemy guns, and the infantry set about dealing with the pillboxes, using a ten-man drill which they had rehearsed during training. They then advanced on the strongpoint at Poggio Lungoe and occupied it at a quarter to nine. The 1st Battalion landed half an hour after the first assault wave and moved inland to take the high ground which overlooked the beach area.

After 1100 hours, the Division consolidated its positions. 7th Infantry continued to disembark vehicles and equipment, 15th Infantry was ordered to push northwards along Highway 123, and the 30th Infantry prepared to move north or west to counter any enemy moves. Truscott established his command post on Yellow Beach just after midday, and then moved it to the north of Licata during the afternoon. His reserve was Combat Command A, less one battalion, and the 20th Engineers; and at midday the 41st Infantry began disembarking in Licata port. Reconnaissance patrols began to push further inland; the bridge over the Fiume Palma was found to be prepared for demolition and was defended.

Before evening the eight-by-fifteen mile beachhead had been secured, and supplies and reinforcements were pouring in through the captured port of Licata. Nearly 3,000 prisoners, predominantly Italian, had been taken, and aggressive patrolling was pushing the area still larger.

Behind the advancing troops, on the landing beaches, the work continued to build up the Allied strength. In the American zone Army Shore Parties, and in the British 'Beach Bricks', turned the sometimes chaotic nature of the beaches into an orderly disembarkation area. With the Beach Bricks were fourteen companies of Pioneers, including men from Bechuanaland and Basutoland, whose task it was to land with, or immediately behind, the assault troops and to unload guns, vehicles and ammunition that were needed quickly, and to build beach tracks and roads, make airstrips and provide smoke cover, collect the wounded and bury the dead and guard prisoners. If necessary, they would also provide a reserve for the assault troops in establishing a firm beachhead. In addition to these there was a Dilution Company of Bechuana Pioneers serving in 209 Heavy Anti-Aircraft Battery, R.A., which was to provide anti-aircraft cover for Syracuse. 'Dilution' companies were manned by Pioneers who were now employed by other arms, such as the artillery. They retained their Pioneer capbadges, but to all intents and purposes became gunners, in some cases providing all of the personnel except the gun No 1 and above. They were swiftly followed by 1977 Company which was to give Syracuse smoke cover as soon as the port had been captured. Pioneer casualties in the initial landings were light, 212 Company suffering most heavily with the loss of four men drowned in the heavy swell in which they were working[23].

At Pachino airfield Pioneers and Royal Engineers of 15 Airfield Construction Group, who had come ashore at about 0930 hours, took charge of some 240 prisoners who had surrendered to the Canadians. They then addressed the problem of restoring the ploughed-up airfield to use, marking out a 'crash strip' which Allied aircraft could use in an emergency, while they awaited the arrival of heavy engineering equipment still to be landed on the beach. Despite an enemy air-raid the following evening which caused some casualties, they had the airfield open for use on 12 July.

Overall, the Allies had succeeded in establishing a foothold on enemy soil, with a minimum of casualties. The Official History calls it a 'coming of age' of British combined operations, for the Navy and Army had, for the first time in five hundred years, worked effectively together professionally to plan and prepare an operation of great magnitude. The authors single out the naval officers and men of the landing craft for special praise, and indeed the contemporary accounts support this acclaim. They authors of the history are less fulsome in their praise of the Air Forces for the part they played in inter-service relations, however, as again are the contemporary accounts. And while the landings were successful, the question was raised by the authors about just how successful the landings would have been had the enemy been prepared to resist more determinedly, and had used their available forces to better effect.

1 Dillon & Bradford.
2 Durnford-Slater.
3 Malony.
4 Moses – Faithful Sixth.
5 Malony.
6 Delaforce.
7 Canadian Operations in Sicily Report No 127.
8 Saunders – Green Beret.
9 Ibid.
10 Morison.
11 Morison.
12 Ibid.
13 Morison.
14 Morison.
15 Morison.
16 Whitlock and 45 Division Report.
17 Morison.
18 Morison.
19 Morison.
20 Morison.
21 3rd (US) Division Report
22 3rd (US) Division Report
23 Rhodes-Wood

CHAPTER SEVEN

THE AXIS REACTION

THE LANDING CAME AS NO SURPRISE to the Axis forces on Sicily; as the war diary of the German liaison staff with the Italian *Sixth Army* reported, they were anticipating it for several hours before it occurred:

July 9th, 6.20 p.m.: Radio message from 2nd Fliegerkorps *indicates the presence of six convoys totalling 150 to 200 vessels in the waters north of Malta and Gozo.*

8.05 p.m.: Radio from C.-in-C. south: 150 landing-craft at 4.30 p.m. in a position north of Malta, steering north.

11.15 p.m. Chief of Staff of Italian 6th Army to General Senger: We anticipate an attack at dawn against Catania and Gela[1].

German intelligence reports had listed the numbers and types of shipping that had been assembling in the Mediterranean for some time; on 1 July, for example, the passage of five hospital ships through the Straits of Gibraltar was interpreted as an indication of forthcoming Allied operations. Two days later, heavy concentrations of troop ships with landing craft aboard, and ten LCTs, were reported at Port Said. What remained unclear, until 9 July, was exactly where the blow would strike – but that fact was now becoming apparent[2].

At 0500 hours on 10 July the first reports arrived of parachute landings in the region of Comiso and San Pietro, between Caltagirone and the coast. News also came in that gliders had landed near Augusta[3].

As dawn broke on 10 July the size and locations of the Allied landings were becoming apparent to the defenders of Sicily. Although details were not always clear, the Italians and their German allies were able to form a picture of events and to begin to plan their countermeasures accordingly. It appeared to them that the main threat was in the south and east, where the landings had occurred that morning; little credence seems to have been given to the possibility that further attacks would come in the west of the island. Even should these happen at some future time or date, the Axis forces had enough on their hands dealing with those invaders that had arrived on the coastline between Licata and Syracuse, and the available resources had to be deployed to deal with this threat. The Axis response was, firstly, to contain the beachheads while their own reinforcements arrived from mainland Italy. Secondly, they would attempt to drive the Allies back into the sea. And finally, in the event that this was unsuccessful, they would fight to keep their escape route off the island – the Straits of Messina – open.

Guzzoni's first action was to order *15th Panzer Grenadier Division*, only recently arrived in the west of Sicily, to move back to the centre of the island ready to be deployed where and when the situation demanded. He also ordered *XIV Corps Headquarters* and the *Livorno Division*, with the *Hermann Göring Division*, less *Group Schmalz* which was in the Syracuse area and therefore already likely to be committed, to counterattack the western beaches before the Americans could establish themselves solidly.

These intentions were all very well, but Guzzoni was in the unfortunate position of not knowing whether or not his orders were being carried out. As previously mentioned, Axis communications on Sicily were patchy, at best, and much depended on the telephone system. Allied bombing and the actions of the scattered American paratroopers had succeeded in cutting telegraph wires across the south of the island, with the consequence that some units failed to receive instructions and instead acted on their own initiatives. Their response was generally in line with the defensive doctrine that had been laid down for Sicily, which called for counterattacks against any landing to buy time for the central reserves to deploy. Many of the first actions carried out by Axis troops would be relatively small uncoordinated actions rather than the synchronized massive assault that the planners had envisaged, because of the inability to communicate effectively.

The situation in *Sixth Army Headquarters* was one of confusion. *Luftwaffe* General Alfred Mahncke, who was visiting Sicily on a fact-finding mission for von Richthofen, recorded that the headquarters looked

> *...very much like a disturbed ant's nest. Soldiers milled around in senseless confusion, a babble of hysterical voices clashed with the noise of motor cars and trucks starting up. Tatty soldiers loitered on street corners, their weapons discarded. Nobody seemed to be in control any more. ADCs rushed between offices, staff cars were packed high with belongings. It looked like a panic evacuation.*

Depressed, he flew off in his Storch, diverting from his journey back to Catania to fly over the landing beaches. His peace of mind was not reassured by what he saw, for over Augusta he saw 'a total route of the Italian forces' which were fleeing, weaponless, and clogging the roads as they went. His day got no better, for shortly afterwards his aircraft was shot down by an Allied fighter and his mechanic killed. Rescued by Italian troops, he made his way to Catania, where he ended the day with a drink. He doubtless felt that he needed it[4].

In the *Hermann Göring Division* General Conrath learned of the landings early in the morning of D Day. The warning came not from *Sixth Army Headquarters* but from Kesselring's staff outside of Rome. The news was confirmed by his own patrols which ran into groups of American paratroops near Niscemi, and by Schmalz, who was moving against the British airborne and sea landings near Syracuse. Conrath decided that he would implement the defence plan by counterattacking against the

Americans at Gela. Using the independent German signals link, he informed von Senger of his intentions, and having obtained approval from that individual, swung into action. At 0400 hours two of his reinforced regiments, one armour-heavy, the other infantry-heavy, began to move down three roads from the Caltagirone area to assembly points south of Niscemi and Biscari. The move took longer than Conrath anticipated, or wished, for the roads were poor and were subjected to Allied air strikes. The ubiquitous American paratroops also hindered movement by setting up obstacles and ambushes, and the Germans were still moving to the assembly areas five hours after setting out.

General Rossi, commanding *XVI Corps*, also reacted. He dispatched *Mobile Group E* forward, with the result outlined earlier – their counterattack failed. Running into about one hundred American paratroops who had established a roadblock, supported by machine guns from an Italian strongpoint which they had captured earlier, the column was ambushed. The three leading vehicles were shot up and their occupants killed or captured, after which the Italians put in a two-company infantry attack which was permitted to approach to within 200 yards before the paratroopers opened a devastating fire. The Italians withdrew and began to shell the position from beyond small-arms range. Unable to respond to this bombardment, the Americans withdrew towards the town of Piano Lupo, just as naval shells – called down by 1st (US) Division troops further to the rear – began to fall on the enemy. Without the paratroops in front of them, the Italians were able to push tanks forward through the naval gunfire to Piano Lupo and onwards towards Gela, where their advance was eventually repelled by the American infantry with naval support.

Gela also came under attack from the *Livorno Division*, which mounted a two-pronged assault from the northwest. Some twenty tanks advanced down the Butera road, losing seven or eight of their number to naval fire as they came. The remainder got into the town where the Rangers engaged them with bazookas and grenades in running fights in the narrow streets. Without infantry support, the tanks were forced to retire to Butera. Too late to either support the tanks, or to benefit from their presence, about 600 Italian infantrymen then mounted their attack on Gela. Advancing in almost parade-ground fashion, they were torn to pieces by American rifle, machine-gun and mortar fire. Having suffered enormous casualties without managing to reach the outskirts of town, the survivors fell back.

Conrath's men were finally ready south of Niscemi at 1400 hours. Their attack on Gela, from the northeast, did not progress very far before it was halted by GIs, once again with the aid of naval gunfire. By 1600 hours, the attack was called off, having achieved nothing in respect of driving the invaders back into the sea. The Axis response to the American landings, on 10 July at least, was little more than mounting probing attacks which were designed to feel out the positions and strength of the invaders.

On the eastern coast, where the British had landed, the widely dispersed *Napoli Division* put up only scattered resistance. The Italians had eventually retaken the Ponte Grande, as we have seen, only to lose it shortly afterwards, but to the north of Syracuse *Group Schmalz* had come down from the Catania area and had contingents in Priolo, south of Augusta. Syracuse fell to the British during the evening of D Day, but Guzzoni, still without adequate communications to the front lines, dismissed this fact as rumour. He was better informed about the situation on the American beaches, and at 2000 hours that day he ordered *XVI Corps* to use the *Napoli Division* and *Group Schmalz* to contain the British while the *Livorno* and *Hermann Göring Divisions* were to mount a strong, and this time coordinated, counteroffensive against Gela on the morning of 11 July. The Italians would attack the American positions from the northwest, while the Germans would synchronise their attack from the northeast to come at the Americans at the same time.

In Rome, Kesselring was kept in the picture by *Luftwaffe* units in Catania and Taormina. He had no means of communicating directly with Guzzoni, but he had no doubt that Syracuse had fallen, and informed the Italian government accordingly. This news, and the realization that the Italian coastal defence divisions had collapsed without putting up much of a fight, confirmed his fears about the ability of the Italians to raise a competent resistance. The burden would fall on the Germans, and he accordingly sent a message to Conrath via *Luftwaffe* channels, ordering him to attack Gela with the *Hermann Göring Division* the next morning.

This message reached Conrath just after he returned to his command post having been briefed by General Rossi on his part in the same operation. Rossi had ordered a concerted attack to commence at 0600 hours on 11 July, in which the Germans would move on Gela from the northeast while the Italians did the same from the northwest. Under orders from both his Italian and German superiors to attack Gela, Conrath was doubly motivated – if, indeed, he needed motivation.

Guzzoni did not receive confirmation of the fall of Syracuse until 0300 hours on 11 July. The news came from von Senger, who in turn had got it from German sources, and it was to provoke a rethink in *Sixth Army Headquarters*. Guzzoni's first concern was now to prevent the British from pushing northwards up the coast to Messina, where they could cut the Axis forces' line of retreat to mainland Italy. He therefore recast his plans to cater for this possibility, by ordering Rossi to move the *Hermann Göring Division* eastwards against the British as soon as its attacks at Gela had proved successful. The *Livorno Division* was to proceed westwards against Licata once the Gela operation had been completed.

For the commanders on the ground, there was now the added complication that they had to prepare to follow their converging thrusts on Gela with diverging movements, leaving the town as soon as they had cleared it of the Allies.

At 0615 hours on 11 July Conrath ordered three *panzer* forces forward. He had been delayed for fifteen minutes, missing the agreed time, but had assumed that the *Livorno Division* was advancing as scheduled. Once again, Axis communications systems did not allow him to confirm the Italian movements. At the same time one of the Italian columns, built around *Mobile Group E*, moved off to commence its assault, and a number of German and Italian aircraft mounted an attack on the beachhead and the shipping lying offshore.

Under heavy fire, *Mobile Group E* fought its way forward for about two hours, until forced back by the unrelenting shelling from naval and field artillery. Meanwhile Conrath's groups of infantry and tanks became bogged down in a series of close-quarter battles. Conrath went forward personally to reorganize his troops and to set them back onto following the plan. The Germans managed to overrun or outflank a number of American positions and by 0900 hours they were poised to thrust forward, when they were struck in the eastern flank by a group of American paratroopers led by Gavin. This action forced Conrath to divert part of his strength to deal with the threat; but the remainder of his force continued to move on the Gela beaches.

General Patton, until now aboard his headquarters ship the *Monrovia*, came ashore at about 0930, complete with polished black riding boots, necktie and his twin ivory-handled revolvers. He made his way towards the headquarters of 1st (US) Division, but took a detour to visit Colonel Derby's Ranger Headquarters, a detour which saved him from running into seven German tanks which were advancing down the road from the opposite direction.

By now, to the west, the *Livorno Division* was putting heavy pressure on the beachhead. Unloading stopped as engineers, infantrymen, Rangers and everyone who could handle a weapon manned hastily-formed defensive positions in the sand dunes and in the streets and buildings of Gela. With tank and naval support, the Italians were brought to a halt, suffering large numbers of casualties. Observing the Italian attack for a while, Patton was impressed by the way the Rangers were handling the fight, and ordered some tanks forward to assist. Naval 6-inch shells took no prisoners, but the infantry and Rangers rounded up about 400 Italians as the *Livorno* withdrew. For the present, the division was ineffective as a fighting formation[5].

To the northeast, those *Hermann Göring Division panzers* that were not involved with Gavin's paratroopers drove forward through the shells and smoke to within 2,000 yards of the shoreline. Ammunition and stores dumps, and landing craft on and close to the beach were bombarded, and it began to look as if victory was in sight. Guzzoni received a signal from the fighting which stated that the Americans had been forced to re-embark temporarily, news that was sufficiently optimistic to cause him – after a brief consultation with von Senger – to order Rossi to wheel the *Hermann Göring Division* eastwards towards Vittoria and thence to Syracuse, to stop the Allied movement which would have cut his escape route through Messina.

It was not to be, however. The Americans were not re-embarking, but were engaging the Tigers and Mark III and IV tanks with Shermans, artillery, and bazookas. Naval gunfire was not practicable here, for the combatants were too close together for observers to clearly identify targets. The Germans were held on the line of the coastal highway, while to their rear confusion set in as the advance stalled and the navy began to drop shells on their reinforcements. Chased northwards by this fire, the Germans started a slow retirement which picked up speed as it proceeded. Sixteen tanks were left in flames on the low land bordering the Moroglio River, more in other locations. Having lost a third of his armour, Conrath called a halt to the attack at 1400 hours, although fighting continued into the hours of darkness.

The resistance put up by the Americans around Gela and the arrival of more Allied troops in Sicily forced Guzzoni to change his plans again. His formations were under pressure in the Vittoria-Comiso area, and the prospect of moving the *Hermann Göring Division* to the east coast via Palazzolo Acreide, which had been his intention earlier that day, was now unpromising. Guzzoni therefore ordered *XVI Corps* to halt offensive operations in the Gela area and to withdraw the *Hermann Göring Division* to Caltagirone. The division would then proceed to Vizzini on 12 July, to move against the British. The *Livorno Division* was to cover the German redeployment by concentrating in the Caltagirone area.

But, yet again, communications between the various Axis formations delayed these orders reaching Conrath. Von Senger was visiting the *Hermann Göring Division* and felt that the American forces blocking the route to Vittoria were incapable of stopping the Germans – the Americans had, after all, taken two days of battering and would surely be unable to take any more. He therefore ordered Conrath to carry out Guzzoni's earlier plan. But the force of paratroopers and infantrymen under Gavin was more than equal to the task of stopping them. The German advance failed to get off the ground, and ignoring von Senger's orders Conrath instead obeyed those given by Guzzoni and withdrew to the hills south of Niscemi as the first stage of his move to Caltagirone.

On the evening of D+1 the Americans had reason to feel that they had done well. In front of 1st (US) Division were over forty destroyed German and Italian tanks. To their right, 45th (US) Division had captured Comiso and its airfield, including 125 German aircraft, of which twenty were serviceable. The town of Ragusa had been captured by GIs, who arrested the mayor and chief of police, and the Italian-speakers amongst the Americans had amused themselves by answering frantic telephone calls from Italian units wanting situation reports. On the west, 3rd (US)

Division had pushed out of its beachhead and some troops had advanced as far as fourteen miles away from Licata. Contact between the three landing areas was well established, and part of 2nd (US) Armored Division was ashore and in action, the navy was still supporting operations with its firepower, and the unloading of further materiel was proceeding to plan.

The situation was not yet as secure as Patton required, however. The enemy had managed to mount threatening counterattacks, and these had delayed some aspects of his plans; the capture of Ponto Olivo and Niscemi, which should have been achieved that day, were still in enemy hands and would have to wait until the 12th.

The Axis counterattacks were only to be expected, and Patton had already made contingency plans for reinforcing the beachheads so that the high ground inland from the landing areas could be taken. Possession of these features would give added security to the disembarkation process.

Using airborne forces to reinforce the beachhead gave Patton a flexible and comparatively swift option. It did have potential problems, however: the drops during the evening of 9 July illustrated these clearly. Poor weather conditions and the nervousness of Allied anti-aircraft gunners had rendered the missions fatal to a large number of parachutists and glider troops, and neither 1 Airlanding Brigade nor 82nd (US) Airborne Division's operations could be regarded as being successful. Before setting out for Sicily Patton had asked General Ridgway to consider the possibility of making parachute drops to reinforce the landings; Ridgway found little difficulty in agreeing to the proposal, providing that the navy agreed an air corridor along which the aircraft could fly free from the danger of being shot at by Allied shipping. From the naval perspective, this was easier said than done, because fast-flying planes suddenly appearing overhead at low altitude demanded a rapid response from men whose training in aircraft recognition was sometimes rudimentary. What gunner was going to risk his ship being sunk?

Several days before the invasion, Admiral Cunningham's staff agreed the corridor with Ridgway. The aircraft would have to follow a closely prescribed route, and the final section of it would have to be over land so as to avoid the shipping in the offshore assembly areas. The route would cross the coast at Samperi, thirty miles east of Gela, and go inland before turning northwest to the dropping zone. The corridor would be two miles wide, and the aircraft would fly at an altitude of 1,000 feet.

When Patton asked, on 11 July, for the operation to proceed, the DZ was to be the Gela-Farello airfield, now in American hands. This fitted in well with the naval demand that the aircraft should make landfall at Samperi. The entire route, from North Africa to the DZ, would be over Allied-held land and sea. It remained to warn off the anti-aircraft teams ashore and afloat that the operation would take place shortly before midnight. That afternoon Ridgway checked that the order had been sent out from Seventh Army, and that it had been received. It was soon apparent that not every gun crew had been informed, but Ridgway was assured that instructions not to open fire would be circulated well before H Hour. As stated earlier, the Axis air forces had mounted several raids against the beachheads on 11 July, nearly 500 sorties in all. Anti-aircraft crews had a busy day, and despite their efforts a transport ship had a hole blown in its side by a near miss, bombs had fallen amongst the vessels anchored offshore, the Gela beaches had been strafed, and the Liberty ship *Robert Rowan*, loaded with ammunition, exploded spectacularly half an hour after being struck by a bomb. The smoke column rising from its ruin made a clear navigation aid for later air attacks. The situation was not designed to relax the anti-aircraft crews, who were understandably edgy.

At 1900 hours that evening 144 aircraft took off from their airfields in Tunisia. The air was placid, and a quarter moon gave sufficient light for the pilots to make out the C-47s leading each 'V' of nine aircraft. After they turned over Malta and headed for Sicily some light anti-aircraft fire was aimed at them from ships below, but no damage was caused. More serious was the German air attack which was launched at Gela at 2150 hours, just as the paratroops were approaching Sicily. The enemy attack involved large numbers of aircraft, which attracted Allied fighters to a dogfight high above the anchorage, where shipping attempted to scatter while pumping anti-aircraft shells skywards. The chaos continued for nearly an hour before the skies became clear – just as the American troop-carriers crossed the coast near Samperi. At 2040 hours the first of the American paratroops jumped from their planes over the Gela-Farello DZ.

As the second wave of C-47s approached Lake Biviere, the final check-point before starting the run-in, a machine gun opened fire on them from the ground. The gun was American, and its fire was sufficient to cause every anti-aircraft gun on land and sea to commence shooting at the slow-flying formation above them. Panic had taken hold on the ground, fuelled by the earlier air strikes on the beachhead.

The 'V's of aircraft broke formation as some were shot down. Most pilots managed to drop their loads, some where they should have done, but many landed elsewhere including into the sea, and eight aircraft returned to their bases with their paratroops still aboard. Six aircraft received direct hits; some of the men aboard them were killed or wounded before they could jump, others were hit as they parachuted to the ground, and some were shot after they landed. The bill for the operation was twenty-three aircraft that failed to return, another thirty-seven badly damaged. Of about 2,300 men of the 504th Parachute Regimental Combat Team that had taken off that evening, eighty-two paratroopers were killed and another 131 wounded, with sixteen missing.

One account, by First Lieutenant C A Drew from the 82nd Airborne Division Report, will illustrate the event:

We jumped into a steady stream of AA fire, and not knowing that they were friendly troops. There was 4 men killed 4 wounded from my Platoon. Three of these men were hit coming down and one was killed on the ground because we had the wrong password. After landing we found that this had been changed to "Think"—"Quickly".

The AA we jumped into was the 180th Infantry of the 45th Division. They also were not told that we were coming. Later we found out that the 45th Division had been told we were coming but word never had got to the 180th Infantry of the 45th Division.

We tried to reorganize but found we didn't have but 44 men including three officers... About 75 yards from where I landed, Plane No. 915 was hit and burned. To my knowledge, only the pilot and three men got out. The pilot was thrown through the window... Another plane was shot down on the beach and another was down burning about 1,000 yards to my front. Altogether there were three planes I know of being shot down.[6]

Although Patton had done everything that he had considered possible to prevent any misunderstanding between the various arms and services, he had been unable to prevent the catastrophe. Some units had clearly not been informed. An angry Eisenhower sent Patton a cable, in which he 'cussed out' the general and ordered that no further airborne operations should be carried out until an inquiry had been held.

The disaster was thoroughly investigated, with inconclusive results. Amongst the culprits blamed by various interested parties keen to attribute blame elsewhere were lack of inter-service coordination, poor discipline amongst the anti-aircraft gunners, unsound planning, poor navigation, the presence of enemy aircraft during the operation, and poor distribution of information. Whatever the truth of the matter, it would appear that it was not only the Axis forces that suffered from bad communications. Ridgway was inclined to draw a line under the event, with the consolation that lessons had been learnt which should mean that there would be no repetition of the mistakes. His optimism was misplaced.

To the east of the American beaches things had gone much more quietly. The Canadians suffered only two officers and thirteen other ranks as casualties (the Diary of the Assistant Director of the Medical Services did not break down the figures into killed and wounded[7]) and the only impact made by an air raid during the night 10/11 July was to encourage the troops to put more effort into their trench-digging. The Royal Marine Commandos of the Special Service Brigade suffered heavier casualties than the Canadians, for in General Simonds' report to Fifteenth Army Group he estimated the total numbers for all of his forces as being a maximum of seventy-five killed and wounded. There were some 700 prisoners taken, mostly from *206 Coastal Division*, with twenty *Luftwaffe* personnel.

On 11 July the Canadians seized Ispica. Prisoners captured during the previous day had reported that the town was empty of both military and civilians, but the first Canadian reconnaissance parties to approach it came under attack from snipers and grenades. Whoever it was that had decided to resist soon vanished, however, for when the Edmonton Regiment moved in at 1450 hours they met no opposition. 'The only difficulties encountered', says the regiment's Diary, 'were enthusiastic greetings of the civilian population and the frantic endeavour of the military population to surrender'[8]. The Seaforth Highlanders of Canada, who passed through the town at 1730 hours, reported: 'Many natives stood in the streets waving and clapping their hands at us. Wine and fruit were passed out to the troops, the hatred of Mussolini and the Germans always being expressed time and time again'. Had the Italians elected to make a fight of it, the story would have been far different, for Ispica stands on a sheer cliff 150 feet high. The town was defended by extensive fields of barbed wire, but Allied bombing had reduced many of the buildings to rubble, which may have been a contributory factor to the inhabitants' willingness to surrender.

All along the Canadian front only token resistance was encountered, if any at all, and the Italians – military and civilian – appeared glad to see the invading troops. While the great majority of Italian soldiers were willing to surrender, those few German units in the area slipped away, as did a number of Fascist officials. At Pozzallo, a small coastal town southeast of Ispica, a naval party went ashore to receive the surrender of two officers and ninety-six other ranks after firing 160 shells to the north and east of the town. A company of the Seaforth took over later in the afternoon, and reported taking ten officers and 250 soldiers prisoner, with much equipment.

On the northern sector of the Canadian advance contact had been made with 51st (Highland) Division, which had captured Rosolini at 1130 hours on the 11th. They handed the town over to the Canadians, and proceeded on their way towards Noto. By the end of the day the Canadians were able to report that the three phases of their original plan had been completed ahead of schedule. They now proceeded to work towards their 'Second Objective' of Modica and Ragusa.

After an overnight march of twenty-two miles, the Princess Patricia's Canadian Light Infantry reached the high ground overlooking Modica at 0500 hours on 12 July. Outside Ragusa, the Royal Canadian Regiment were also in position, having been sent forward on a motley collection of vehicles, which included tanks and captured trucks.

51st (Highland) Division, which had landed with little difficulty on BARK East and South Beaches, were within three miles of Vizzini by nightfall on 11 July, an advance of twenty miles. The following day 1st Battalion, The Black Watch came under heavy shelling in the Bucheri Hills – from Canadian artillery – but the division's real blooding would come later.

Further north, 50th Division had experienced a very successful D Day, even if the landing had not gone precisely to plan. For the majority of soldiers, the biggest challenge of the day had been marching inland and climbing slopes across ploughed fields divided by stone walls, in the heat and burdened with heavy loads. Commandeered Italian vehicles, including bicycles, carts and even prams were at a premium. During the night of 10/11 July patrols had penetrated 4,000 yards inland without making contact.

At dawn on 11 July carrier patrols were sent forward, and reported that Canicattini Bagni, twelve miles west of Syracuse, was clear. In the south Noto was occupied and contact was made with XXX Corps. There were isolated contacts with the enemy – five miles east of Palazzolo a patrol from 8th Battalion Durham Light Infantry was ambushed and two carriers destroyed, a loss which the battalion felt to be serious, given the problems it was having with transport[9].

During the night of 12/13 July, Augusta fell into British hands. In a successful attempt to seize it quickly a daylight landing was made late in the afternoon, against naval advice. Once again, it was Paddy Mayne's Special Raiding Squadron which carried out the task, having been briefed that it was to be little more than a mopping-up operation. As far as the Italian defenders were concerned, it was, for Admiral Leonardi, the port commander, ordered the guns destroyed and the fuel and ammunition supplies demolished. Colonel Schmalz reported disgustedly that the Italian officers deserted their men, and many units of *206 Coastal Division* surrendered meekly. *Group Schmalz*, however, was made of sterner stuff. In the town and on the hills around the port, the Germans opened fire on the landing craft as they left *Ulster Monarch* at about 1930 hours. Under machinegun and artillery fire the LCAs landed their passengers in neck-deep water, supported by naval gunfire. The SRS troopers then cleared the town of Augusta, fighting house-to-house until 5th Division arrived early in the morning of 12 July[10].

To understand the advance northwards from the Eighth Army landing beaches to Catania, and thence to Messina, it is necessary to take a brief look at the terrain and the road system. A coastal plain some seven miles wide lies between Cassibile and Syracuse. North of the Syracuse-Floridia-Solarino road, which runs roughly west from Syracuse, the country is very broken and hilly, extending north for ten or twelve miles to the Plain of Catania. There were two roads northwards, the good coastal road along which 5th Division advanced, and the inland road from Floridia to Sortino. These two roads met at Lentini, on the edge of the plain, and from there the road became one, crossing the Leonardo River and then running along a low but commanding ridge until it descended to the Simeto River and the Primasole Bridge. North of here the road ran over flat countryside to Catania. The inland road up which 50th Division was to advance passed through valleys above which were steep hills some 200-300 feet high. The road was not Sicily's best; it wound through tightly-confining stone walls with hair-pin bends, and through constraining villages. It was really only suitable for one-way traffic, and certainly not best fitted for the vehicles of a modern army with its tanks, trucks, and self-propelled guns.

As Montgomery's plan to advance to Messina fell into place, 51st (Highland) Division moved into positions that had been captured by 50st Division, while it in turn moved to take over those captured by 5th Division and was then to be ready to go on to Lentini. 5th Division was to push northwards along the coast. Transport shortages started to bite, with the RASC only being able to supply 50th Division as far as Sortino, and units were ordered to unload all food and ammunition and send their vehicles back to Avola to shuttle supplies forward to a dump near Floridia.

The division sent forward a mobile column consisting of a squadron of tanks with carriers and self-propelled artillery with the aim of blocking the road from Solarino to Palazzolo and then attacking enemy positions facing Solarino from the rear. The column was late in setting out, and was further delayed by difficult country. Although it had some fighting and took a number of prisoners, it never seriously engaged the enemy, who were able to mount two counterattacks, one of which – with four or five Italian-crewed French R35 light tanks from the *Napoli Division* – broke through the position held by 2nd Battalion The Wiltshire Regiment. All but one of the tanks was halted by anti-tank fire, and the survivor dashed on alone, firing all weapons and getting as far as Floridia before knocking down a telegraph pole and crashing into a Sherman tank, when its crew was taken prisoner[11]. At least some Italians were prepared to put up a fight.

The enemy positioned in front of 50th Division had to be dealt with. They were a potential threat to the division's communications, and could not simply be bypassed and left at liberty to decide where and when to move next. Divisional orders were issued late that evening, to the effect that 69th Brigade would continue the advance through Sortino to Lentini, while 151 Brigade would mop up the enemy. Once this task had been completed, the latter formation would relieve 69 Brigade in Sortino. It was also to patrol the plateau overlooking the Sortino road from the east.

69 Brigade opened operations against Sortino that evening, 12 July. 5th Battalion, The East Yorks Regiment, passed through the lines held by 6 DLI north of Solarino and were in sight of their objective by 1820 hours. Subjected to heavy mortar and machine-gun fire when a mile south of the village, they were forced to take cover off the road before deploying to clear the enemy from the high ground to the north. At midnight the defenders partially withdrew, and the East Yorks were able to occupy the high ground on each side of the village. At 0600 hours 6 DLI passed through and occupied Sortino. It became clear that the enemy, Germans from *Group Schmalz*, had withdrawn at about two in the morning. It was also becoming clear that the enemy was stiffening its resistance as the Eighth Army moved northwards.

With the high ground around Solarino firmly in British hands, it was now essential to take the heights overlooking the Plain of Catania before the enemy could coordinate their defences in this difficult country. The divisional commander, Major General Kirkman, had not long issued his orders to achieve this, when he was summonsed to Montgomery's headquarters to be briefed on the next plans for the advance on Catania.

The orders from Montgomery read as follows:

(a) *5 Div, having captured AUGUSTA were to concentrate in area NW of AUGUSTA.*

(b) *50 (N) Div during night 13/14 July, to capture CARLENTINI and LENTINI.*

(c) *One airborne brigade, during night 13/14 July, to be dropped to capture PRIMASOLE Bridge.*

(d) *3 Commando to land during night with the object of capturing the bridge over the LEONARDO River some 3,000 yards North of LENTINI.*

(e) *50 (N) Div on 14th July to take over PRIMASOLE Bridge from the airborne brigade.*[12]

Montgomery had appreciated the strength of the defences Schmalz had managed to assemble. His thoughts were directed in two directions, the first of which, as outlined above, was to leap over the enemy positions to secure the bridge crossings. This would prevent their demolition, so keeping the route to Catania open, and would cut off some of the enemy forces. His other thought was to look westwards and to use XXX Corps to outflank the enemy by pushing through Caltagirone, Enna and Leonforte, swinging around to Mount Etna's western slopes and getting behind the German and Italian troops blocking his entry to Catania.

There was a major difficulty with this proposal. The only feasible road up which XXX Corps could move quickly enough to put the plan into operation was Highway 124, which had been assigned to the Americans.

Montgomery merely ignored this difficulty: he ordered Lieutenant General Sir Oliver Leese to advance up Highway 124. In doing so, he violated the boundary between the Eighth and Seventh Armies and denied the Americans a road which they had planned to use. XXX Corps was directed across the right flank of the Seventh Army advance. The decision to do this was to widen the split between the Allied partners, and was probably to extend the length of the campaign.

While the Eighth Army had been working its way northwards towards Catania, Patton's Seventh Army had been steadily expanding its foothold on Sicily. 1st (US) Infantry Division had taken the Ponte Olivo airfield, 45th (US) Division had captured Biscari, and 3rd (US) Division anchored the army's left flank at Licata. Having achieved these objectives, Patton had no specific orders on which to act next; Alexander had not given guidance other than that the Americans should 'prevent enemy reserves moving eastwards against the left flank of Eighth Army'. Patton, however, was not content to sit idly by, and had ordered Truscott to mount a reconnaissance in force along the coast towards Agrigento. Bradley was also ordered to move inland with 1st and 45th (US) Divisions, towards Caltagirone.

When Alexander visited Patton during the morning of 13 July, he gave broad approval to Patton's actions. Patton explained that possession of Agrigento and Porto Empedocle would greatly ease the logistic problems he was facing without adequate port facilities; and if Bradley were to capture Caltagirone, Enna and Leonforte, he would prevent *15th Panzer Grenadier Division* and the *Hermann Göring Division* from linking up and increasing the opposition to Montgomery's advance on Catania. Bradley would also be in a good position to continue his move northwards, pushing around the western side of Etna to Randazzo. This would work well in coordination with Eighth Army's drive through Catania to Messina.

Although Alexander agreed to the capture of Agrigento – providing it was not too costly in men or equipment – he preferred to keep 3rd (US) Division firm on the left flank of Seventh Army to block any possible incursion from the west by *15th Panzer Grenadier Division*, which had been reported in the area by aerial reconnaissance.

Alexander then moved off to visit Montgomery, who persuaded him to place Highway 124 in British hands. For 45th (US) Division this ruling caused serious difficulties. The division was already shoulder to shoulder with XXX Corps, and there was a danger that sooner or later one ally would accidentally fire on the other. Even before Alexander agreed to place the road in British hands, orders had been issued by Montgomery to use it for an attack that evening. Some hours after the attack started, shortly before midnight, Alexander radioed Patton to inform him that Highway 124 was no longer his.

The immediate impact of this ruling, for the Seventh Army, was that 45th (US) Division would have to move clear of the road. This was not as straightforward an operation as it might sound, for the question than arose as to where it was now to be deployed; Patton's decision was that the division should move westwards and take up position on the left of 1st (US) Division. II (US) Corps would now advance to the west rather than to the north. To get to this position, 45th (US) Division had to return to the Gela beaches and move west, behind 1st (US) Division.

The change of ownership of the road had other implications for operations. When the orders came through for the Americans to relinquish it, they were in an excellent position to break out of the beachhead and to capture the towns of Vizzini and Caltagirone, or so Bradley believed. If 45th (US) Division were to be allowed to do so, they could have moved to the west of 1st (US) Division without having to retire all the way back to the sea, by using the Vizzini-Caltagirone road. But it was not to be. Patton refused Bradley's pleas to argue the case for this possibility with Alexander[13].

The surrender of the road was to have deeper implications than moving a division unnecessarily. The Americans felt, with some justification, that they were being relegated to little more than observers of a British operation, which was being run to further enhance Montgomery's standing – and that the whole affair was yet another example of Montgomery's arrogance. Beneath this belief lay the fear that Alexander had little faith in American military competence. After North Africa, both British and American generals were inclined to distrust each other, with the British being sceptical about the battle-worthiness of the US Army. Alexander seemed fixed to this viewpoint, and the Highway 124 episode was to have long-lasting repercussions, which were to last well up to the end of the war. Relationships between Bradley, Patton, Montgomery and Eisenhower were uneasy from here on; in some instances they had not been warm beforehand, but now they were positively cool.

Patton received Alexander's order without protest, despite being unhappy about it – he could not have welcomed such a decision, which required a major reorganization of his plans and which was, in American eyes, a deliberate snub. But Patton was still wounded by the blast he had received from Eisenhower after the debacle of the airdrop on 11 July; Bradley felt that Patton dared not protest too strongly now, lest Eisenhower fire him[14]. On the ground, the ridiculous situation developed wherein the Canadians of XXX Corps did not initially receive support from the Americans, a mile away, when they ran into enemy opposition on nearing Vizzini. American troops had been ordered not to fire within two miles of the highway, but chose to ignore the order to assist the Canadian advance[15]. Bradley, according to one study, refused to agree the details of the hand-over of the road to General Leese[16].

The move of 45th (US) Division took the pressure off the *Hermann Göring Division*, which was moving eastwards to contest Montgomery's advance onto the Catania Plain. It also allowed *15th Panzer Grenadier Division* to link firmly with the *Hermann Göring Division*, which would have been a more difficult endeavour had Bradley been permitted to continue northwards. The possibility of driving a wedge between the two German formations and exploiting the gap which was covered only by the battered remnants of the *Livorno Division*, was missed while the Americans withdrew to allow the Canadians use of the road.

Montgomery had ordered the Canadians to take two days of rest and reorganization in the vicinity of Ragusa and Giarratana (12 – 14 July). The division's supply lines were stretched to the limit of the available vehicles' capabilities and many of the men had had no more than eight hours' sleep since landing. There were other reasons, however. Montgomery considered that they were a 'bit soft' and that their 'operational discipline was not good' and that they needed a break to get into form.[17] After nearly a month aboard ships, before which the division had been almost three years in the rather cooler climate of the United Kingdom, it is perhaps unsurprising that the Canadians felt the heat and dust, not to mention the lack of transport, more than did some of their comrades in the Eighth Army.

Following their rest, the Canadians were sent north-westwards along Highway 124 to Caltagirone, while 51st (Highland) Division, having captured Vizzini during the night of 14-15 July, turned north, were ordered to form a firm base on XIII Corps' flank. In fact, the division continued to press northwards on the corps' left, almost without pause[18].

The Allied armies were not the only forces to build up their presence on the island. On 13 July Advanced Headquarters, Western Desert Air Force established itself at Pachino airfield. No 244 Wing, with three of its four Spitfire squadrons, flew in from Malta to continue operations over Sicily. The following day the fourth squadron arrived at Pachino, and three squadrons – also Spitfires – from No 324 Wing landed at Comiso airfield. The Americans also arrived: three squadrons of Kittyhawk fighters of the 33rd Fighter Group and the American 111th Tactical Reconnaissance Squadron, with Mustangs, based themselves at Gela-Farello. The Advanced Headquarters of XII Air Support Command had been at Gela since the 12th. On 15 July the remaining two squadrons of No 324 Wing arrived, and two Kittyhawk squadrons of the US 31st Fighter Group flew to Ponte Olivo, and a third to Licata. The available airfields were now pretty much fully occupied, not only by aircraft but also with their supporting units, which provided fighter control and air raid warning facilities, and which included No 40 Air Stores Park, which performed maintenance, and which was in situ eleven days ahead of schedule[19]. Until the Gerbini group of airfields were captured, no further Allied aircraft could be accommodated.

1 Von Senger.
2 Canadian Army HQ Report, Information from German Sources.
3 Von Senger.
4 Mahnke.
5 Blumenson.
6 US Army 82 Airborne Report.
7 Canadian Operations in Italy Report No 127.
8 Ibid.
9 Lewis & English.
10 Dillon & Bradford.
11 Moses – Faithful Sixth.
12 Kirkman.
13 D'Este – Bitter Victory.
14 D'Este - Patton.
15 Whitlock.
16 D'Este – Bitter Victory.
17 Canadian Operations in Italy Report No 127.
18 Maloney.
19 Ibid.

CHAPTER EIGHT

PALERMO

O N 14 JULY ALEXANDER signalled Sir Alan Brooke outlining his intentions for the way in which the campaign would progress. He envisaged a thrust from Catania to Messina by XIII Corps, while XXX Corps would push to Santo Stefano on the north coast before swinging eastwards to Messina, going around the western side of Etna. Once the island had been split in two, Seventh Army would be directed onto Palermo and Trapani. That same day Patton visited Truscott and discussed his desire to capture Porto Empedocle, but in order to do this Agrigento had first to be taken. Excluded from Highway 124 and having lost the opportunity to be the ones that drove the wedge between the eastern and western halves of the island, the Americans were left with little more to do than to be passive observers while the glory went to Montgomery and his Eighth Army. Patton's eyes were on Palermo, the largest of the Sicilian cities. While there was no real strategic reason to capture the city for it could have been left isolated while the Allies secured Messina, after which it would have fallen of its own accord, it was nevertheless an attractive target for propaganda purposes – and to restore the bruised pride of the Seventh Army.

Before Palermo, however, Agrigento and Porto Empedocle would have to be taken. Alexander had already authorized a reconnaissance in force to these towns, and Patton was not slow to take advantage of this. Truscott was ordered to get on with capturing the two objectives. Agrigento was the gateway to western Sicily; Porto Empedocle would provide port facilities which would assist the Americans to resolve the difficulties presented by the limited capacities of Gela and Licata.

While Truscott set out on his mission, Patton restructured Seventh Army. There would now be two corps, the first – II (US) Corps, under Bradley, comprised 1st (US) and 45th (US) Divisions. The second, entitled the Provisional Corps, was to be commanded by his deputy army commander, Major General Geoffrey T Keyes, and would have 3rd (US) Division once Agrigento had fallen, 82nd Airborne Division and those elements of 2nd (US) Armored Division that had already disembarked. Bradley would drive northwest towards Caltanissetta, then to the coast, cutting the island into two. Keyes would go for Palermo.

During the afternoon of 17 July Patton appeared unannounced at Alexander's headquarters in North Africa. He made the visit to appeal for a greater American role in the campaign, and brought with him the argument that the Eighth Army was obviously having severe difficulties in crossing the Catania Plain. While XIII Corps was stalemated there, the Anglo-Canadian XXX Corps was having similar problems in the central highlands, where the road system was not up to supporting the advance. Patton successfully argued for his plan to use II (US) Corps to drive on Termini, while the remainder of Seventh Army would clear western Sicily. Patton deliberately omitted to mention Palermo, or that his thoughts went beyond the capture of that city, to taking Messina by advancing along the north coast – the route that Alexander had intended XXX Corps to take. Nor did Patton mention that he intended to get to Messina first. Perhaps feeling that he had given Montgomery a degree of independence and that Patton could not be denied the same leeway, Alexander agreed to II (US) Corps advancing to the coast[1].

While Patton was in Tunis Eisenhower's representative with Seventh Army, General Lucas, went to see Eisenhower in Algiers to brief him on developments. Eisenhower's response was to direct Lucas to inform Patton that he must stand up to Alexander – and that if he failed to do so, then he would be removed from command. Patton had the green light.

Truscott dispatched the 7th Infantry Regimental Combat Team to Porto Empedocle. The most direct route was along the coastal road, Highway 115, but this was overlooked by Agrigento, which stands on high ground and was reportedly well defended by artillery. To isolate Agrigento and to ensure that it was not reinforced before capture, the regiment's 2nd Battalion (2/7th) was to take a hill commanding the northern approaches to the town. The 3rd Ranger Battalion would take a position a mile or so northwest of the town, and then with Agrigento cut off from these directions 1/7th would cross the Naro River and take the town from the east. The Rangers passed through the American front lines at 1900 hours on 15 July and advanced along Highway 112, the road from Favara to Agrigento. Although fired upon by both artillery and machine guns, they proceeded unscathed until they ran into an Italian roadblock at about midnight. They attacked it half an hour later, and after a sharp skirmish took both the roadblock and some nearby emplacements, and captured 165 Italians. Too many for the Rangers to handle, these were marched back to Favara and handed over to the 7th Infantry. No Rangers were lost or wounded during the action, and after a few hours of sleep they set off at 0600 hours, crossing a mile-wide valley through which the highway ran, to Montaperto. Again they came under ineffective artillery fire, but managed to ambush an Italian motorized column consisting of ten motorcycles and two troop-carriers, killing many and taking forty prisoners. And again the Rangers escaped the encounter without casualties.

At 0800 the Rangers entered Montaperto, from where they were able to overlook the valley leading to Porto Empedocle and the sea. They could also see four enemy artillery batteries, which they brought under mortar and automatic weapons fire. Some of the artillerymen fled south, but the majority raised their hands and climbed up the hill in surrender. Descending the valley, the Rangers captured the command post of the local Italian artillery, but lost their only fatality – the commander of Company F, Lieutenant Campbell – when he led the attack on a machine gun position. A mile outside the port they paused in an almond grove to plan their move before advancing with three companies on either side of a gulley which ran into Porto Empedocle. The attack started at 1420; by 1600 hours the Rangers had overcome the enemy – resistance was offered from a walled cemetery and by German troops manning coastal positions – and had started to establish a perimeter defence of the town[2].

2/7th had moved around the north of Agrigento while 1/7th crossed the Naro River north of the main highway. 3/7th attacked towards Porto Empedocle that afternoon. Despite communications problems between the units, the tactics succeeded largely because of the speed with which the operation was carried out. 2/7th's unexpected appearance on the high ground north of the town surprised the defenders and 3/7th met little opposition when it advanced on the highway. By 0300 hours on 17 July Agrigento was in American hands[3].

Five Congressional Medals of Honor were awarded to American servicemen during the Sicilian campaign. For his actions on 17 July, one of these went to First Lieutenant David C Waybur of 3rd Reconnaissance Troop who led a three-vehicle patrol on a volunteer mission behind enemy lines to contact an isolated group of Rangers. Under cover of darkness, on heavily mined roads which were defended by road blocks, his patrol was halted at a destroyed bridge where it was cut off by four enemy tanks. Waybur ordered his men to disperse and open fire with their machine guns, but he and three of his men were wounded. Despite his wounds, Waybur stood in the bright moonlight firing at the leading tank with a Tommy gun, killing the crew members and causing the tank to crash off the bridge and into the stream. After sending one of his men for assistance he rallied the rest and continued to fight off the enemy until relieved the next morning[4].

Patton's decision to take Palermo might have been countermanded but for the decision of his chief of staff, Brigadier General 'Hap' Gay, to withhold a signal from Alexander which appeared to limit his activities. Alexander seemed to have had second thoughts about the freedom he had given Patton and was now holding him back. Gay replied the message was garbled and could not be deciphered, and asked for it to be repeated. But by the time the repeat message arrived it was too late to halt Patton, who did not hear about the affair until later.

At 1800 Hours on 17 July JOSS Force was dissolved and 3rd (US)

Division became part of the Provisional Corps. Its strength was augmented by a *tabor* – about a battalion sized unit – of Moroccan *Goumiers*, and it received its first orders from the new Provisional Corps Headquarters, which were to send it on its way towards Palermo. The objective was a hundred miles away, at the far end of a dusty road where water was scarce and difficult to supply. Truscott ordered his men to be there in five days. In the July temperatures it was not going to be an easy stroll. The plan to get to Palermo was seemingly straightforward, but it was to cause tremendous difficulties for the logistics staff.

With the 15th and 30th Infantry Regiments and 3rd Ranger Battalion leading, Truscott's division set out for Palermo. The 15th marched north of Aragona towards Casteltermini, encountering scattered resistance and some artillery fire. A series of blown bridges and tunnels south of Castelermini caused brief delays, but the advance was not slowed for long. The 30th moved from Aragona towards San Stefano Quisquina, also running into demolitions. One of these, a section of road running along a cliff, required hard work by the 10th Engineer Battalion to make it passable by jeeps, but the job was completed by midnight.

The training for Truscott's Trot paid dividends. The division made remarkable advances across terrain that included mountains rising to over 4,000 feet in height, on roads that wound through position after position where ambushes and demolitions could be laid. One battalion, 3/30th, marched fifty-four miles cross-country to capture the high ground northeast of San Stefano Quisquina in thirty-three hours. Unable to bring forward water or rations because of the lack of roads, and in the Sicilian summer heat, it was an outstanding performance, which may not have been equalled by any force during the war.

With 3/30th positioned to the northeast of San Stefano, 1/30th moved cross-country on the west of Highway 118 to attack the town from the western side, and 2/30th advanced along the highway to a position to its south. Artillery units came forward to support the operation, which started at 1130 hours on 20 July when 3/30th reached the eastern outskirts of the town, having overcome intermittent resistance on the way. Now the enemy began to put up a stiffer performance, bringing machine gun and artillery fire to bear on the battalion.

The advance guard of the regiment – a reconnaissance platoon from 2nd Armored Division and two infantry platoons from the 30th – reached a spot a hundred yards from the town outskirts. Before them was an Italian roadblock, where two enemy artillery batteries were preparing to come into action. The regimental commander of the 30th, Colonel Rogers, organised all of the weapons available in the reconnaissance party – a collection of small-calibre guns, machine guns, mortars and rifles – and opened fire. Taken by surprise, the enemy gunners and some thirty-two machine-gun crews abandoned their weapons and fled into the town.

Pressure on 3/30th was eased, and Rogers ordered 1/30th to attack east of the highway and to assist in clearing the eastern slopes of the mountains bordering San Stefano.

Now Rogers ordered his artillery to concentrate their fire onto the highway north of the town to prevent the enemy escaping; numerous vehicles were destroyed by the shelling. 3/30th entered San Stefano Quisquina at 1700 hours, closely followed by 1/30th; over 750 prisoners were taken, together with more than a hundred vehicles, the more serviceable of which were pressed into service to move the regiment on its way. 2/30th was ordered forward towards Prizzi while the other two battalions held the mountains arching from the northwest to the northeast of San Stefano.[5]

During the same day, 20 July, the 15th Infantry Regiment continued to advance on the right, against light resistance, passing through Castelermini and Castronuovo. Numbers of prisoners and equipment were captured.

On the 21st, the 7th Infantry Regiment took the lead and led the advance towards Palermo. With two battalions abreast the regiment captured Prizzi and the ridge behind it by 0930 hours, taking 500 prisoners. 3/7th, followed by 1/7th, moved on Corleone. By 2100 the entire regiment was concentrated to the north of the town; an hour later 2/7th started to advance on Marineo. 15th Infantry, with the 4th *Tabor* of *Goumiers* attached, followed the 7th.

By 0300 hours on the next morning the 2/7th Regiment was positioned two miles south of Marineo, when the order was issued for the advance on Palermo. 1/7th embussed and passed through 2/7th; 3/7th then leapfrogged through 1/7th; and the supporting artillery units moved up for the attack. The swift advance kept constant pressure on the enemy, and 3rd Division maintained its rate of progress, pushing units forward to take their turn in the lead, throughout the morning.

At 1445 hours orders were received from Patton that until further notice no troops other than patrols were to cross a line running a mile or so south of Palermo. By now 7th Infantry motorised patrols were already in the city, but the rest of the regiment halted as ordered. At 1900, civilians representing the city offered its surrender to Brigadier General William W Eagles, the assistant divisional commander, who declined to accept. An hour and a half later, 3/7th entered the town to secure important installations.

While the 7th rounded up thousands of Italian and German prisoners, the 15th and 30th Regiments cleared out pockets of enemy resistance in the areas around the city. The Germans had sunk forty-four vessels in the port in an attempt to deny its use to the Americans, but the engineers had it working at nearly two-thirds capacity within a week.

Patton had achieved his aim, and Palermo was his. The local

population welcomed the Americans effusively, showering them with flowers, and even the two Italian generals who were captured claimed to be pleased 'because the Sicilians were not human beings, but animals'[6], and the lower-ranking prisoners appeared to be well content with their lot, for when Patton drove past a group of them they rose to their feet, saluted and then cheered. Patton also formed a better impression of the Italian prisoners here, who were 'better looking... bigger and older.' They were not necessarily more hygienic, however, for the Royal Palace which he commandeered for his headquarters had to be cleaned for 'the first time since the Greek occupation'.

Patton was well content with his actions. He believed that the operation would go down in history as a classic example of the proper use of armour, certainly at Fort Leavenworth, the Army Command and General Staff College, and that the Provisional Corps would prove to have advanced faster, against heavier resistance, and across worse roads, than had the Germans during their blitzkrieg campaigns. While he may well have believed that his achievement surpassed anything that Guderian and Rommel did during the blitzkrieg, he rather neglected the part that the American infantry had played. Truscott's men had, after all, got to Palermo before Patton's beloved tanks.

While Patton was satisfied, Bradley was less happy. He could not see the need to capture Palermo, when Messina was the objective which would achieve the aim of isolating large numbers of enemy troops and rendering them incapable of continuing the war. Although the port facilities of Palermo would help the Seventh Army's logistical difficulties, the situation was not serious enough that it could not be overcome in other ways. Bradley saw Patton's ambition to capture the city as self-aggrandisement. Moreover, it did not concentrate on II (US) Corps and the role Bradley wanted for it – more prominence in seizing Messina. On the positive side, the event was a morale-booster for the American servicemen. The headlines which were published at home praised the achievement and gave the GIs a sense of pride.

Bradley's corps had been steadily working its way to the north coast of Sicily, 45th (US) Division cutting the island in half on 23 July. It did this without the attendant publicity that was given to the capture of Palermo.

On 13 July 157th Infantry Regiment, from 45th (US) Infantry Division, had advanced from its positions near Chiarmonte to south of Vizzini against light resistance. 179th Regiment had continued to move towards Grammachile, but the third regiment, the 180th, was delayed in its progress to Biscari by a blown bridge across the Acate River. The following day the advance continued in all three areas, with 157th Regiment being ordered to halt two miles south of Vizzini while the British took the town. The 180th Regiment mounted a surprise attack on Biscari airfield, and captured it at 0630 hours after hand-to-hand fighting and beating off a counterattack. The enemy were not giving up ground easily, and on 15 July another counterattack was mounted, this time against K Company of 3/179th at 0550, supported by Mark IV tanks. The attack was beaten off with fixed bayonets, one tank being put out of action with a rifle grenade and another suffered a similar fate when a 4.2-inch phosphorous mortar shell dropped through the open hatch and killed the crew.

On 18 July Guzzoni decided to withdraw from western Sicily. He left a regiment from the *Aosta Division* in Palermo for the short term, to supervise the removal of supplies, and the German flak and administrative units were withdrawn from the city with no difficulty. Much of the 15,000 tons of stores had to be abandoned, however. As we have seen, the morale of most of the Italians in Palermo collapsed, and the city was surrendered with little resistance. For the Headquarters of the Provisional Corps, 2nd (US) Armored Division and 82nd Airborne Division, the campaign was over, and their role became that of occupation forces in western Sicily.

In II (US) Corps, 45th Division had advanced northwest on Highway 121. 180th RCT reached the outskirts of Palermo on 22 July, while the other two regiments turned north the previous day. 157th RCT arrived on the northern coast road at Cerda Station on the 23rd, and turned eastwards. Despite some sharp clashes with rear parties from *29 Panzer Grenadier Division*, 1st (US) Division had also moved swiftly. The regiments leap-frogged forwards, reaching Enna on the 20th, overrunning Alimena on the 21st, Bompietro and Petralia on the successive two days.

As the Official History comments, in five days Seventh Army had succeeded in achieving Alexander's directive to bisect Sicily, and had practically cleared the western part of the island. Had Alexander given permission for its actions sooner, Patton's army might well have finished the job at an earlier date.

The Axis was also experiencing strains. Fascist propaganda had ceaselessly rolled out the message that the Italian nation would become revitalized and united in defence of the homeland once the Allies invaded, and the first bulletins after the landings in Sicily continued in the same vein. By 12 July, however, the tone changed and the message was now about containing rather than throwing back the Allies. Although the Italian forces engaged in the fighting were praised, the bulletins acknowledged that the Sicilian coastline from Licata to Augusta was in Allied hands. Particularly hard for the Italians to understand was the fact that the Syracuse-Augusta naval base had fallen so swiftly.

Hitler was unsurprised by the turn of events. By 11 July, D + 1, he had determined to reinforce the Sicilian defenders. His reasoning was that the Allies might use the island as a springboard from which to strike at the Balkans, and that Sicily would give his enemies bomber bases from which they could more easily reach the industrial areas of Italy and Germany.

With Italy visibly wavering, Hitler needed to bolster his ally's confidence before it withdrew from the war altogether. Kesselring was ordered to move 1 Parachute Division to Sicily from its base in France, and 29th Panzer Grenadier Division was to move from Calabria across the Strait of Messina. Additionally, XIV Panzer Corps Headquarters was to go to Sicily to take command of the German units on the island.

Flying to Sicily on 12 July, Kesselring found that both Guzzoni and von Senger were pessimistic about defending the island. It was already clear that further counterattacks against the Allied beachheads could not be mounted until reinforcements arrived, and therefore the Axis would have to fight a defensive battle. Nor was the thought of reinforcing the troops universally welcomed; extra units would place a strain on the available transport and supplies, and would only add to the problem when it became time to evacuate the island[7].

The only realistic option open to the Axis commanders was to shorten the defensive front to a line which ran across the northwestern corner of Sicily. This line would be held as long as possible, and would secure the escape route across the Straits of Messina. The first step in carrying out this strategy was to stop the Allies from entering Catania, and this objective was already in the capable hands of Schmalz. He, however, was in need of reinforcements; his battle group, with help from the battered Napoli Division, was under pressure. Guzzoni had ordered the Hermann Göring Division across to join him, while the Livorno Division screened the gap between it and 15th Panzer Grenadier Division coming from the western side of the island.

That evening, 12 July, Comando Supremo decided that the possibility of pushing the Allies into the sea was out of the question. The Italian coastal defences had collapsed, and Allied air and naval superiority meant that they could land forces on Sicily faster than the Axis could. The only possible way to weaken the Allies was to strike at their sea lanes, thereby hindering the movement of troops and materiel from North Africa. But this could only be done with air power, of which the Italians had no reserves. There was no alternative but to ask Hitler for assistance. This request was presented the following morning.

At the same time Kesselring was telephoning the findings of his Sicilian visit to Colonel General Jodl at OKW. The situation on the ground he described as critical – there was no opportunity to launch another counterattack against the beachheads. The only alternative was to fight a delaying action, which was essential if Italian morale was not to plummet further. Kesselring wanted the remainder of 1st Parachute Division and the whole of 29th Panzer Grenadier Division deployed to Sicily immediately. Furthermore, he wanted the Luftwaffe reinforced, and submarines and E-Boats brought into increased action against Allied shipping.

At OKW the question of what to do about Sicily was debated. Jodl was of the opinion that it should be abandoned, and that emphasis should be given to defending the Italian mainland and Germany. Hitler ordered that Kesselring's view be sought, and a telephone call to him elicited the opinion that the island should be held as long as possible to stiffen Italian morale. Hitler agreed, and approved sending the rest of *1st Parachute Division* to Sicily; *29th Panzer Grenadier Division* was to move to the tip of Calabria, ready to cross the straits if transport and supplies were to be found available; Hube's *XIV Panzer Corps Headquarters* was to go to Sicily; and *Luftflotte 2* in Sardinia and Southern Italy was to be reinforced.

The role of German forces in Sicily, as laid down by Hitler, was to delay the enemy advance as much as possible, and to halt it in front of Etna along a line which ran approximately from San Stefano through Adrano to Catania.

His support of the Italians was not without reservations, however. Hube was secretly ordered to exclude Guzzoni and other Italian commanders from German planning. Command of all operations in Sicily, including those involving whatever Italian formations might still be of use to him, was in his hands. He was to ensure that as many Germans were saved as possible.

On 15 July *XIV Panzer Corps Headquarters* arrived in Sicily. Its immediate role was to take command of the two German divisions when they met. At 2030 hours the following day, Kesselring ordered Hube to take over command of all German troops on the island. This happened shortly after midnight, and problems soon emerged, for German battalion commanders arriving without transport were ordered to commandeer vehicles of Italian troops who were no longer in the fighting. This led to some clashes and shooting, with fatal casualties on both sides.

Other difficulties were to surface later, for Guzzoni was still in command of the Italian forces on the western front.

The unease with which the Germans now regarded their allies was not without foundation. In Italy General Vittorio Ambrosio, the Chief of the Comando Supremo, the Italian High Command, advised Mussolini that there was no longer any hope of winning the war. He saw no military justification for continuing the struggle, and urged Mussolini to withdraw Italy from the war. Without the means or will to fight the Allies on sea or in the air, as evidenced by the events in Pantarella, Lampedusa and Sicily, the Italians could not prevent the enemy from approaching the coast. Once ashore, the Allies had little to face but inadequate armament and weak, thinly spread defences, and reserve divisions with limited mobility and equipment. After three years of war, which was started with scanty means and during which the few resources were burned up in Africa, Russia and the Balkans, there was little future in continuing. Mussolini was left in no doubt that the military hierarchy wanted him to withdraw from the Axis and to make a separate peace with the Allies.

OKW also wanted things clarified with the Italians. Unhappy with what they saw as feeble Italian resistance in Sicily and the friction between themselves and *Comando Supremo*, together with the ineptitude of Mussolini's government, on 14 July they updated the plans they had prepared some time previously. If Mussolini or the Italian government collapsed or sought a way out of the war, then German forces would enter and occupy northern Italy. Hitler could not run the risk of the Allies coming so close to Germany without having to fight for the opportunity.

1 D'Este - Patton.
2 King.
3 Taggert.
4 Citation, Congressional Medal of Honor.
5 Taggert.
6 Patton.
7 Kesselring.

CHAPTER NINE

PRIMOSOLE

TO THE EAST, MONTGOMERY'S PLAN to make a bridgehead across the Simeto River at the Primosole Bridge was launched, with the objective of capturing the bridge by the evening of 14 July. The Malati Bridge which carried the road from Lentini to Primosole was to be captured by No 3 Commando which would land from the sea, while Primosole Bridge would be secured by 1 Parachute Brigade parachuting in. Both operations would be carried out during the night 13-14 July. Within a few hours 50th Division was to arrive at the respective bridges and to continue to drive northwards.

The enemy managed to frustrate the operation, not through having any plan to deal with the possibility that it might happen, but rather by chance and through the competence of the German commanders on the ground. Colonel Schmalz with his battle group from the *Hermann Göring Division* had established delaying positions on Mount Pancali just south of Carlentini on 11 July, which, as has been seen, slowed 50th Division's movement northwards. The following day German reinforcements began to arrive at the Catania airfields, in the shape of *1st Parachute Division*.

As soon as news of the Allied landings in Sicily had been received in Berlin, the 30,000 airborne troops of *Fliegerkorps XI* were placed on alert to reinforce the Axis forces on the island. Lieutenant General Richard Heidrich, commander of *1st Parachute Division* was ordered to Rome from his headquarters near Avignon in France by Kesselring, who told him that his formation was destined for Sicily; the following day Heidrich received an order from Göring himself to dispatch a parachute regiment to reinforce the *Hermann Göring Division*[1]; as may be imagined from the division's title, Göring had an interest in its wellbeing.

Colonel Heilmann's *3rd Parachute Regiment* spearheaded the division's move to Sicily. Having flown into Catania on 12 July to carry out his reconnaissance, he selected an area south of the city between the Simeto and Gornalunga Rivers for his regiment's drop zone. No sooner had the details been transmitted back to Avignon, than *3rd Parachute Regiment* took off in their Junker 52 aircraft. During their flight, they came under attack from about twenty P-38 Lightnings as they passed over the Straits of Messina – but the incident was short-lived as the American pilots were low on fuel and had to break off to return to their bases in North Africa. The transports were extremely vulnerable – not least because the flight was carried out in daylight hours – but fortune was on the Germans' side. At 1815 hours the paratroops made a textbook drop[2].

Waiting for them was transport organized by one of Heilmann's officers, who had flown out on the morning's reconnaissance. *3rd Parachute Regiment* was quickly on its way to Lentini to reinforce Schmalz. The *2nd Battalion* was destined for Francofonte, and the remainder of the regiment was to defend the area between Carlentini and the sea.

The next day, 13 July, the *1st Parachute Machinegun Battalion's* aircraft landed at Catania airfield. The battalion moved south, crossing the Primosole Bridge and took up positions about a mile south of the Simeto River, to the west of Highway 114. On the edge of an orange grove and hidden from the air, the paratroops were well-placed to interfere with any attempt to capture the bridge from the south[3].

Meanwhile the British 50th Division was working its way northwards on the inland road on the same day. 6 DLI, with a troop of tanks and artillery support, completed the capture of those enemy troops that had held positions astride the Solarino-Palazzolo road. The enemy were well dug in and the British had to mount a deliberate attack, which – as it turned out – was against greater numbers than expected. Resistance was not very determined, however, although considerable fighting took place and it was estimated that 100 to 150 enemy were killed and 400 captured. Amongst the latter was the commander of the *Napoli Division*, General Gotti-Porcinari, and his staff, who were duly driven off into captivity on a Bren carrier. Amongst the equipment captured, much of it burnt out or destroyed by artillery fire, were fifteen much-needed lorries which were pressed into service. Of less immediate use were six R35 tanks and an assortment of artillery and anti-tank guns.

As 69 Brigade continued its advance the opposition gradually became stiffer, and shortly before nightfall Brigadier Cooke-Collis reported back that the situation was no longer as promising as it had been when Montgomery had issued his orders. The leading troops from the brigade were about three miles south of Carlentini, facing a strong enemy rearguard which was bringing machine-gun fire on them from two features, one astride the main road and the second on Mount Pancali, which lay a little further on, and to the left of the road. Both of these positions overlooked the road for some distance. It seemed clear to both General Kirkman and Brigadier Cooke-Collis that capturing Lentini that night was very unlikely.

Unlikely it may have been, but at this late hour it was too late to propose a postponement of the plan. As happens so often in war, events assume a momentum of their own, and although the armchair historian can ponder at ease the ways in which things might have been done better, for those heavily involved in preparing for action at the time, things are rarely so cut and dried. Although the radio links from brigade, through corps and to Eighth Army Headquarters via HMS *Bulolo* were working, which would have allowed him to request that the operation be delayed,

General Kirkman ordered 69 Brigade to continue working forward through the night. The artillery support for this advance could not be as effective as hoped, because the Gunner regiments had only just come into action and the enemy locations were only broadly known. Nevertheless, it was felt that if the brigade was facing Italians (and there was some evidence that this was the case) then the arrival of shells amongst them might be sufficient to scare them away.

During the night the 6th Battalion, The Green Howards pushed on and took the first of the enemy-held features, capturing a dozen German soldiers despite the expectation that the enemy rearguard was at least partly Italian. Any further movement was held up by the enemy on Mount Pancali, but on the positive side, word was received that No 3 Commando had landed without difficulty as part of the plan to capture the bridge over the Leonardo River.

The 7th Battalion, The Green Howards was ordered to attack Mount Pancali at 0700 hours, but the operation was delayed for an hour and a half after communications difficulties with one of the supporting Gunner units, 124 Field Regiment. As the infantry was about to set off a number of enemy tanks mounted their own attack, succeeding in knocking out a machine gun. They withdrew under artillery fire and the Green Howards moved off, clearing the objective by 1000 hours. Pancali had been held by about a hundred Germans, many of whom were killed in the battle. Twenty-nine German machine guns were captured on the mountain, many of which had been kept in action until the end.

Off to the east 4 Armoured Brigade, under command of 5th Division, was advancing on the coastal road towards Lentini, where the two north-bound roads converged. In front of them, they encountered ten German tanks and some 88mm guns, which they drove off after inflicting losses of one tank and two guns on the enemy. 69 Brigade was by now extremely tired, and the troops were slow in regrouping after their exertions. In front of them German tanks and guns were identified south of Carlentini and brought under artillery fire, as 151 Brigade prepared to pass through and to take up the lead once Lentini fell. During the early afternoon both Carlentini and Lentini fell into the hands of 69 Brigade, and the weary soldiers were welcomed with scenes of celebration from the inhabitants. Behind them, along the road that they had advanced up from Sortino, burnt-out and burning vehicles were littered, blocking the way in several places. Enemy aircraft had managed to carry out a number of attacks during the afternoon, causing several casualties. On the 4th Armoured Brigade front, the first demolition of the campaign was encountered: a bridge had been blown near Carlentini. By 1700 hours, however, the tanks had succeeded in by-passing the obstacle and were moving through Lentini. At nightfall 4 Armoured Brigade and 9 DLI were a mile south of Primosole Bridge.

It is now time to take a look at events there.

Primsole Bridge

Montgomery's plan to leapfrog forward across the bridges at Malati and Primosole bears uncomfortable similarities to his attempt to do much the same thing, albeit on a grander scale, the following year in Holland – Operation MARKET GARDEN. On both occasions the objective was to capture bridges by special forces (in Sicily's case, commandos and paratroops; in Holland, paratroops) to secure a route forward for the slower-moving earth-bound armoured and infantry formations before the enemy could stiffen up their defences. The broad planning concept apart, there were other similarities, for 1 Parachute Brigade under Brigadier Gerald Lathbury was tasked with capturing the bridges at both Primosole and Arnhem.

On 13 July Lieutenant Colonel Durnford Slater, CO No 3 Commando, was summonsed to Syracuse to be briefed on the operation by Generals Montgomery and Dempsey, and Admiral McGrigor. On the bomb-damaged quay, he was told that 3 Commando was to land from the sea at 2200 hours that evening, ten miles behind enemy lines. The unit would then march seven miles inland and seize the Malati Bridge which crossed the Leonardo River two miles north of Lentini. 50th Division would relieve the commandos and cross the bridge on the road which continued north to Catania. Dempsey advised Durnford Slater to leave the bridge and hide up, should the division not appear by dawn the following morning. Durnford Slater had little time to brief and prepare his men. The *Prince Albert* sailed immediately he returned aboard, and there were only two or three hours in which to plan and get organized[4].

The trip to their landing site, in the bay of Agnone, was not without incident. An E-boat emerged from the darkness and fired two torpedoes at the *Prince Albert*, which fortunately failed to hit the ship because of the quick-wittedness of her captain, who steered his vessel out of danger. On arriving at the disembarkation point, the commandos had to be put ashore in two waves, for the landing craft available could not take the whole unit ashore in a single run. As the assault boats were being loaded, the commandos could see Catania being bombed, along the coast to the north, and above them was the sound of the aircraft bringing the airborne brigade to the Primosole Bridge DZs.

Intelligence had indicated that the operation might be opposed by Italian troops on the coast, but thereafter it should be a clear run to the bridge. The opposition bit they got right, for the landing craft came under machine-gun fire from several pillboxes as they came ashore, after which the commandos were subjected to showers of grenades – a different affair from the unit's landing on D Day. Durnford Slater was the first ashore, and was to be alone there for a while for the officer who was next in line to land, and who was carrying a Bangalore torpedo, managed to jam his load across the exit from the landing craft, preventing anyone else from leaving it until he had disentangled himself. The CO was exposed to the fire from four pillboxes while he waited for his men to catch up, but he was not unsupported, for the commandos were firing as their craft neared the shore. Having pushed their way through barbed wire entanglements as the troop commanders sounded their rallying calls with a hunting horn and whistles, the commandos proceeded to make their way inland. Durnford Slater was soon presented with a prisoner taken by his men. He was in German uniform, which went some way towards explaining the strength of the resistance that had been put up earlier. A series of what Durnford Slater called 'violent little battles' occurred over the next mile as the Commando advanced through the village of Agnone. German machinegun posts were well distributed in the area, and it was apparent that intelligence had not got the whole picture.

Once through the village progress became easier as the enemy outposts thinned out. Making their way inland along a railway line, the 160 officers and men from the first wave that had made it through the coastal defences (thirty had been left behind on the beach) continued towards their destination in the dark. On their way, they came across paratroops who had been dropped away from their DZs for the Primosole Bridge; these men declined an invitation to join the commandos, and made off to rejoin their airborne comrades. Leaving the railway the commandos progressed across country through low hills strewn with rocks and thorny bushes until they reached the river a mile or so below the bridge. Wading through the river to the north bank, so as to approach the bridge from the unexpected direction, they found it to be protected by four pillboxes. Within a few minutes these had been cleared of the enemy, Italian troops, the commandos attacking with grenades. They were now astride the main supply route for the Germans who were facing 50th Division.

Having established a defensive perimeter around northern end of the bridge, Durnford Slater's men settled down for the remainder of the night to await the arrival of 50th Division from the direction of Lentini. The next arrivals at the bridge were not British, but Germans, however. One troop of commandos was sent off to re-cross the river to the southwest of the bridge, but it was soon held up by heavy enemy opposition. The Germans to the south of the river began working their way around the left flank of the Commando. For the next hour or so until dawn broke, the Germans increased the pressure.

The defenders of the bridge were subjected to a mortar bombardment which lasted for some hours. By now their strength had risen to about 350 men as the second landing wave arrived, far too many to cram into the pillboxes for shelter. With the ground too stony to dig trenches, the exposed commandos began to suffer casualties. To add to their problems, a Tiger tank emerged from a group of trees south of the river and proceeded to add its weight to the bombardment.

Despite the battle going on around the bridge, German lorries continued to approach it from the north, only to run into a troop of commandos which Durnford Slater had positioned a hundred yards up the road. The ammunition exploding in the burning vehicles added to the noise and chaos of the fighting. A young officer dispatched a lorry with his PIAT, at too close a range, for the ensuing explosion killed him as well as the enemy soldiers aboard it. Captain Bill Lloyd, with both legs broken by the mortar bomb which had landed at his feet, continued to fight, supported on a bicycle by two of his men until he was killed leading an attack on a German machinegun post[5].

With casualty numbers steadily mounting, Durnford Slater took the decision to order an attack on the Tiger tank. A troop of men moved into a house flanking it, under enemy fire; but the tank was beyond the effective range of their PIAT and the attempt failed. Little option remained for the commandos but to make their escape before they were all wiped out, but they had, at least, removed the demolition charges which had been laid on the bridge. Falling back to the hillsides to the west of the bridge, from which they hoped to be able to dominate it and hinder German activity in the area, they were pursued by shells from the Tiger which had crossed the bridge, and it became obvious that they could not stay[6].

Splitting up into small parties, the surviving commandos made their way back towards the Agnone-Lentini road through the remainder of the day and following night. A number were taken prisoner, most of whom eventually returned to the unit in one way or another, some being freed when the Allied advance overran the locations in which they were being held. Casualties numbered twenty-eight killed, sixty-six wounded, and fifty-nine missing[7].

No 3 Commando had not managed to hold the bridge until the arrival of 50th Division, but its activities had distracted German forces from delaying that formation, and the bridge had not been blown. Some while later, Montgomery ordered Durnford Slater to find a stonemason and have the inscription '3 Commando Bridge' cut into a stone, to be built into the bridge. It is still there, as are some of the pillboxes.

At the Primosole Bridge, the intention of 1 Parachute Brigade was to land two platoons of the 1st Battalion The Parachute Regiment and 1st Field Squadron Royal Engineers as close to the bridge as possible, and seize it by *coup de main*. Five minutes later, two platoons from the 3rd Battalion would land to capture the anti-aircraft battery which was situated nearby. The remainder of the 1st Battalion would then organize themselves in positions to defend the bridge, while 3rd Battalion would take up positions about a thousand yards north of Primosole, in a loop in the River Simeto. The 2nd Battalion was to take the high ground south of the river and capture three hills, codenamed Johnny I, II and III. Four DZs were to be used, two to the north and two south of the Simeto; a landing zone close to the southern end of the bridge was to be used by three gliders.

The parachute elements of 1st Airborne Division (as compared to the glider-carried Airportable Brigade which was involved in the Ponte Grande operation on D Day) had been waiting in North Africa for their call to action. A proposed drop by 2 Parachute Brigade near Augusta had been cancelled once it had become clear that it was unnecessary, but eighteen hours later 1 Brigade was warned off for the Primosole operation, code-named FUSTIAN.

At sunset 105 Dakota aircraft of the American 51st Troop Carrier Wing and eleven Albemarles of No 296 Squadron RAF, carrying paratroops, took off from six airfields between Kairouan and Sousse, with Halifaxes and Stirlings towing gliders with the Royal Artillery's anti-tank guns and their crews. Six aircraft, three of paratroops and three pulling gliders, failed to make the trip because of mechanical problems, but the remainder flew to Sicily by way of Malta. The next leg of the journey was northwards, five miles off the coast of Sicily, to the mouth of the Simeto River, where the aircraft turned inland to the DZs. As was now fast becoming a habit, the aircraft experienced trouble, being fired upon by Allied vessels. Fifty-five aircraft reported being shot at, and twenty-six aircraft had to return to base without dropping their loads because of damage from anti-aircraft shells and other causes. Eleven aircraft were shot down, and three more came down for other reasons. As pilots sought to avoid the flak, navigational mistakes were made, and some went adrift – thirty aircraft dropped their loads on the DZs, nine dropped near them, and forty-eight dropped their paratroops off-target by between half a mile and over twenty miles from the DZs. Only four of the gliders landed accurately, and another seven without undue damage but off the LZs. The strength on the ground, from the 1,856 men and twelve anti-tank guns that set out, was twelve officers, 283 men and three anti-tank guns[8].

The DZs and LZs were marked by a radar device known as 'Eureka' which was set up by 21st Independent Parachute Company, dropping half an hour before the main body arrived. Eureka sent out signals which were received aboard the aircraft by 'Rebecca', and which should have guided the pilots accurately to their objectives. The device was in its infancy, and although it was later to prove its worth, at this time it was not entirely reliable[9]. To add to the problems, as if they were not enough already, the 3rd Battalion paratroops were dropping for the first time with kitbags attached to their legs which were to be lowered on cords once they had jumped, and the pilots' violent action as they sought to avoid the flak threw many men to the aircraft floors in disarray. Among those whose jump was disrupted was Brigadier Lathbury, whose pilot dropped his passengers at a height of only 200 feet onto high ground three miles south of the DZ. Fortunately for Lathbury, he landed on ploughed soil which cushioned his fall, and he set off with his batman – the only other paratrooper in sight – for the bridge[10].

Arriving at his intended DZ Lathbury found his brigade major and a depleted number of his staff, with few wireless sets. With the area illuminated by the fires of burning haystacks, the brigadier and his small party made their way to a ditch about 500 yards away from the bridge. After a few minutes Lieutenant Colonel Frost, limping from a twisted ankle which he had suffered on landing, appeared at the head of some fifty men of the 2nd Battalion, on their way to the high ground which they were to occupy to the south. They were amongst the comparatively small number of men who had landed on their intended DZ, but they were few in number. Frost went on his way, and more men began to arrive until Lathbury was able to form four groups, each of ten to twelve men. Three of these were briefed to rush the southern end of the bridge while the fourth was to provide covering fire.

As the party approached the bridge, which lay silently in the moonlight, a paratrooper emerged from the darkness to inform Lathbury that the 1st Battalion had already captured it. A small group of Lieutenant Colonel Pearson's men had stormed it from the northern side, but they evidently had not cleared it of the enemy, for as Lathbury moved across it, a lorry towing an 88mm gun – which the brigadier assumed had been captured – burst into life as its driver started throwing grenades at the paratroops. One of these wounded Lathbury in the back and both thighs. He received some cursory first aid, which included a large tot of whisky, and was able to carry on, albeit rather more slowly than hitherto, to the north bank. Here he found about 150 men, including some Sappers who had removed the demolition charges from the bridge.

By daybreak the bridge was being defended by some 250 men from the 1st and 3rd Battalions, supported by three anti-tank guns manned by three sergeants of the 1st Airlanding Anti-tank Battery, Royal Artillery, aided by some glider pilots. The defenders also had two 3-inch mortars and a Vickers machine gun. In a farmhouse half a mile southeast of the bridge, a surgical team from 16th Parachute Field Ambulance had set themselves up. They were to carry out seventy-two operations during their time there, unhindered by patrols of German paratroops. A number of casualties were carried under fire to the main dressing station from the forward aid station in a mule-drawn cart, led by Staff Sergeant Stevens, RAMC.

To add to the confusion, groups of Italian soldiers were wandering about the battlefield looking for the opportunity to surrender. A solitary British sergeant had been approached by an Italian commando captain,

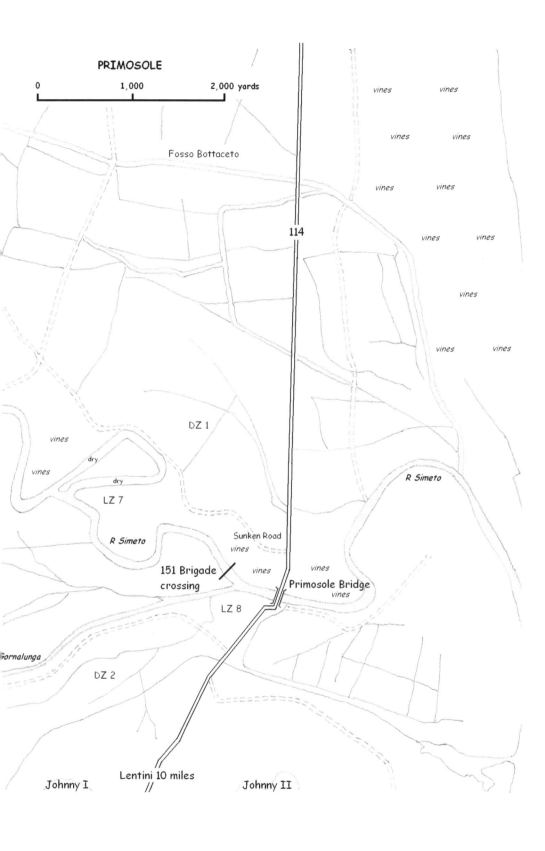

PRIMOSOLE

0   1,000   2,000 yards

Fosso Bottaceto

vines   vines

vines   vines

114   vines   vines

vines   vines

vines

vines   vines

DZ 1

vines

dry

vines   dry   R Simeto

LZ 7

R Simeto   Sunken Road

vines

151 Brigade   vines   vines

crossing   Primosole Bridge

vines

LZ 8

Gornalunga

DZ 2

Lentini 10 miles

Johnny I   //   Johnny II

who pleaded with him to accept the surrender of himself and his sixty men. The sergeant told them to get lost, which they did. The War Diary of the 3rd Battalion recorded that at 0700 hours Italians were emerging from all over the place, with their baggage in hand, and waving white rags. In the 2nd Battalion positions, over 130 had surrendered, and were proving to be an embarrassment, for the paratroops had more important things to worry about than crowds of docile prisoners. They were herded into a farmyard and left, unguarded. Eventually their numbers swelled to more than 500[11].

The German response was not long in coming. Firstly a group of Messerschmitts strafed the bridge, without causing much damage, and then an attack was launched, not from the north as expected, but from the south. The German paratroops (*Fallschirmjäger*), supported by mortar fire, kept up pressure from that direction throughout the day, and were only held off with difficulty. Their presence in the area, it will be remembered, was as a result of the move of elements of *1st Parachute Division* from France; those attacking the bridge from the south were from *1st Parachute Machine gun Battalion*, which had only arrived in the area the previous day.

To the north of the river, news of the British landing had been taken to Catania by a German motorcycle despatch rider who had approached the bridge at about 1030 hours, only to come under a hail of fire. He reported back to Captain Stangenberg, one of the officers who had arrived on the reconnaissance, who went to look for himself. Having confirmed the report, Stangenberg gathered twenty men together and returned to the bridge, only to be seen off by the defenders. Not content to let matters rest there, he assembled the only available troops, a company of signallers from the *1st Parachute Communications Battalion*, commanded by Captain Erich Fassl. With these and a collection of clerks, cooks and headquarters personnel, some 350 men in all, he set off to mount a counterattack at Primosole. To support this, he arranged for a heavy anti-aircraft battery (comprising one 88mm gun and an old 5cm artillery piece) to provide artillery cover. With his motley headquarters collection advancing down the road leading from Catania and the signals company ordered to cross the river to the east of the bridge and to turn the British right flank, Stangenberg opened his attack shortly after 1300 hours. It was repelled with little difficulty, but the Germans were soon able to augment their artillery with a self-propelled 88mm gun and some anti-tank guns, with which they pounded the British positions[12].

Around the bridge British spirits were high, and rose still further when some casks of wine were discovered in a pillbox. At about 0930 hours one of the wireless sets had displayed a brief spell of life and permitted contact with Eighth Army, giving the information that 4th Armoured Brigade was fighting its way towards the bridge against stiff opposition. The wireless then gave up the ghost and died.

The hours passed, but the brigade did not arrive. German *Fallschirmjäger* attacks continued, and were repelled with increasing difficulty. In their slit trenches and the captured pillboxes, the British paratroops held on, but it was becoming apparent that it was only a matter of time before they were driven off. By 1700 hours the situation was such that it was necessary to withdraw the defenders from the north end of the bridge to support those at the south, who were under continuous and increasing fire. The *Fallschirmjäger* had also crossed the river lower down and were trying to turn the defenders' flank.

An hour later the Germans brought up an 88mm gun with which they shelled the two pillboxes at the southern end of the bridge, on which the defence was based. With their positions becoming untenable, casualties mounting and ammunition decreasing, and as yet no sign of 4 Armoured Brigade, it was readily apparent that the time was fast approaching to leave. From the south, where Frost's 2nd Battalion was supposed to be holding the high ground of Johnny I, II and III, there was no sound. Lathbury determined to pull back to these positions to join Frost – or if he should prove not to be there, to the positions that he was to have taken. Here the remaining paratroopers would make a last stand, hoping to hold out until relieved from the south. With German tanks beginning to make their appearance on the battlefield, there was no alternative.

In small groups the survivors of 1 Parachute Brigade slipped away, but the field ambulance fell into enemy hands.

On Johnny I, men from the 2nd Battalion held a defensive perimeter throughout the day. It had been captured, together with 130 Italians, by an officer and twenty-five paratroops, but the message that they had sent advertising this fact had not got through. By 0215 hours, Frost and his group which had passed Lathbury earlier, now enlarged with A Company, were making preparations to attack the position. Fortunately the state of affairs became clear at about 0530 hours, and a 'friendly fire' situation was avoided. Johnny I was secure, but Frost's battalion had no heavy weapons, and could not retaliate when the enemy began to fire on them from Johnny II, which the paratroops had not been able to capture.

The battalion, such as it was, came under attack by *Fallschirmjäger* from three directions. A patrol sent out to deal with enemy machine guns was badly mauled by three armoured cars, and the decision was taken to withdraw the forward troops. Under pressure, subjected to sniping and hindered, as has already been noted, by Italian prisoners milling around, some relief came when Captain Vere Hodge, RA, the forward observation officer, succeeded in contacting HMS *Newfoundland*, a six-inch cruiser, which brought down heavy fire on the advancing Germans.

The British paratroops and German *Fallschirmjäger* continued to battle it out until about 1930, when the first Sherman of 4 Armoured Brigade appeared south of Johnny I. Two hours later the first infantry arrived, a company of 6 DLI. They had covered some twenty miles on foot, marching through the heat of the day which had reached ninety-five degrees Fahrenheit in the shade, and were in poor shape for continuing the fight.

With the Shermans of 44th Royal Tank Regiment on the scene, the Germans on the south of the Simeto withdrew to the area of the bridge. Although the opportunity to keep the momentum of the advance going by pushing quickly ahead might have taken the Primosole Bridge, the troops were in no condition to carry out such an operation, and the British settled down for the night.

The tanks leaguered on the heights overlooking the Catania Plain, at the far side of which was the city of Catania, about twelve miles away and just visible in the evening light. Beyond it rose Etna, the sight of which drew a number of spectators, who were shortly driven away by shells from a German tank below, the occupants of which were evidently unhappy with the British presence.

Crossing the Simeto

At first light on 15 July A and B Squadrons of 44 RTR moved down the slopes towards the Primosole Bridge, which was strewn with the debris of the previous day's fighting, particularly around the south end where a subsidiary road joined the highway. Here the destroyed pillboxes stood among felled telegraph poles and wire, and the dead bodies of seven or eight mules from an Italian pack train. In the heat, the smell was unbearable and the place was soon dubbed 'Dead Horse Corner'. The 400-foot long bridge lay in the middle of a horseshoe loop in the Simeto River, the open end of which was to the north, and at this point the water was about thirty yards wide with a muddy bottom and banks, on which grew patches of tall weeds. At that time of year the river, slow-moving, was about waist deep, although in places hollows in its bed brought the water over a man's head. At a distance of 700 yards to the west of the bridge the Gornalunga River joined the Simeto from the south. It was embanked, and canal-like. To the east of the bridge the Simeto wound its way to the sea, about a mile and a half away, through marshy flats with little cover. For a distance of a thousand yards to the east and somewhat more to the west of the bridge, the north bank had a belt of vines, fruit trees and olives which extended about 500 yards northwards. At the far side of this vegetation, running parallel to the river, was a track which in places was sunken and which contained the occasional farm building. The ground is described in the Official History as 'a hole-and-corner area' full of 'lurking-places'.

Still further north of the river lay the Catania Plain, which was comparatively bare but across which ran a number of drainage ditches, the biggest being the Fosso Bottaceto, a dry irrigation channel ten feet deep on the southern outskirts of the Catania airfield defences. Highway 114 ran northwards from Primosole to Catania over this flatland.

The German forces around Primosole were strengthened during the night of 14-15 July. After the appearance of British armour the initial response had been to pull back to the Catania defences, but Captain Stangenberg managed to get this plan reversed, and to persuade the powers that be that the Simeto crossing should be held. At last light on the 14th more aircraft appeared over Catania airfield to drop three companies of the *1st Fallschirm-Pionier Battailon*, the parachute engineers, onto Sicilian soil. These 450 men were immediately sent south to the bridge. Two companies were deployed south, the third north, of the river. The machine gun battalion that had fought throughout the 14th took up positions to the west, on the north bank of the river, and Fassl's company from *1st Parachute Communications Battalion* was positioned along the sunken road. In addition, there were the scratch force of headquarters personnel, part of a parachute artillery battery armed with 7.5mm guns, at least two 88mm anti-aircraft guns, and a couple of Italian battalions. Schmalz's group and a battalion of *1st Parachute Regiment* had fallen back to the Catania area, having disengaged themselves from the front further west, and to add to the German strength building against 50th Division, various other reinforcements were beginning to arrive[8].

With A Squadron to the right of the road and B to the left, 44 RTR advanced with 9 DLI as the battalion mounted its attack on the bridge at 0730 hours. 24th and 98th Field Regiments RA provided artillery support. The infantry moved forward in open formation across the open ground, as heavy machine-gun fire was brought down on them from the vineyards on the other bank of the river. Casualties were heavy and only the odd platoon was able to cross the Simeto. Once there, they engaged the Germans in hand-to-hand fighting, but to no avail. Forced to turn back, the survivors dug in on the south bank, from which position they were able to stop the enemy from laying demolition charges on the bridge. It was all they could do under the circumstances – casualties numbered over one hundred men, including eleven officers. Any attempt by infantry or armour to cross the bridge was met by fire from mortars and 88mm guns. The Shermans suffered losses as well: several were knocked out by 88mm fire and one went up on a minefield that had been laid to the right of the road.

As 9 DLI advanced to attack, their sister battalion, 8 DLI, moved to the area around Dead Horse Corner, followed by 6 DLI. General Kirkman arrived at Brigade Headquarters at about 1000 hours, and it was decided to renew the attack at 1630, with 8 DLI. The battalion would get even heavier artillery support than before. However, this intention was put into abeyance after General Dempsey appeared just before noon, with a wider plan. 50th Division was still to cross the Simeto, but in concert with troops from 17 Brigade and two Royal Marine Commandos which were to attack Catania from the sea during the night of 16/17 July. Once the bridge had been captured, 5th Division was to pass through. Kirkman therefore decided that 151 Brigade should renew its attack by moonlight in the early hours of the 16th. More artillery would be available by that time – two field regiments and one medium battery would join the Gunner units already present.

Meanwhile, the infantry and tanks continued to exchange fire with the enemy. Accurate sniping made even the most basic of functions difficult, and the RTR history records that at one stage a troop commander was conferring with one of the DLI battalion commanders in the shelter of a tank, when a hand emerged from the flap above the co-driver's position bearing a used shell-case. The case was tipped, to discharge a steady stream of yellow liquid onto the colonel's steel helmet, a christening which was unappreciated and which led to a temporary cooling of infantry-tank cooperation[14].

With 9 DLI engaged on the riverbank and 6 DLI stationed two miles to the rear to cover the brigade's open flank, it fell to 8 DLI to mount the assault. Two companies were to wade the river half a mile west of the bridge, swing right and outflank the bridge defences from the northern bank. The rest of the battalion would then cross the bridge, to extend the penetration a thousand yards northwards.

At 0230 hours on 16 July A and D Companies forded the river and established a foothold. Their route had been identified with the assistance of Lieutenant Colonel Alistair Pearson, CO of 1st Parachute Battalion, who had appeared – unshaven, dirty, tired, with no badges of rank and in plimsolls – at 8 DLI's headquarters when the Durham's CO, Lieutenant Colonel Lidwell, was outlining his plan. The reconnaissance Lidwell had carried out had been unpromising, for he had failed to find a suitable place to ford the river. A direct assault on the bridge appeared suicidal, for the enemy had their weapons concentrated to stop any such attempt, but Pearson had found a possible way across further upstream and was prepared to lead the Durhams to the place despite having already spent more than twenty-four hours in battle.

For an hour and twenty minutes before the infantry attack, the artillery laid down a barrage in the area of the bridge and the vineyards immediately north of the river, extending for 500 yards left of the bridge. The last ten minutes of this concentration were on the bridge, and was supported by fire from a squadron of tanks and machine-gun fire from a platoon of the Cheshire Regiment stationed on high ground overlooking the bridge. On such a narrow front, the noise was deafening.

Led by their commanding officer, the two companies waded into the water at points about fifty yards apart. They crossed without serious difficulty or opposition, although several men temporarily disappeared into holes in the river bed. Both of the companies' wireless sets 'drowned' in the crossing, presenting the CO with the problem of communication back to the troops on the southern bank.

Gathered on the far bank, the two companies proceeded to work their way eastwards towards the bridge. Pushing their way through the vineyards would have been a difficult enough task in daylight, and was more so in the darkness. Contact had to be maintained by soldiers calling out their section and platoon numbers to each other as they advanced. Fortunately for them, the Germans had pulled back some three or four hundred yards northwards. Although a certain amount of machine-gun fire was directed at the Durhams from the enemy positions, the fact that tracer was being used made it simpler to avoid the streams of bullets which were being fired 'blind'.

At the north end of the bridge, the few defenders that had not already withdrawn or that had not become casualties of the artillery barrage were quickly dispatched with the aid of grenades, bayonets or Tommy-guns. D Company established itself near the bridge, while A Company pushed about 500 yards further along the river bank to the east and dug in a hundred yards north of the Simeto, where it turned sharply left. In the vineyards, thickened by tall grass, shrubs and trees, where visibility was very limited, they were constantly harried by Spandau fire and attempts to infiltrate the position by *Fallschirmjäger*.

Lidwell now had to summons the rest of his battalion from the south. His wirelesses were dead, the sole 2-inch mortar flare which had been successfully fired – most of the remainder had gone astray in the dark – was not seen by the reinforcements. As a back-up to these methods two officers had been ordered to station themselves at the south end of the bridge in a Bren carrier, but when Lidwell reached it he found that the carrier had suffered a direct hit which had killed one officer, the driver and the wireless operator, seriously wounded the second officer, and rendered the wireless set useless. The only remaining option was to use one of the Sherman tanks to relay a message, but when Lidwell climbed aboard one and tapped the commander on the head to attract his attention, the man disappeared and closed the hatch, refusing to emerge.

At this stage, almost surreally, a War Office observer pedalled up on a bicycle. He was immediately sent back to order the rest of 8 DLI forward. All of this delay meant that B and C Companies did not set out until just before dawn. Advancing on either side of the road, they ran into the enemy about 300 yards north of the bridge.

The leading men got to within a few yards of the Spandaus before the Germans opened fire. The forward sections of both companies were cut down, the leading platoon of B Company being practically wiped out. Disappearing into the ditches along the roadside the Durhams returned fire. B Company, to the left, brought their Bren guns into action, while C Company outflanked the Germans on the open country to the right. A handful of men rushed the enemy position and forced the Germans to retire, but the party was shot down almost on top of a machine gun emplacement. B Company then went into the vines after the *Fallschirmjäger* with bayonets fixed. In the close vegetation, in the shadows, the Germans were waiting, and a deadly game of hide-and-seek developed in which it was hard to tell friend from foe. It was every man for himself, with no quarter asked or given, and within twenty minutes both sides had fought themselves to a standstill. The Germans and the leading half of B Company suffered nearly a hundred percent casualties, and the only men left in the area that had been fought over were the dead or wounded. Some of the Durhams, including the company commander, had reached the sunken road four hundred yards from the river, but after a fierce exchange of bullets all were killed or wounded. The paratroops retained possession of the position.

The rear part of B Company, about forty men with no knowledge of the existence of the sunken road, attempted to advance to their original objective but in fields just in front of the enemy positions they came under automatic fire and showers of grenades, which forced them into the vineyards. As the breaking dawn improved visibility, the existence of the sunken road became clear – as did the vulnerability of their situation. With difficulty they withdrew to the shelter of an embankment surrounding a farmhouse to the rear.

C Company, to the right, had been whittled down and by first light was without officers. The survivors occupied scattered locations. A Company had a comparatively quiet night, but just before dawn enemy activity ceased – an indication that an attack was to be expected shortly. As soon as it became light the two platoons on the right of the company position came under attack and were overrun. The *Fallschirmjäger* had worked their way up under cover of the vines, and fierce fighting took place in the section positions. Casualties were high on both sides, and the surviving Durhams were pushed back to the river bank. Some of them swam across to safety. The third platoon and A Company Headquarters were forced to retire to the bridge.

At 0600 hours 8 DLI held a salient some 300 yards deep and wide on the north bank. The bridge was under constant enemy fire and could only be crossed by armoured vehicles. The brigade commander, who had gone forward to see conditions for himself, was marooned on the north bank where he had to stay until a Bren carrier became available to carry him back. It was a precarious position, and the battalion had suffered heavily. An attempt to bring two Shermans across the bridge in support came to nothing as they were forced to retreat by an 88mm gun, firing on them from a range of eight hundred yards. At 0630 the Battalion Carrier and Mortar Platoons were ordered forward across the bridge, and provided welcome support – as did the self-propelled artillery pieces, Priests, stationed to the south. Fire from these removed one of the 88mm guns, but others remained. Two anti-tank guns followed across the river, and a second attempt was made to bring Shermans forward. Three crossed the bridge, two of which were soon knocked out by the 88mm gun[15].

At 1330 hours Generals Montgomery and Dempsey came forward to assess the situation. What they saw convinced them that the planned amphibious operation against Catania had to be postponed until the night of 17/18 July. They also ordered General Kirkman to mount another attack that night, to enlarge the bridgehead.

This time the attack would be a larger-scale affair. With 8 DLI holding the salient on the north bank – however precariously, because the Germans were maintaining their pressure on the bridgehead at short range – the other two battalions in the brigade, 6 and 9 DLI, would make the same river crossing upstream and then advance on the left and right sides, respectively, of Highway 114. Their objective was a line running east-west across the northern end of the loop in the river. The attack would be supported by 3rd City of London Yeomanry, which would exploit the breakthrough with their Shermans, and by an artillery concentration laid down by six artillery regiments – a total of 159 guns. The attack was scheduled for 0100 hours on 17 July.

The Germans were not caught napping. As the two battalions moved across the river and into their attack positions astride the road, they came under heavy machine-gun fire, the tracers criss-crossing the road in the night. The *Fallschirmjäger* stood their ground until they were shot down, even in positions in the sunken road after the advance had passed through them. The weight of the attack decided the issue, however, and when the Shermans crossed the Primosole Bridge at 0700 hours the end was in sight.

Deployed on both sides of the road, the tanks pressed through the vineyards, shooting at everything before them. German soldiers began surrendering, white handkerchiefs waving, and by mid-morning mopping-up operations were complete. Not all of the *Fallschirmjäger* surrendered gracefully, however. One, wounded, managed to throw a grenade before being dispatched. Another, who was camouflaged and in the branches of a tree, was ordered to climb down and surrender. Without ammunition, he nevertheless continued his resistance by spitting at the two soldiers who waited at the foot of the tree. They shot him[16].

The performance of the *Fallschirmjäger* at Primosole Bridge was held in high regard, even by their opponents. The *London Times* of 27 August 1943 stated:

> *They fought superbly. They were troops of the highest quality, experienced veterans of Crete and Russia: cool and skilful, Nazi zealots to a man and fanatically courageous. To fight against them was an education for any soldier.* [17]

As he was being led into captivity, the German commander was approached by the CO of 9 DLI, who shook his hand.

During the fighting for the bridge the three battalions of the Durham Light Infantry suffered some 600 casualties. More than 300 German dead were found in the area. Although the fighting for the bridge was over, the Germans continued to interfere with Allied traffic across it, for they shelled it with a heavy gun from some miles away, causing a number of casualties.

At the junction of Highway 114 and the sunken road, re-named 'Stink Alley' (or variations, all of which reflected the stench of bodies that had to lie there awaiting burial), the Durham Brigade later erected a memorial. The words upon it read:

This memorial has been erected
To keep fresh the memory of
the soldiers of 151 Durham Infantry
Brigade who gave their lives for their
Country
and the cause of the Freedom during the
Sicilian Campaign 10 July - 17 August 1943

It is placed here because it was
during the actions round the
Porte Primosole 14 - 17 July 1943
that the Brigade experienced the fiercest
fighting in which it took part during the Campaign

HQ. 151 Durham Infantry Brigade
151 Durham Brigade Support Company
6th Battalion The Durham Light Infantry
8th Battalion The Durham Light Infantry
9th Battalion The Durham Light Infantry

1 D'Este – Bitter Victory.
2 Ibid.
3 Ibid.
4 Durnford-Slater.
5 Ibid.
6 Ibid.
7 Molony.
8 Ibid.
9 Saunders – Red Beret.
10 Ibid.
11 Ibid.
12 D'Este – Bitter Victory.
13 Ibid.
14 Honniball.
15 Lewis & English.
16 Moses – The Gateshead Gurkhas.
17 Lewis & English.

CHAPTER TEN

THE PLAIN OF CATANIA

THE DECISIONS TAKEN BY ALEXANDER on 13 and 16 July dictated the form that the campaign would take. By giving Montgomery the use of Highway 124 he had made the Eighth Army the principal agent by which Messina should be captured, and relegated the Seventh to a secondary role. With XIII and XXX Corps advancing on two fronts towards Catania and Enna respectively, the expectation was that Catania would quickly be occupied; but a stalemate developed as the German defences stiffened south of the city. Montgomery's attempt to broaden his front there by moving 51st (Highland) Division up on the left of XIII Corps, which might have outflanked the enemy, was too late. On 16 July Alexander took the decision to move both of the British corps eastwards – only for them to run directly into the Axis defence line known as the *Hauptkampflinie* which Kesselring had agreed with Generals Hube and Guzzoni. The Axis forces in Sicily were now, *de facto*, under the command of the Germans, and General Hube was an effective instrument to carry out their policy – which was not wholly communicated to the Italians – of fighting a defensive battle which would lead to eventual evacuation of the island[1].

As outlined earlier, on 16 July Hitler ordered further reinforcements into Sicily. The one-armed *General der Panzertruppen* Hans Valentin Hube's *XIV Panzer Corps Headquarters* arrived and took firm control of the German forces, which now included the remainder of *1st Parachute Division* (less one regiment), which arrived from Avignon, and much of *29th Panzer Grenadier Division* which crossed the Messina Straits from Calabria. The *Luftwaffe* flak batteries were brought into action as field artillery. Whatever Kesselring may have told Hube about the potential for driving the Allies back into the sea, Hube was clear in his own mind that a progressive withdrawal was the only feasible strategy. He had also received secret orders to keep the Italians out of planning, and was to gain control of all Italian units still in Sicily. His task was to save as many German forces as possible for future operations. By 2 August, Hube would be in control of all Sicilian operations[2].

Every move that the British made on the Catania Plain could be observed from the slopes of Mount Etna. Hube had sufficient forces to counter any advance XIII Corps could make, but no proper reserves. While 5th and 50th Divisions attempted to progress northwards, the

Hermann Göring Division and the *Fallschirmjäger* dug in firmly.

The first of the defence lines which the Axis command established to protect the withdrawal to the Straits of Messina, the *Hauptkampflinie*, ran along the route of the road just west of Santo Stefano, south to Nicosia and Agira, then east to Regalbuto before heading south again to Catenanuova, eastwards along the Dittaino River, and ran across the northern edge of the Catania Plain, reaching the coast about six miles south of that city. The line therefore ran all of the way from the northern to the eastern seaboards, taking advantage of the mountainous terrain, a river bank, and the Catania Plain with its broken countryside.

Fifteen miles behind this line the Germans planned the *Etna Line*, from San Fratello south to Troina and then east to Adrano (which was also known as Aderno in some accounts) and along the road which ran eastwards along the southern edge of Etna to the sea at Acireale. Behind this, the innermost defence line which protected the north-eastern evacuation sites ran from Mount Pelato through Cesaro and Bronte to the sea near Riposto.

The three lines were based on natural features which lent themselves to defence, and which could be strengthened by demolishing roads and bridges and by the laying of minefields and booby-traps. The defences were beginning to be established, albeit not yet firmly, by 17 July. The anchor of the *Hauptkampflinie* was Catania – and it was here that Montgomery pressed XIII Corps to attack.

Between 16 and 22 July the Axis operations were focused on three, largely independent, areas. In the east, forces largely made up from the *Hermann Göring Division* held the line of the Dittaino River from Dittaino Station to the sea, forty-two miles to the east and four miles south of Catania. Alongside the *Hermann Göring Division* were elements of *1st Parachute Division*, part of the *Livorno Division*, and *76 Infantry Regiment* from the *Napoli Division*. Facing them were XIII Corps and 51st Division from XXX Corps.

In the centre of the Axis front, *15th Panzer Grenadier Division* was withdrawing from a line which ran through the towns of Caltanissetta, Pietraperzia, Barrafrance, Piazza Armerina, and then north-westwards to the Leonforte-Nicosia area. Here, 1st Canadian Division was in contact with the enemy at the eastern end of the twenty-mile line. At the western end of this sector, 1st (US) and 45th (US) Divisions were in pursuit.

The westernmost section of the *Hauptkampflinie* was the most fluid. Here the Italian *XII Corps*, comprising the *Assietta* and *Aosta Divisions*, most of the Corps artillery and three Mobile Groups, had been ordered back to defend a forty-five mile length of line on Highway 120 running from Cerda through Petralia to Nicosia. Harassed in their retirement by American troops and aircraft, some of the Italian columns were destroyed as they moved along the narrow roads.

The defence line was very long, and was not continuous. Formations were not firmly linked together, and the forces were thinly stretched; in theory, it should have been possible for attackers to feel out weak spots through which to thrust deep into enemy territory. In practice, however, the terrain dictated otherwise, and the climate did not help. The road-bound Allies were tied to the narrow, winding routes which were frequently even more constrained by the stone walls which bordered them.

The most practical directions along which to advance were generally the most obvious – and the most obvious places to concentrate the defences. The Allies were further hindered by their lack of animal transport. During the planning stages for HUSKY seven companies of pack-mules were included in the Eighth Army's Order of Battle, but these were not included when priorities were established for shipping men and materiel to Sicily. On 17 July, Eighth Army signalled to Middle East that 'No Pack Transport Units are required by 8th Army in Sicily'. Although local mule trains were organised, they were too small and too untrained to achieve anything more than small tasks[3].

From Alexander's perspective, the Eighth Army appeared to be the formation best situated to achieve the objective of seizing Messina and sealing off the enemy's escape route. Not only were the British well-positioned – on the map – to push up the eastern coast of Sicily, but there was also the legacy of the performance of the Americans and British in North Africa, which left a lingering mistrust of Seventh Army's reliability. Alexander had confidence, built upon evidence of past performance, in Montgomery. But Monty's assertion, on 12 July, that Catania would be in his hands two days later failed to materialise – as did his revised target of reaching the city on the 16th. Alexander's faith in Montgomery had led him to accept the redefinition of the Anglo-American armies' boundary; the failure to push 45th (US) Division rapidly northwards on Highway 112 had cost him the opportunity to split Sicily in two quickly and to forestall the Germans' window of opportunity to inject fresh forces into the island and to stabilise their defence lines.

Montgomery's strategy, accepted by Alexander, effectively sent the Eighth Army in diverging directions to objectives forty-five miles apart – XIII Corps towards Catania, and XXX Corps towards Enna – while the American Seventh Army was left without a real role in achieving the objective of securing Messina, other than protecting the British left flank. As the Catania front became stalemated, so Monty tried to extend it by bringing 51st (Highland) Division from XXX Corps up on the left of XIII Corps, but he was too late to affect a decisive blow against the enemy defences. Alexander's decision to push both corps eastwards, taken on 16 July, was also too late to bring about the desired result. By this time the Axis defences had become sufficiently well knitted together to prevent the success of the strategy.

On 18 July Montgomery decided that 50th Division would hold fast in the Primosole area, while 5th Division would strike about three and a half miles west of the bridge, towards Misterbianco. The line of attack was to cross the Gornalunga and Simeto Rivers; any further west and it would have had to cross the Dittaino River as well. On the night of 18-19 July 13 Brigade succeeded in making a shallow bridgehead across the Simeto, through which 15 Brigade mounted an attack at 0130 hours on the 20th. The attack faded out, partly because the infantry battalions' positions were unclear to the supporting artillery – all eight field and one medium regiments of it – and they were unable to bring effective fire down to assist the advance. In fact the infantry had advanced about three thousand yards before being brought to a halt by machine guns and mortar fire from the enemy who were situated in the gullies and ditches which criss-crossed the ground north of the river. A later attempt to restart the assault came to nothing when enemy defensive fire caused confusion and delay, and the division was ordered to consolidate where it was, pending changes in plans.

Further west again, by another eleven miles, Montgomery had hoped that 51st (Highland) Division would be in Paterno by the night of 20 July. General Wimberley intended to reach that town at speed, using his 'Arrow Force' on the right and 154 Infantry Brigade on the left. Arrow Force was an all-arms battle group based on Headquarters 23 Armoured Brigade, with 50th RTR (less two troops), 11th (Honourable Artillery Company) Regiment RHA, 243rd Antitank Battery RA, a company from 1/7th Middlesex Regiment – the Division's medium machinegun battalion – and 2nd Battalion The Seaforth Highlanders. As such, it was a self-sufficient formation capable of acting relatively independently.

Paterno, however, was difficult to approach tactically, being on the far side of three rivers, the Simeto, the Dittaino and the Gornalunga. To get there, either the enemy defences at Sferro or Gerbini had to be penetrated; the two towns protected alternative routes. Arrow Force succeeded in making a shallow bridgehead over the Dittaino at Stimpano, on the Gerbini route, by 18 July, while 154 Brigade advanced through Ramacca with 152 Brigade behind it as the reserve which would exploit whichever route proved most promising. 153 Brigade was to the right moving on Sferro. Now Wimberley changed the direction of his advance, sending 154 Brigade through the Stimpano bridgehead towards Motta Station and 153 to Sferro with the intention of forcing a bridgehead across the Dittaino.

Both brigades ran into more opposition than expected. 154 Brigade was unable to cross the Simeto by dawn on 19 July. At Sferro, 153 Brigade's 5th Battalion of The Black Watch made a bridgehead and dug in with mortars and antitank guns. The battalion was supported by machineguns from the Middlesex, and the guns of 127th Field Regiment RA. The defenders of

Sferro brought down heavy fire on them from artillery, tanks and mortars, causing some sixty casualties, including the regimental sergeant major, who was killed when the battalion headquarters was hit. With enemy *panzers* in evidence ahead, and with only a single field artillery regiment in support, a rethink was necessary. Wimberley elected to try to enlarge the Sferro bridgehead that night, and 1st Gordon Highlanders and two companies of 5/7th Gordons moved forward through the fiercest bombardment they had ever endured to do just that. They crossed the railway line and then the main road, and 1st Gordons established their headquarters in the station yard, packed with goods wagons. The 5/7th Gordons' companies forced their way into the village, but lost wireless contact when their radio sets were knocked out in the street fighting. They stayed, isolated, and were shot up by German 88mm guns and armoured cars when dawn broke. The Gordons were to remain in the bridgehead, unable to expand it in the face of stubborn enemy opposition, until 24 July[4].

Wimberley began to feel that his division was over-extended. On his right, the enemy defences appeared to be the strongest, and not the place to attack. However, he did not wish to redeploy his troops away from there, for to surrender the ground which they had already seized would mean that XIII Corps would have to retake it, should they find it necessary to move through the area. A renewed attack at Sferro was an option, but it was becoming clear that the enemy defences were firmly anchored on the area of Gerbini airfield, two thousand yards north of the positions now occupied by 154 Brigade. Wimberley decided that Gerbini should be taken during the night of 20/21 July by the brigade, supported by a squadron of tanks from 46 RTR and three artillery regiments.

1st Battalion Black Watch, followed by the 7th Battalion and the 7th Battalion Argyll & Sutherland Highlanders led the attack. 1st Black Watch became pinned down in front of the heavily defended barracks. 7th Black Watch, supported by the tanks, attacked the airfield, again against stiff opposition. The Argylls attacked Gerbini along the railway line, with artillery assistance, and after three hours of hard fighting gained their objective. The Argyll carriers and mortars, covered by a squadron of Shermans, moved up to join them, but the enemy – probably the *Reconnaissance Unit* and most of the *2nd Battalion Panzer Regiment*, and two battalions from *2nd Panzer Grenadier Regiment*, all of the *Hermann Göring Division* quickly responded with heavy fire and infiltration. The Argylls' A Company was surrounded by enemy with tanks and was forced to surrender.

Before dawn most of the 1st Battalion of The Black Watch were also committed, and finally reached the barracks, which had by now been abandoned by the Germans. By 1030 hours a German counter-attack regained the ground they had lost. The action cost the Argylls eighteen officers, including the CO, and 160 men. 46 RTR lost eight Shermans, and the squadron commander dead.

Eight miles to the northwest of Sferro, XXX Corps planned the capture of a bridge over the Dittaino at Catenanuova that same night. The unit which was to carry out this task was 7th Battalion Royal Marines, a force which had provided the now redundant Beach Bricks, the troops that had administered (with medical, signals, ordnance, service corps, anti-aircraft units and the Royal Naval Commandos) each of the British landing beaches on D Day, but which was now reunited. With inadequate transport resources, much of the battalion had to hitch-hike its way sixty miles inland to join XXX Corps. The battalion was extremely tired – its work on the beaches had been very strenuous, and many men had been working in salt water for long periods during that stage of the landings. Their feet had become softened, and the long march to their present location had added to the difficulties. Furthermore, because of the limitations on transport, much equipment had yet to be brought forward. This included digging tools.

As the two wings of XXX Corps were on divergent courses, a dangerous gap was emerging at Catenanuova through which enemy armour might infiltrate. Two companies from 7 RM provided cover for the Corps Headquarters from this threat, and on 19 July fresh orders were given to the Marines which placed them under command of 51st Division, with the primary task of establishing a roadblock at Lennaretto, which would cover the division's left flank. A further task, to establish a bridgehead over the Dittaino and the railway line beyond it, was also ordered. Once this had been achieved, the battalion was to advance of Catenanuova[5]. The codename LEOPARD was given to this crossing, with 153 Brigade's bridgehead at Sferro being named JAGUAR. A third bridgehead to the east, through which 152 Brigade was advancing, was christened LION.

The Royal Marines were supported in the attack to gain their bridgehead by a troop of Shermans, two batteries of 6-pounder antitank guns, a medium machine gun platoon of the Middlesex, and a battery of 3.7 inch howitzers. At 1400 hours, 19 July, two of the marine companies reached the battalion rendezvous south of two mountains which lay about 3,000 yards south of the intended river crossing site. They prepared a hot meal for the remainder of the battalion, which arrived two hours later. With reassurance from the Carrier Platoon of 4/5th Gordon Highlanders that the track ahead was suitable for mechanical transport, the plan was firmed up for one Marine company with an antitank gun to establish the roadblock at Lennaretto, while the remainder of the battalion made a night march and assault to secure the bridgehead over the Dittaino. The Gordons' brief reconnaissance had indicated that no enemy were present south of the river, but that some movement had been seen on the north bank.

At dusk, 2000 hours, two companies moved forward and occupied the pass between the two mountains immediately north of the rendezvous point; a third passed through them and crossed the river without incident until Italian troops in a building near the railway raised the alarm. The position was taken at the point of the bayonet and several prisoners were taken. To the right, the first of the companies that had secured the pass moved up and crossed, again taking prisoners, and the third company advanced into the centre. By 0500 hours the far bank was secure, and some 100 Italian and fifty German prisoners were in the bag.

The infantry may have been on the north bank, but behind them the supporting antitank guns were having difficulties in coming forward to the position. The track between the two mountains was poor. It had never been used for motorised transport and the edge was crumbling, and a Bren carrier and two portees carrying 6-pounder guns went over the edge into a deep ravine; there was no possibility of tanks or artillery using the track. The Marines were without support apart from those few antitank guns which had made it to a ridge south of the Dittaino.

To compound their problems, the ground which the Royal Marines occupied was hard and rocky, and impervious to digging. Moreover, it was overlooked by two features to the north, Razor Ridge and the Fico d'India. Enemy on the second of these could enfilade British troops huddled in the only cover available, the railway embankment and the banks of the river. Soon the Marines came under very heavy fire from an assortment of weapons, directed from observation posts beyond the range of anything the British had. Self-propelled guns, *Nebelwerfers* (multi-barrelled mortars) heavy machine guns and 88mm guns firing airbursts, together with snipers, all pitched in. One 88mm gun was destroyed by the antitank guns south of the river before they in turn were put out of action by the *Nebelwerfers*. Four carriers attempted to bring the battalion's 3-inch mortars across the river, but one bellied down on the approach, and although the other three came into action they were soon knocked out.

The 3.7 inch howitzers gave what support they could, as did the Middlesex' machine guns from the south of the river, but at extreme range they had little affect. The Shermans, despite efforts by the engineers to make the track suitable, were unable to move forward. By 1100 hours withdrawal was inevitable. This was far from easy because of the exposed positions, but seven hours later the battalion was back, some 200 yards across the river[6].

The other crossings to the east, at LION and JAGUAR, had some initial success but XXX Corps was not able to exploit forward from the bridgeheads. AT LION, the Highland Division had reached the outskirts of the Gerbini airfield, whereupon they had been counterattacked by tanks and driven back. This setback caused the British advance to be paused for a week to allow time for reorganisation and to give the troops time to gain a second wind.

Montgomery visited Wimberley at midday on 21 July. With the strength of the opposition facing the Highland Division and XIII Corps, he had come to the decision to stop attacking on these fronts, and was ordering 78th Division to Sicily from North Africa. Once they had arrived, the offensive would be resumed using the 78th and the Canadian Division. Meanwhile, the right flank of the Eighth Army would go on the defensive[7].

To the west, 1st Canadian Division had been moving on Leonforte and Assoro since 15 July. Its route had been through mountainous country, where the enemy had made good use of the small villages which sat astride the tortuous roads to make easily defensible redoubts. These were strengthened by use of demolitions, road blocks and mines, and had to be reduced by a series of small battles.

On 17 July 231 (Malta) Brigade was given the independent role of covering the gap between the 51st (Highland) and 1st Canadian Divisions, and moved northwards towards Raddusa. Its advance was held up by enemy demolitions, but the route was soon cleared and by 1900 hours that day contact was made with German forces on the line of the Gornalunga River, a mile or so south of Raddusa.

To the Canadians' left, Seventh (US) Army advanced against less opposition, the Germans having abandoned any thought of defending the west of Sicily, and many of the Italians having no other thought but to surrender. On 17 July 1st (US) Division was abreast of the Canadians about eight miles to the west of Piazza Armerina, approaching Caltanissetta. 45th (US) Division was further west again, approaching the same town from the southwest. The race was still on between the Americans and the Canadians for Enna. The latter had the main road leading to the town from the southeast, but enemy resistance was stiffening, and was much more determined than the Canadians had experienced hitherto.

General Simonds directed 3 Brigade towards Enna and the 1st northeast towards Valguarnera. 3 Brigade were delayed at a narrow pass, the Portella Grottacalda, for some fourteen hours on 17 July until they attacked the enemy frontally with the Royal 22e Regiment, and from the flanks with the Carleton and Yorks, and the West Nova Scotia's. At Valguarnera 1 Brigade entered the town, against resistance, after nightfall. The two encounters cost the Canadians 145 casualties.

The enemy – the *2nd Battalion* of *1st Panzer Grenadier Regiment* was thought to have been reinforced by the regiment's *1st Battalion* – held a position on a road junction southwest of Valguanera. Having had their advance held up by a blown bridge, 3 Canadian Infantry Brigade encountered the Germans here, and came under mortar and machine-gun fire. The infantry disembarked from their transport, the tanks took up hull-down positions to the west of the road, and the enemy were forced to retire, leaving three Italian guns and three small tanks out of action behind them.

At this stage Simonds decided to by-pass Enna. On 19 July he broadened his front by taking advantage of the road fork north of Valguarnera, sending 2 Infantry Brigade towards Leonforte and 1 Brigade to Assoro. The Canadians did, however, send a patrol from the Reconnaissance Squadron to try to enter Enna before the Americans, who were rapidly approaching it from the southwest. Halted about five miles from the town by a badly cratered road which prevented any further motorised progress, a group consisting of a sergeant, two corporals and a trooper proceeded to complete their mission on foot.

They had a walk of some four and a half miles to do uphill, but became 'browned off' after a short while, so commandeered a donkey to help them on their way. A patrol comprising a man mounted on a donkey, leading three others, proceeded with the mission of capturing Enna for the Canadians. In front of them they saw two truckloads of troops, but it was a little while before these were identified as being Americans rather than Germans. The GIs had just arrived, and gave the Canadians a lift into town, whereupon one of the Canadian corporals later claimed to be the first to dismount from the jeep in the town centre – thus claiming the honour of the capture for Canada. No doubt the Americans disputed this[8].

Leonforte sat at the western end of the Etna Line before it turned northwards to the sea. Three battalions of the *104th Panzer Grenadier Regiment* of *15th Panzer Grenadier Division* held the town and Assoro. The German defences were centred on demolitions and minefields, and small stay-behind parties armed with machine guns and mortars were deployed around destroyed culverts and cratered roads to further delay the Allied troops. The Canadian approach to the two towns had to cross the Dittaino valley, in full view of enemy observation posts, and artillery fire on them was continuous.

The route forward was hazardous. Although no enemy were encountered at close range, the Canadians were harassed by artillery, and C Squadron, 12th Canadian Tank Regiment (The Three Rivers Regiment) drove straight into a minefield, where nine tanks had their tracks blown off before the crews realised their predicament. They had to stay in their Shermans for nearly five hours while the Germans rained down mortar and artillery fire on them. The danger increased when the stubble on the ground around them caught fire, setting off petrol and ammunition dumps nearby. The Sappers distinguished themselves by starting to clear the mines while under fire, and it was yet another unpleasant experience in the campaign for those involved.

The lead battalion nominated for the attack on Assoro, the Hastings and Prince Edward Regiment, lost both its commanding officer and intelligence officer while carrying out a reconnaissance for a night assault on the village. The Canadians' approach had been impossible to carry out unannounced, and the Germans were ready. The light was fading, but the Canadians could see that all along the horizon stretched an escarpment running from Leonforte through Assoro and on eastwards to Agira. Directly ahead the Assoro feature dominated, and it was clear that the Germans would have the only direct approach, a winding road, well covered. Major The Lord Tweedsmuir (the son of John Buchan, the author and former Governor-General of Canada) took command of the Hastings. He identified a route up a steep slope on the east of the feature to the 12th Century Norman castle which dominated the village, which might be practicable, and determined to attempt it. To divert the Germans' attention from the Hastings' approach, three carriers of the 48th Highlanders were sent down the road at dusk, with orders to swing about and return as soon as they came under fire, and artillery laid on harassing fire.

At 2130 hours Tweedsmuir led a hand-picked group of twenty men, followed by the rest of the battalion, up the terraces to the summit. Armed with no more than rifles and a few Bren Guns, they scaled the heights in bright moonlight, on their way awakening a sleeping boy on the back of a donkey, who closed his eyes and went straight back to sleep, not realising how tense the men around him were, and how close he might have been to being shot. The Hastings gained the summit a quarter of an hour before dawn, and the position was taken without a casualty. The enemy expected no-one but their own men to be there, and were completely surprised by the manoeuvre. The Germans mounted two counterattacks in attempts to dislodge them, but the Hastings held on until, on the morning of 22 July, the 48th Highlanders fought their way into the village through its western defences, which had been weakened in an attempt to dislodge the Canadians on the castle heights.

The fall of Assorto made it more difficult for the Germans to defend Leonforte. They had to hold the whole ridge, or withdraw from it altogether.

On 21 July the Seaforth of Canada had been halted in the steep approaches to Leonforte, but towards 2100 hours the Edmonton Regiment succeeded in gaining a foothold in the town. House-to-house fighting continued through the night, and early the next day the Canadians managed to repair a bridge over a ravine below the town, allowing four tanks of the Three Rivers Regiment, a troop of antitank guns and a company of the PPCLI to enter. After a morning of hard fighting the Germans were driven out. They retired to two hills, from where the PPCLI removed them at about 1730 hours. Leonforte cost the Canadians 175 casualties; Assorto nearly a hundred.

The Divisional Intelligence Summary of 23 July made the following statement:

For the first time, the Germans fought all three battalions of 1 Pz Gren Regt as one tactical formation. After the fall of ASSORO the coys (3 Bn?) fighting there were moved in to defend LEONFORTE. During 22 Jul all three bns were identified in and about the latter town. At first light 5 tks and about 75 inf penetrated back into LEONFORTE. This resolute defence is something new. Hitherto the German rearguard has pulled stakes cleanly and retired some 8 or 10 miles to a new posn. The fact that they are not voluntarily retiring from their latest strong point but are fighting for every yd of ground indicates that we are nearing something like a serious defence zone. Beyond doubt they would have held LEONFORTE had they not been driven out of it[9].

The point regarding nearing 'a serious defence zone' was not far off the mark. Ahead lay Agira.

While the Eighth Army was engaged in the events described above, Alexander was giving consideration to the future. On 19 July he signalled Montgomery, pointing out that the enemy defences stretching from the northern to the eastern coasts (in effect, the *Hauptkampflinie*) might prove to be too strong for the Eighth Army to pierce. He suggested placing one of the American divisions under Monty's command, which would work in the northern sector. He still saw Seventh Army's task as being to occupy western Sicily, very much a secondary role.

Montgomery's reply enumerated the four thrusts that he had launched: Catania (which was now called off), Misterbianco, Paterno, and Leonforte-Adrano. He considered these to be very powerful, and if his troops could be in Misterbianco the following night (20 July), and Adrano the next day, he thought that he would be in a strong position to move around either side of Etna. The Americans, he suggested, might provide one division to push along the north coast towards Messina. This would stretch the enemy's defences and might divert them.

After visiting Montgomery on 20 July, Alexander reported to Brooke that the Catania offensive was to be suspended because it would prove too costly. However, Agira had fallen, the Canadians had captured Enna and Leonforte, and the Americans were expected to be in Petralia that day. They would then provide one division to cut the northern coast road and to work to the north of the Eighth Army. His intention was for the Seventh Army to be based on Palermo, before operating to the north of the Eighth in the final thrust for Messina.

One has to question where Alexander got his information. Leonforte did not fall until the 22nd, and Agira on the 28th. Whether it was Montgomery's over-optimistic view of things, or Alexander's, is debatable – but the Eighth Army situation reports for 19 and 20 July gave the correct state of affairs, and it would appear that Monty's rosy assessments were not checked before Alexander reported to the CIGS[10].

During the evening of 21 July Montgomery again signalled Alexander, reporting that enemy resistance around Catania and in the foothills about Misterbianco and Paterno was 'very great'. Although he 'had won the battle for the plain of Catania... heat in the plain is very great and my troops are getting very tired'. He was therefore going to hold his right wing, while continuing operations against Adrano. XXX Corps would be strengthened by 78th Division, to assist in operations north towards Bronte.

Meanwhile the Americans should thrust along the northern coast road towards Messina, and the full weight of Allied airpower from North Africa should be brought to bear on the enemy in the northeast corner of Sicily. The four-thrust strategy which he had outlined only two days previously was no longer mentioned; the prospect of extending the battle on both sides of Etna with the assistance of an American division had gone. Instead, he was calling forward his reserve, 78th Division, from Africa, and XXX Corps would be committed to a 'blitz attack' on the line Adrano-Bronte-Randazzo, northwards up the western side of Etna. Possession of Adrano would put Etna between the two halves of the Axis forces, robbing them of their lateral communications on the southwest and south of the mountain. What Monty now wanted was more commitment from the Americans on the northern coast road.

Alexander accepted Montgomery's fresh strategy. Patton had already been ordered to bring pressure against the enemy on Highways 113 and 120, the coast road and that some twenty miles inland, running west to east through Nicosia and Troina to Randezzo, On 23 July Patton was given directions to transfer his supply lines through Palermo, and to use the maximum strength he could maintain to thrust along these two roads, striking at the enemy's northern flank while the Axis communications system in the north-eastern corner of Sicily was subjected to a bombing campaign.

He ordered the remainder of his reserve, 9th (US) Infantry Division, to the island (39th RCT had been brought over on 15 July, landing at Licata, and had been attached to 82nd Airborne Division to assist in clearing western Sicily). On 24 July, Alexander visited Montgomery, and the following day the two generals held a conference with Patton – the first time during the campaign that the land force commanders met together.

It is notable that the conference was held at the instigation of Montgomery rather than Alexander. Monty signalled an invitation to Patton and his chief of staff to attend the meeting, in Syracuse, to discuss the capture of Messina. Despite the campaign now being two weeks old, there was still no strategy agreed for its completion. Montgomery was coming to recognise that the enemy facing the Eighth Army was too strongly ensconced to push through, and that a greater degree of coordination was needed between Patton and himself to resolve the impasse. Alexander, on the other hand, was continuing with his 'hands-off' style of leadership, refusing to become involved in the detailed direction of the campaign. This may have been acceptable in North Africa when he let Montgomery run Eighth Army's battles as he saw fit, but in Sicily there were two Allied armies operating, and thus far Alexander had rather ignored the American role in the campaign.

Patton's – understandable – suspicions notwithstanding, the two army commanders quickly agreed that Seventh (US) Army was to have the exclusive use of Highways 113 and 120, and Montgomery even proposed that it should be Patton who was to have the privilege of taking Messina, and striking through Randazzo to Taormina, across the north of Etna. If necessary, the Americans were given full permission to cross the inter-army boundary in pursuit of this aim, which if successful would mean that two German divisions would be cut off from their line of retreat. With the legacy of Monty's commandeering Highway 124 from the Americans only eleven days earlier, it was not surprising that Patton should be suspicious of Montgomery's motives. But the Eighth Army commander was aware that his strategy of launching separate attacks by various divisions along the Catania front was proving unsuccessful and that the campaign needed greater inter-Allied cooperation.

Three days later Montgomery paid a return visit to Patton in Palermo, narrowly avoiding disaster when the airfield proved too short for the B-17 bomber in which the British delegation was travelling. An accident was prevented only by the skill of the pilot. At last, Allied strategy – at least on the ground – was coming together. But Alexander appeared to be taking little part in this, for he arrived late at the Syracuse meeting, to be told by Montgomery that everything had been settled by Patton and himself. In Palermo, the Montgomery-Patton agreement was confirmed, although Patton remained mistrustful. With memories of Anglo-American problems since TORCH, he had little faith in Monty's good intentions, and saw Messina as the prize that must be competed for, as a way of establishing American military prestige.

1 Malony.
2 D'Este – Bitter Victory.
3 Malony.
4 Delaforce.
5 Royal Marine Business.
6 Ibid.
7 Delaforce.
8 Canadian Operations in Sicily Report 135.
9 Ibid.
10 Malony.

CHAPTER ELEVEN

THE PERSPECTIVE FROM THE AXIS' SIDE

FROM THE AXIS SIDE, the view was – naturally – somewhat different from the opinions of Alexander and Montgomery. For a start, Hube did not see that the Eighth Army was in control of the Plain of Catania; it was not until 26 July that he felt that it was becoming necessary to withdraw from the *Hauptkampflinie*. Nor was the picture Montgomery painted of the enemy being hemmed into the north-eastern corner of Sicily, waiting to be bombed into submission by any and every available aircraft, quite correct. On 21 July, Kesselring was reporting that the Allies had not yet embarked on any significant offensive, and on the 25th *29th Panzer Grenadier Division* had reinforced the northern end of the defence lines.

That night, 25 July, news was received that Mussolini had fallen. After years of promising the Italians glory, but only leading them into overextending their military capability and into suffering a series of setbacks which had now led to their country being invaded, they had had enough. After a vote of no confidence in him had been passed by the Grand Council on 24 July, King Victor Emmanuel told him on the following afternoon that the game was over and that he was to be replaced by a caretaker government under Marshal Badoglio. When Mussolini left the royal villa, he was arrested and whisked away to a secret location.

The divisions between the Axis partners had become more apparent. Although Badoglio immediately announced that the war would go on, behind the scenes moves were afoot to agree a separate armistice with the Allies. On the island of Sicily, however, Guzzoni and the headquarters of the Italian *Sixth Army* continued to cooperate fully with the Germans, and at a later date von Senger was able to testify to this effect when the German-sponsored Republican-Fascist Government – which continued fighting the Allies after the Italian armistice – wanted to execute Guzzoni as a traitor[1].

German suspicions of Italian intent with regard to future participation in the war had been present for some time, and had underlined Hitler's policy for the defence of both Sicily and the Italian mainland. Now that it was clear that the partnership between the two nations was in danger of crumbling, the Germans took immediate steps to protect their own interests, and the contingency plans which they had prepared in the event of Italian collapse were brought out and dusted off. At Hitler's evening conference on 25 July he announced to his service chiefs that the 70,000 German troops on Sicily must be evacuated from the island. Kesselring was ordered to halt any further movement of forces to Sicily, and to draw up plans to withdraw.

On 27 July Kesselring called a conference to consider the matter, by which time Hube had decided that the *Hauptkampflinie* had outlived its purpose. Allied strength on the ground and in the air made holding the line impractical. Around the Straits of Messina the Axis anti-aircraft defences had already been built up, and by 29 July assembly points and reception areas were being allocated to the German divisions in readiness to abandon the island. On 1 August *XIV Panzer Corps Headquarters* issued written orders for the actions to be taken once the evacuation code-word was received.

Consideration of the transport links across the Straits of Messina had not waited for the decision to prepare for evacuation, of course. The despatch of German reinforcements across the waterway had been underway for some time, under the supervision of the German Sea Transport Leader (*Seetransportführer*) Messina Strait, *Fregattenkapitaen* von Liebenstein, who had been in post since the end of May. He had found the transport links between the mainland and Sicily to be a chaotic and inefficient operation based upon a number of commercial ferries which plied their way across the Straits between Messina and two Italian ports. Each ferry was capable of carrying up to twenty-five railway carriages, but the system was vulnerable to Allied air strikes, which had already disrupted rail links to the ports. Even before von Liebenstein's appointment, the Germans had commandeered a number of smaller vessels to run on three minor routes, but this would not be enough to ensure a smooth evacuation. Among other failings, the *Luftwaffe* and army engineer units which ran the ports had individual ferry fleets which acted completely independently of each other and with complete disregard for each other's requirements.

Von Liebenstein wasted no time in bringing the separate flotillas under a single command, an efficiency-saving measure that increased their capacity by a factor of ten. A thousand tons of supplies, several hundred vehicles and thousands of personnel could be transported daily. He also increased the number of ferry routes, so that they operated from twelve separate locations on each side of the Straits, and improved the dock facilities and the road networks that led to them. His re-organised loading procedures allowed the port staff to ship as many as a dozen pre-loaded vehicles onto a ferry in twenty minutes, which would drive directly to depots on the far side of the crossing. During the move of the *Hermann Göring Division* to Sicily, 610 vehicles, 750 tons of supplies and 3,600 men were ferried across the Strait in one day. In addition, the service had sufficient built-in surplus capacity to cater for the eventuality that some ferries would be lost to Allied action.

On 14 July, Kesselring had appointed Colonel Ernst-Guenther Baade as German Commandant, Messina Strait. Baade was one of the more colourful officers in the German army: an accomplished pre-war international show jumper, whose eccentricities included a taste for wearing a kilt and a dagger. Fluent in English, when in North Africa he was known to send messages to the British on their own radio frequencies telling them to stop firing, for he was on his way back. Eccentric at times he may have been, but he was possessed of great organisational abilities.

Baade had been given wide powers by Kesselring. His task was to defend the evacuation routes across the Straits from Allied air strikes, and to provide the means for carrying out the movement of German forces to the mainland. To achieve these aims he established six anti-aircraft sectors, three on each coast, comprising some sixty flak units – a total of eighty-two heavy and sixty light guns on the Italian side, and forty-one heavy and fifty-two light guns on the Sicilian. Some of these weapons were mounted on barges. To protect the crossings from naval attack, he positioned 150 mobile 3- and 4-inch guns along the shorelines, which were also capable of being used in an anti-aircraft role. Four batteries of 280mm, two of 152mm, and one of 170mm guns were situated to interfere with enemy shipping. Supply dumps to sustain troops pulling back from Sicily were established, which included stocks of food, cigarettes and brandy. No detail appeared too small for Baade and his staff.

On 2 August, Baade was able to inform Kesselring that the evacuation plan was ready, a message that was passed on to *OKW* the next day. In essence it meant moving personnel as a priority, after which as much equipment and supplies as possible would be taken. The combination of Baade's plan and von Liebenstein's ferry service gave the Germans at least a fighting chance of escaping from Sicily with as many men and as much equipment as possible, and indeed all inessential personnel had started leaving the island as soon as the Allies landed. Despite a degree of pessimism in *XIV Panzer Corps Headquarters* that the escape could be pulled off, von Liebenstein told Hube that he could bring 12,500 men back every day – and he proposed taking all of their equipment as well.

While the Germans were occupied with their plans for evacuating Sicily, the British were also giving thought to the future direction of the war once this particular campaign came to a close. On 22 July Churchill informed Alexander that he was to visit Roosevelt on 15 August. His message made it clear that his intentions were to convince the President that Italy would be the next objective, but the details of where and how the war would be taken to the mainland would rest with Alexander and Eisenhower, who were best placed to weigh up the alternatives.

Alexander's reply outlined the situation as it was at the time, and how it might be developed once Sicily had fallen. He laid out three possibilities, starting with a jump across the Straits, and continuing with reference to two other plans which had been drawn up under the codenames BUTTRESS and GOBLET, for landings at Reggio and Crotone respectively. As far as the British were concerned, the Mediterranean Theatre would continue to play a decisive part in the war.

As far as the progression of the battle for Sicily was going, Alexander reported that the enemy bottled up in the north-east of the island was the subject – almost exclusively – of the Allied air power in the region. As the RAF and USAAF fighter, fighter-bomber and photographic reconnaissance squadrons had occupied the captured enemy airfields in the south of Sicily, they had freed up space on Malta for British and American Baltimore and Boston bombers. These were easily within range of any targets on the island, and their missions were supplemented by aircraft based in North Africa. By day American Fortresses, Mitchells, Marauders and Bostons flew; at night RAF Wellingtons, Bostons and Baltimores, and some USAAF Mitchells, operated. To add to the Italian misery, sorties were also made against the mainland: over 500 by Fortresses and smaller bombers from North Africa, and 337 Lancasters flew from the United Kingdom to make three bombing attacks on northern Italy. Although the Sicily sorties outnumbered those against the mainland by a factor of three to one, the weight of bombs dropped was comparable because of the greater capacity of the aircraft operating against Italy. The round-the-clock attacks focused on airfields, road and rail communications, and military and industrial targets; on Sicily Messina, Catania, Palermo and Randazzo were hit, as were locations lying in the path of the Allied armies. On 19 July the marshalling yards in Rome were bombed.

The decision to bomb the Eternal City was not taken lightly, but the railway hub there was vital to the Axis' lines of communication. Any attack which might damage the cultural, historic, and religious city – and which might consequently prove to be a propaganda disaster – deserved very careful preparation, and indeed consideration of the antiquarian importance of sites was to be of importance throughout the whole of the Italian campaign – as witnessed by the furore that was raised the following year when the monastery at Cassino was bombed. The night preceding the bombing of Rome, RAF Wellingtons leafleted the city to warn the population of the impending attack; the crews manning the Fortresses and Liberators which were to target the two marshalling yards were hand-picked, carefully trained and briefed, and the actual bombing proved sufficiently accurate that very little damage was caused outside of the target areas. Nevertheless, some 700 people were killed and a further 1,600 wounded. Combined with attacks on the railway yards in Naples, a 200-mile hole was created in the Italian railway system for several days. The trains no longer ran on time, despite Mussolini.

From the standpoint of Axis air missions, after the initial offensives against the beachheads, the frequency of attacks diminished rapidly.

Daytime sorties were generally abandoned in favour of the less hazardous night-time attacks, but even these could not be maintained, and there was little or no air support for ground operations. With the great majority of Axis aircraft having to be based on the mainland because of the damage or capture of the Sicilian airfields, the *Luftwaffe* and the remnants of the *Regia Aeronautica* could do little more[2].

Back on the ground in Sicily, the Allied plan (codenamed HARDGATE) to break the *Hauptkampflinie* was about to be launched. The focus was on Adrano, on which the main thrust was to be directed, and involved three and a half British divisions. To the north, on the left of the Allied front, four American divisions on a two-divisional front were to bring their weight to bear on the enemy defences.

The tactical air forces were tasked by Coningham to disrupt the enemy supplies by sea, road and rail; to give direct support to the ground operations; and to provide round-the-clock fighter protection for forward troops and Allied shipping.

General Leese's XXX Corps was to make the push on Adrano. 78th Division landed at Cassibile during the period 25-28 July and concentrated at an assembly area south of Scalpello, and was assigned to the corps. Eight separate, synchronised operations were to be mounted during the nights of 29/30 July and 1/2 August. During the first, 1st Canadian Division was to seize Regalbuto, on the left, and 78th Division was to take Centuripe in the centre. As a preparatory move for the Centuripe operation, 3 Canadian Infantry Brigade (temporarily attached to 78th Division) would capture a bridgehead over the Dittaino River at Catenanuova. To the right 51th (Highland) Division was to capture another bridgehead over the Dittaino between Catenanuova and Sferro before moving on to take Mount Serra di Spenza. These gains would secure the dominating features on the approaches to Adrano, and should be completed by nightfall on 1 August. Once these positions were secured, the corps artillery would be moved forward to support the next night's operations, which would concentrate on Adrano, to be attacked from the west by the Canadians and from the south-east by 78th Division. To the north, II (US) Corps would be reinforced and would push along Highways 120 and 113, the former route passing through Troina, the latter along the coast.

The Axis forces facing the advance were by now boosted by *15th Panzer Grenadier Regiment*, which arrived on 18 July to join the two battalions of *29th Panzer Grenadier Division* which were already in Sicily. On 24 July the divisional commander, Major General Fries, arrived. Under his orders were *15th* and *17th Panzer Grenadier Regiments*, an artillery regiment, flak and engineer battalions, and an anti-tank company. These were a welcome addition to Hube's strength, and had been sent to Sicily because Kesselring wished to defend the island at all costs until the political situation resolved itself. With the removal of Mussolini from power, of

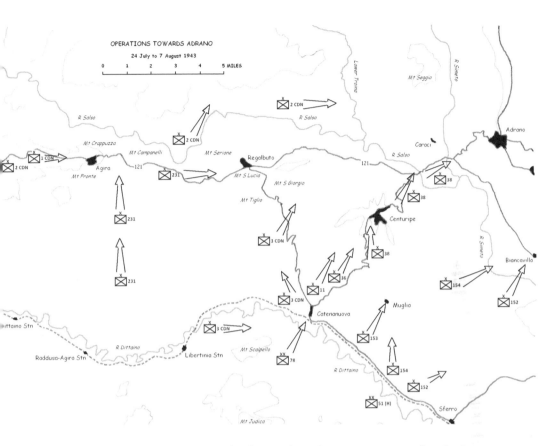

OPERATIONS TOWARDS ADRANO

24 July to 7 August 1943

0   1   2   3   4   5 MILES

course, the situation was much clearer, but the troops were already in Sicily and would be employed to delay the Allies as long as possible.

The Canadian Division had regrouped after taking Assorto and Leonforte before advancing on Agira, which was to be taken by 1 Brigade in co-ordination with 231 Infantry Brigade in a pincer movement. The enemy they faced were, once again, from *15th Panzer Grenadier Division.* 231 Brigade had crossed the Dittaino during the night of 18/19 July and pushed as quickly as possible towards its objective. It soon became clear, however, that the enemy were occupying the heights commanding the southern approaches to the town. General Simonds ordered the brigade to take these positions and to exploit forward to within about a mile from Agira, the maximum range at which the divisional artillery could support it. On 23 July the brigade captured its objectives, but the 1 Canadian Brigade's attack was delayed until the following day. 231 Brigade was ordered to prevent the German withdrawal by seizing a height to the east of town.

The route 1 Brigade was to take to Agira ran through the town of Nissoria, to the east of which lies a ridge which commanded Highway 121. During the late afternoon of 24 July the ridge was attacked by the Royal

Canadian Regiment and a squadron from the 12th Canadian Tanks, supported by the fire from five field and two medium artillery regiments. The artillery fire-plan advanced too quickly for the infantry, which could not keep up and so lost the cover it was supposed to provide. Ten of the tanks were knocked out by enemy anti-tank guns, which they could not manoeuvre around because of the narrow road. The Germans, a battlegroup based on *2nd Battalion* of the *104th Panzer Grenadier Regiment*, successfully beat off the attack, and a second which was mounted by the Hastings & Prince Edward Regiment at midnight. Still led by Major Tweedsmuir, the battalion attempted to advance south of the road, but as the night drew to a close and it began to get light, it came under fire from fourteen machine guns and three Mark III tanks. Having taken heavy casualties, and running out of ammunition, the survivors withdrew through Nissoria.

A third attack, this time by the 48th Highlanders of Canada during the evening of 25 July, did no better. All three of the brigade's infantry battalions had been pushed into the battle, and on the evening of 26 July the Princess Patricia's Canadian Light Infantry, from 2 Brigade, entered the fray supported by an eighty-gun artillery barrage, each gun firing 139 rounds, and by fighter-bombers. This proved sufficient to break the defenders.

While the Canadians had been attacking along the line of Highway 121, the Hampshires from 231 Brigade had managed to cut the road east of Agira, but had been forced to abandon their gains when the Canadians were held up. They retook the position when the 48th Highlanders mounted their assault, only to have to leave it again when the Canadians proved unsuccessful. For three successive nights they took the road, only to have to give it up in the hours of daylight because it was overlooked from Agira. On the fourth attempt, on 26/27 July, they stayed but were unable to intercept the retreating enemy. It had taken five days to capture Agira. A combination of tenacious defenders and rugged terrain had denied the Canadians the swift advance they had hoped for, costing them 438 casualties. 231 Brigade sustained over 300[3].

Led by 231 Brigade, the Canadian Division now continued its painful advance towards Regalbuto until it was halted about a mile short of the town. By 31 July the defenders had withdrawn into the town itself. They were to hold out until 2 August.

The approaches to Regalbuto from the west ran between Monte Serione and the Regalbuto Ridge, lying north and south of the road respectively. A ring of heights protected the town, which was defended by the Engineer Battalion from the *Hermann Göring Division*, supported by more than a company of tanks, the *4th Battery* of the Division's Artillery Regiment, and a company from *3rd Parachute Regiment*. The defenders were ordered to hold the position at all costs. On 29 July 231 Brigade led the attack. 1st Battalion of the Hampshires ran into heavy machine-gun, mortar and *Nebelwerfer* fire, which stopped its advance, although to their right the 1st Dorsets fared rather better. During the night of 30/31 July the 2nd Devons put in an attack from the northwest, supported by 144 artillery pieces; at 0235 hours they signalled their success. The battalion had been severely weakened during the campaign thus far, having suffered some 200 casualties, and was unable to hold off a strong counterattack which pushed them back off the eastern end of the ridge. The reserve company managed to regain the position, and the enemy was also attacked by Kittyhawk fighter-bombers.

To the north of Highway 121 the Dorsets took Monte Serione in close-quarter fighting; relieved by the 48th Highlanders of Canada, the Dorsets prepared to move into the town itself. Fighting patrols from the battalion pushed into Regalbuto on 1 August, and that night a patrol from the 48th Highlanders discovered that the enemy had gone. General Conrath had ordered the withdrawal to commence at midnight; in defending the town the *Hermann Göring Engineer Battalion* had been virtually destroyed. They had inflicted considerable casualties on the British and Canadians: the Devons lost twenty-seven killed and a further eighty-two wounded during the fighting[4].

Now the Canadian Division, with its 2nd Brigade acting as flank guard, moved towards Adrano.

During the night of 31 July/1 August, 51st (Highland) Division had crossed the Dittaino to the right of 78th Division. 154 and 152 Brigades attacked the Iazzovecchio ridge, a mile beyond the river, which was defended by the *1st Battalion* of the *2nd Panzer Grenadier Regiment*. To the east of the road to Centuripe, up which 78 Division had advanced, lay a tangle of hills, one of the summits of which was Monte Serra di Spezia. Covered with cultivation – olive and almond groves, lemon and orange trees – and divided by terraces and with hedges of cactus and prickly pear, as well as the omnipresent stone walls, the ground was cut up by river valleys. It was infantry country, and the defenders made good use of it. The Highland Division engaged in confused fighting as they pushed their way onwards.

On 1 August a counterattack was attempted against the highlanders, but unsuccessfully. The enemy began to withdraw, and the Highland Division pressed onwards towards the Carcaci-Paterno road. 154 Brigade advanced rapidly towards the mountains, including Serra di Spezia, and then spent the next two weeks either on the hillsides or in orange groves near the River Simieto. The former location had no shade and was very hot; the latter had mosquitoes and malaria. 153 Brigade secured the Serra di Spezia feature and rested in the area of Muglia, to the west of the mountain. To all intents and purposes the campaign was over for 51st (Highland) Division[5].

3 Canadian Infantry Brigade, which had not participated in the action for Agira, reached the outskirts of Catenanuova on 26 July and had then

captured Monte Santa Maria and Monte Scalpello which dominated the Dittaino valley and the western and southern approaches to the town. A counterattack the next day pushed them off Monte Santa Maria, but the Germans only stayed for a day before withdrawing. On 29 July the brigade was placed under command of 78th Division for the attack on Catenanuova, and took the town that night against little resistance from the German *923rd Fortress Battalion.*

To the right of the Canadian Division, 78th Division moved onto ground vacated by 51st (Highland) Division. Their route to Catenanuova had to be prepared by the Sappers, for there was no road forward from Castel di Judica. On 30/31 July, the division's 11 Infantry Brigade enlarged the bridgehead made by the Canadians, despite resistance from troops of the *Hermann Göring Division* and the *3rd Parachute Regiment.* During the fighting Lance Corporal Chadwick of the East Surrey Regiment won an immediate Military Medal for capturing a wounded German officer from the *Hermann Göring* who had the entire plan for future German operations in Sicily in his attaché case. The information was promptly sent to Divisional Headquarters for analysis; General Montgomery arrived to visit the Divisional Commander, General Everleigh, as it was being translated, and it was passed to the two generals paragraph by paragraph. From this document it became clear that the Germans regarded Centuripe as the pivot on which this part of their defences was hinged; it was also clear that it was to be held at all costs. (An alternative version exists of how this information came to fall into Allied hands: that it was deciphered from enemy signals – ULTRA - and that the story about the contents of the German officer's attaché case was embroidered to cover the real source.)[6]

The landscape between Catenanuova and Etna is a confusion of ridges interspersed with rocky gorges and gullies. Much of it is bare of cover, offering sweeping views of countryside over which nothing can move undetected. In other areas, to the north of Centuripe where the ground drops down to the Simeto and Salso Rivers before the town of Adrano, the ground is covered with fruit trees. To appreciate the fighting for Centuripe there is no substitute for a visit, for it is difficult to describe the ground adequately. Perched atop a precipitous ridge, the town is reached by a winding road which snakes its way around the edge of a deep gully. The slopes on which Centuripe stands are at angles sharper than forty-five degrees, in places terraced for crops and pasture with stone walls more than six feet in height. In other places the slippery grass and loose rocks have made even this rudimentary cultivation impossible. The visitor invariably questions what reason people have for living in such an inaccessible location, and what – over the centuries – they do to make a living. But make a living they do, housed along the narrow, winding streets which challenge the passage of vehicles.

The position was defended by troops from the 2nd Battalion and a field battery and anti-tank troop from the *Hermann Göring Division*, and the *1st Battalion of the 3rd Parachute Regiment*. Every time the approach road twisted around a bend it came in sight of the defenders, and there were only brief intervals where the slopes offered cover. The road had been mined, cratered, and demolished. The plan for capturing Centuripe was for 11 Infantry Brigade to take and hold a covering position north of Catenanuova while 36 Infantry Brigade would move under cover of darkness during the night of 1/2 August to capture an outlying feature from which they would make the attack at first light. The third of 78th Division's brigades, the 38 (Irish), was to stand ready to pass through Centuripe once it had been taken, and then to descend into the valley beyond, to the Salso River.

Secreted on the hillsides between Catenanuova and Centuripe, German paratroops allowed the 1st East Surreys from 11 Brigade to move forward without hindrance, emerging from their bolt-holes after dark to attack the 5th Buffs of 36 Brigade as they advanced. Their actions caused considerable confusion, and as the Germans leapfrogged back from one delaying position to another they brought down mortar and sniper fire onto the British troops. 36 Brigade's advance was carried out despite this interference, but by dawn on 1 August the Buffs and the 6th Royal West Kents came under a barrage of fire from mortars and light machine guns. The assault ground to a crawl as minor actions were fought for small gains of ground, and the day passed slowly.

At last the 8th Battalion of the Argyll & Sutherland Highlanders passed through the Buffs and reached the slopes south of the town, where their advance was brought to a halt; a night attack was then mounted, with the Argylls on the right aiming for the town, while in the centre the 1st East Surreys (of 11 Brigade) went for the cemetery which lay 500 yards west of the town, and separated from it by a gorge. On the right the Royal West Kents went up the spurs from the southwest. Daylight found the East Surreys pinned down short of their objective, but sufficient gains had been made for a final assault to be made.

The position on which Centuripe stands has been likened to a capital letter 'E', with the three horizontal strokes pointing in the direction up which the British were attacking, and the down-stroke on the far side, above the river valleys below. The westernmost of the three ridges led to a series of heights to the north of the town, the centre ridge to the cemetery, and the last to the centre of Centuripe. The advance by 36 Brigade was stalled, but a number of points to the west of the main approach road from Catenanuova had been secured, which gave some protection to troops advancing by that route; but it was still overlooked from the east, which meant that stretches of the road were hazardous. It was not clear, moreover, whether or not a series of heights to the west of town were in British hands. If they were not, an attack from that direction was out of the question.

It was time for Evelegh to bring up his reserve, the Irish Brigade. The plan was for a silent night advance in two phases, with the entire divisional artillery – seventy-two 25-pounder guns – on call. The first phase was for a reconnaissance in force by two battalions, the 1st Battalion, Royal Irish Fusiliers (the 'Faughs') and the 6th Battalion, the Royal Inniskilling Fusiliers, which would also place them within attacking distance of Centuripe. The Inniskillings were to advance on the right to seize points which overlooked the road, while on the left the Faughs were to ascertain whether the western heights were free of the enemy. If so, they were to be ready to move onto the town.

The Inniskillings moved towards their objective in single file on the steep mule tracks, climbing over two thousand feet in nearly four miles. With no mules available, their supporting weapons, entrenching tools and even water had to be left behind. By 0845 hours one company was on the final crest in front of Centuripe, but under heavy mortar and rifle fire from the enemy dug in before them. It was clear that a frontal attack in daylight would be a dangerous venture.

What had started as a brigade offensive quickly developed into a series of smaller actions at battalion, company – even section – levels. By early afternoon the brigade commander had finalised his plan. It involved two attacks, the first by the third of the brigade's battalions, 2nd Battalion London Irish Rifles, supported by the artillery, to capture points to the west of the town. Once these were secure, the Inniskillings and Faughs would attack the town itself. The Faughs would advance by way of the cemetery into the northern end of Centuripe, the Inniskillings from the right flank and up the steep slopes towards Point 708, which dominated the ridge south of town.

The intent was for the attack to commence before nightfall to allow sufficient light for the street fighting which was considered to be inevitable. The Inniskillings moved forward at 1630 hours, anticipating the brigade plan. One of their companies had come under 'friendly' fire from troops of another brigade half an hour previously, but enemy fire appeared to have stopped and the spur before them looked deserted; it was decided to attempt to enter Centuripe through the 'front door'. This entailed scaling a hundred-foot high cliff before getting into the town. C Company did so with the artillery providing covering fire; A Company, following, had no such support and came under fire from both flanks before moving through 'C' and into the streets. Here the Germans put up determined resistance as the fight moved from house to house. The Skins had to deal with a Mark III *panzer* before they reached the town square.

While the Inniskillings' C Company moved right to secure the ridge east of town, the London Irish took two of the heights which were their objectives on the west before attacking Centuripe from that direction. The third battalion, the Faughs, launched their assault late, and darkness was falling as they advanced on a single-company front towards the cemetery.

The company came under machinegun fire which killed its commander. A second attack by another company was ordered, and elements of both entered the German positions at the same time, to find them abandoned. They found only the bodies of enemy dead mingled with those of long-deceased Sicilians whose tombs had been destroyed by artillery fire.

The capture of Centuripe attracted a good deal of attention. When Montgomery visited the scene later, he was alleged to have uttered the single word, 'impossible!' when he was shown the cliff up which the Inniskillings had attacked. In London, Churchill made much of the victory in a speech in the House of Commons, and news reports rated the storming of the town as one of the greatest achievements in storming almost impregnable heights. Much of this has to be explained by the success of the operation after so many disappointments over the past days, for Centuripe did not bring the strategic benefits that were claimed of it. The Germans had no intention of holding Sicily indefinitely, and the speed of their withdrawal was unaffected by the loss of the position. Nevertheless, it was a fine achievement by the Irish Brigade against determined resistance by the German paratroopers.

The Germans retired in good order, leaving 38 (Irish) Brigade in possession of Centuripe, which was to be known as 'Cherry Ripe' by those who were unable to get their tongues around the Italian pronunciation. The brigade's tasks were not yet over, however. The original plan had been for 36 Brigade to take the town, after which 38 (Irish) Brigade would pass through and force the crossings of the Rivers Salso and Simeto, a few miles north. Now, despite having fought the town battle, the Irish were ordered to carry on to the rivers, for the road system was incapable of allowing another formation to leapfrog through them. A rapid follow-up was necessary to ensure that the enemy had no time to reorganise and to stiffen up the next line of defence with their typical efficiency.

After fighting a battle that had lasted for thirty-six hours, the brigade was on the banks of the Salso River by midday, and fighting patrols crossed that night, 3 August. Behind them the divisional artillery deployed on the Centuripe heights to provide covering fire, having to bring forward ammunition by jeeps and manhandled with ropes, but having a superb standpoint on which to situate their observation posts which had magnificent views across the valleys below. In the distance rose the heights of Etna, and lying in front of it the road which ran from Adrano to Paterno was completely dominated, making it unusable by the enemy. Further support was given by the guns from 51st (Highland) Division and the Corps artillery.

On the afternoon of 4 August the London Irish and the Royal Irish Fusiliers waded the river and attacked the bluffs on the north side; by nightfall all three battalions were between the two rivers, except for transport which could not cross the Salso until the engineers had filled in craters on the road – the largest taking about twelve hours to make passable – and brought forward heavy equipment to span the hundred-foot gap blown in the bridge. This had to be transported along the tortuous roads leading up to Centuripe from the south, and then down the forward slopes to the river valley.

By daybreak on 5 August the Faughs had established two companies on the far bank of the Simeto, an advance in which both company commanders were wounded and two platoons were forced back. The bridgehead was far from secure, and preparations were being made to cross in strength. On the Salso, the Sappers had finished their bridge, working at night and under shellfire, and their reconnaissance parties were assessing the task on the Simeto. This was a different matter to the first river because the banks were much steeper, and the water flowing through the gulley was deeper and swifter.

On the southern bank the London Irish held the left flank of the line, while the Inniskillings moved up to the Simeto from their positions between the two rivers. In the face of stubborn resistance from the enemy a third company from the Faughs crossed the Simeto to support their comrades. German troops concealed in caves on the far bank had to be winkled out, and a brigade attack was decided upon, to be carried out by the London Irish and the Faughs, with a company of the Inniskillings attached. It was launched at 1530 hours, with the support of the divisional artillery and a further four batteries of medium guns, as well as two platoons of 4.2-inch mortars of the 1st Battalion, Princess Louise's Kensington Regiment. Ahead of them were a number of strongpoints, including two well-built stone houses known as the Casino and the Palace. By nightfall all of the objectives had been taken, and by 2100 hours the bridgehead was safe, the two aforementioned houses having been knocked out by antitank guns and a PIAT.

Having advanced twenty-five miles and having fought three battles in the period between the afternoon of 1 August until the night of 5 August, men of 38 (Irish) Brigade was permitted an opportunity to rest while 78th Division's other two brigades captured the towns of Adrano and Bronte. Led by the armoured cars of the 56th Reconnaissance Regiment ('Chevasse's Light Horse', so named after their commanding officer), 78th Division advanced towards Adrano. The route from the Simeto was contested by small rearguards, and three armoured cars were lost to mines and artillery fire. The attack was halted to allow Allied bombers to raid the town, followed by a heavy artillery barrage. At daybreak on 7 August, 11 Brigade entered Adrano unopposed[7].

The following day Bronte was taken. A night advance from Adrano had brought 11 Brigade to a position a mile south of the town, which was seized by capturing the hills on either side of the town while an attack went in from the centre. Again, the defenders put up a stiff resistance, employing mines, machine guns and *Nebelwerfers*, but without success.

The lead was now turned over to 36 Brigade for the advance on

Randazzo, nine miles further on. The road then swung around the base of Etna, and now ran somewhat to the east of north. In this phase of the fighting, the Germans displayed their obstinate best, buying time for the evacuation across the Straits of Messina. The village of Malleto sat astride the road to Randazzo, overlooked by high ground which dominated the approaches. To the left, 1st Canadian Division was moving parallel to the 78th, and further left again, 9th (US) Division was approaching Randazzo from the west. The two Eighth Army divisions would be pinched out of the attack once the town had fallen, for the Americans were to take the lead for the advance on towards the Straits of Messina.

On the morning of 9 August 36 Brigade opened its attack on Malleto. A company of the Buffs occupied the high ground to the left of the village, which gave them command of the road. On the small mountain to the right, however, the Germans threw back an attack by a second company, and another by a third. Later in the day the Royal West Kents, supported by three tanks, were more successful. The following day 8th Argylls occupied Mount Macerone, which overlooked the heights which had been recently fought over. It was hoped that this would give control of the positions dominating the village, but when the Irish Brigade moved up to take its turn to attack Malleto they came under fire from the hillsides. They mounted a night attack to clear the enemy, but slow progress was made – it was not until the following night that the village was finally occupied, and the Argylls began clearing it of pockets of Germans while 11 Brigade pressed on towards Randazzo.

Pursued by the Royal Irish Fusiliers, the enemy withdrew along the road. Towards dawn the battalion came under American artillery fire from the west, but pressed on; and at 0930 hours contact was made with 9th (US) Division just south of Randazzo. The German defenders left the town in haste, destroying everything of possible use to the Allies as they went.

The advance to the north of Etna was an American affair, and for 78th Division the campaign was effectively over.

1 Von Senger.
2 Malony.
3 Canadian Operations in Sicily Report 135.
4 Malony.
5 Delaforce.
6 Ford.
7 Ibid

CHAPTER TWELVE

THE AMERICANS IN THE NORTH

WHILE XXX CORPS was operating to the west of Etna, the Americans had set out on their mission to get to Messina. The Provisional Corps was scattered across western Sicily, and on 22 July Bradley's II (US) Corps was divided, with 45th (US) Division moving northwest towards Termini Imerese and 1st (US) Division involved in taking Enna. These objectives achieved, they were now moving eastwards, with 45th (US) Division on the northern coast road, Highway 113, and 1st (US) Division and 39th RCT from 9th (US) Division on Highway 120, some ten miles north of the Canadians.

45th (US) Division, once completing its task of cutting the island in half, had turned right onto the line of the coastal highway which clung to the coast, above which the hills rose to heights of 3,500 feet or more. It wound its way – as roads seemed to do all over the island – through areas where the advantage lay with the defender, able to demolish it with little difficulty and to set ambushes and obstacles which demanded the best that infantrymen and engineers alike could produce. While 157th RCT broke through Italian defences at Campofelice and Cefalu before being temporarily halted by a blown bridge and minefields further east, the 179th covered its right flank by advancing through the hills and mountains inland.

Late on 24 July the 180th RCT passed through the 157th to cross the Malpertugio River, before encountering stiff German resistance at Pizzo Spina, a 3,000-foot high peak which dominated the way east. *29th Panzer Grenadier Division* put up a determined fight, and the GIs had to scale steep cliffs in their fight to dislodge the enemy. Pushing on, they ran into a series of ridges at the mouth of the Tusa River, lying to the west of the next large town, San Stefano di Camastra, which were so steep that several mules carrying supplies died from exhaustion when trying to climb them. During the night 26/27 July the 157th again moved into lead position, and advanced into the most intense enemy fire the division experienced during the Sicilian campaign. At a point west of San Stefano which was to become known to the GIs as 'Bloody Ridge', they encountered a complexity of strongpoints including pillboxes, mines, booby-traps and wire entanglements.

2/157th skirted the obstacle from the south to threaten it from that

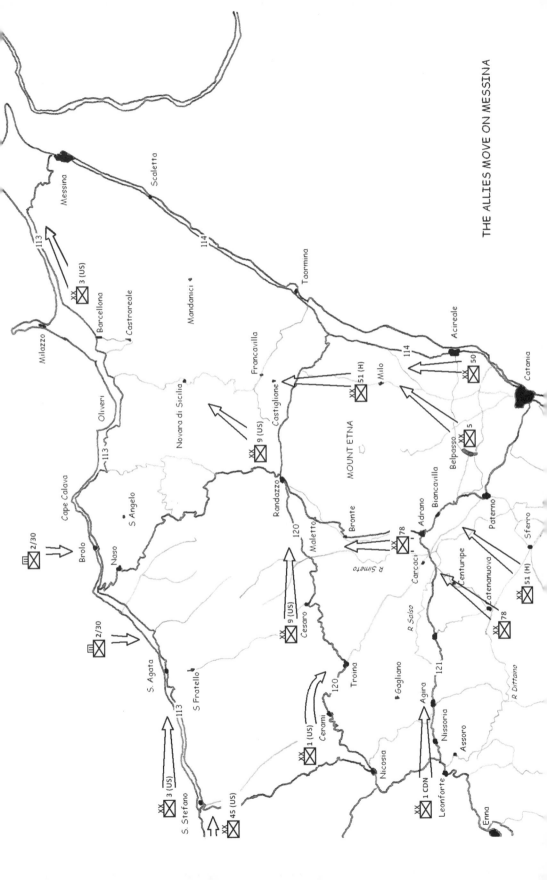

THE ALLIES MOVE ON MESSINA

direction while the other two battalions advanced from the northwest. The first attack was made by 1/157th, but although the Americans destroyed two pillboxes they were forced back by a counterattack supported by artillery and mortar fire. On the rocky ground the shells threw shards of stone to add to the shrapnel cutting down the GIs. In an attempt to neutralise the defences, a Chemical Mortar Company brought its weapons forward through a railway tunnel and laid down 4.2-inch white phosphorous shells on the enemy. The battle lasted throughout the day of 28 July and into the next. On the 29th, all four divisional artillery battalions laid down a fifteen-minute barrage to support another attempt to dislodge the Germans, but yet again the Americans were forced to fall back in some places. To cover their retreat, four machine gunners remained behind; Privates First Class Olsen, McGee, and Howe, and Private Blanco were all awarded the Distinguished Service Cross, posthumously, for this action.

The enemy were not driven from their defences until a US Navy destroyer began to bring down fire on them, after which the Germans withdrew towards Reitano. The 2/180th pushed along the coast to San Stefano, fighting all of the way, finally taking control of the town on 31 July. The battle had cost the division 163 killed and wounded in five days of combat[1].

That day 45th (US) Division, having lost 275 men killed, 573 wounded and a further 141 missing in action since landing in Sicily, was withdrawn from the fighting for a period of rest. Truscott's 3rd (US) Division came forward to replace them on the coast, moved to the front by rail once the engineers had repaired the system.

While 3rd (US) Division fought its way along the coast, inland the 1st was progressing on the line of Highway 120, which ran through Nicosia, Triona, Cesarò and Randazzo. Between this road and that on the coast ran the Caronie Mountain range, with few lateral roads linking the two highways. The first major town on 1st (US) Division's route, Nicosia, was a highly defensible point but Hube withdrew his forces from there on 27 July. His action was criticised by Guzzoni, but Hube convinced the Italian general of the correctness of his decision by explaining that his primary mission was to preserve the German forces and to prepare them for evacuation, should that become necessary. In the Catania area the *Hermann Göring Division* appeared able to prevent the British from advancing to Messina, but *15th* and *29th Panzer Grenadier Divisions*, with support from *1st Parachute Division* and the remnants of the Italian forces, were having difficulties in holding against the American and Canadian advances in the north and centre. Guzzoni accepted the need to shorten the line, and Nicosia fell into American hands, with 700 Italian troops who were willing to surrender. Agira also fell, to the Canadians.

It began to appear that the Germans were preparing to fall back to make a final stand, possibly with the intention of fighting to retain a bridgehead in the northeast of the island, much as they had attempted to do in Tunisia. It seemed that they would establish a defensive line somewhere to the east and surrender everything west of it without contest. The Germans appeared to be tired, low on ammunition, and suffering from poor morale.

The American intelligence appreciation of the German intentions for Troina was well off-target. General Hube's concept of the battles his forces would engage in as they retreated towards Messina and their embarkation points for the evacuation, was to defend a series of mountain strongpoints until the Allied pressure on each site dictated a withdrawal. The *Etna Line* was not a continuous belt of defences, but concentrated upon key features. At Troina the intention was to hold a chain of hills that crossed Highway 120. The Americans, however, believed that the Germans would fall back through the city to positions five miles further east near Cesarò, and had failed to discover that *15th Panzer Grenadier Division* had halted its withdrawal beforehand. Intelligence also underestimated the morale and the fighting capability of the enemy – any that were to be found at Troina were expected to do no more than to continue to employ delaying tactics with comparatively few troops.

Holding Troina would protect the *Hermann Göring Division* in the event that the Canadians succeeded in capturing Regalbuto. It was also a strong position, which had limited lines of approach, and Highway 120 could be controlled from hilltops around it. The ground across which an attacker had to move was dominated by gun positions and offered little cover. To defend the area Hube had the greater part of *15th Panzer Grenadier Division*. To the north were units from the newly arrived *29th Panzer Grenadier Division* and the *Aosta Division*. To the south were units of the *Hermann Göring Division*. General Rodt, the commander of the *15th*, had formed two regimental-sized bodies from his division: *Group Fullreide* was positioned in Troina and in the mountains to the north, *Group Ens* covered the southern approaches. Around Troina was a concentration of troops which included four battalions of the *Aosta Division*. Troina protected the western flank of the Etna Line, and the Axis forces were going to hold it as long as possible.

1st (US) Division was by now battle-weary. It was also considered ill-disciplined by some senior American officers, and plans were in hand to replace it with 9th (US) Division in the push eastwards, but the Sicilian roads did not easily allow a change-over that was swift enough to maintain pressure on the enemy. Any delay would give the Axis time to regroup and stiffen the defences, a possibility that was to be avoided, and so for the time being the 1st would continue to lead.

The battle for Troina started on 31 July, when the 39th Infantry from 9th (US) Division, temporarily under command of 1st (US) Division, captured

Monte dell'Annunziata, some five miles northwest of the city. 1/16th Infantry, to the southeast of Highway 120, captured Hill 1209 despite enemy fire from Monte Acuto, the highest point overlooking the city and the highway. These gains were sufficiently encouraging to persuade General Allen, the 1st Division commander, that Troina was not going to be seriously defended. His optimism was soon demolished, however, for although a battalion of the 39th advanced to capture Hill 1034, only a mile west of the city, it was driven back by the first of *15th Panzer Grenadier's* counterattacks. The GIs had taken the hill only because the German commander, Colonel Ens, had not completed his preparations for defence. He was not long in rectifying his omission, and 1/39th was pushed back to the position it had held that morning.

The repulse caused Allen to mount a major assault on 2 August, in which the 39th Regiment, with the 26th Regiment to its left, and the *Goumiers* further left again, tried to capture Troina and the mountains to the north from which the Germans were able to dominate the highway. Despite the support of nine artillery battalions the only success was an advance of half a mile by one battalion of the 26th; none of the other attacking units were able to move forward through the overwhelming German artillery fire.

The following day one of the 26th Regiment's battalions lost its way on the hillsides and wandered around, playing no part in the battle, but another battalion reached its objective of Monte Basilio.

That afternoon the *129th Panzer Grenadier Regiment* mounted a major counterattack which was driven off, but the Americans on Monte Basilio were kept pinned down for the next two days by small-arms and artillery fire; continued German pressure nearly resulted on the 26th being cut off from the rest of 1st (US) Division. With ammunition and food running low, attempts were made to resupply them by air, with only partial success. Casualties were mounting, and one company could only muster seventeen men fit for duty.

During the night of 2/3 August Allen attempted to break the defence by attacking right along the 1st Division's front, believing that the Germans were not strong enough to resist everywhere. This assault brought the Americans a little closer to Troina, but the defenders clung tenaciously to their positions. Counterattack after counterattack stopped the GIs from moving forward.

On the fifth day of the battle Troina was pounded by an eight-battalion artillery bombardment and an air strike by seventy-two A-36 fighter-bombers, each of which deposited a 500-pound bomb on the enemy. Notwithstanding this assault, the Germans held on. Their counterattacks came close to throwing the Americans back to the west, and desperate fighting was endured by both sides. On 5 August a German attack on the 26th Infantry threatened a one of the company positions where Private

James Reese, the acting leader of a 60mm mortar squad, brought his team forward the better to engage the enemy, and contributed greatly to breaking up their counterattack. When his position became untenable, he ordered the rest of his team to the rear but stayed with his weapon, moving it again to fire on an enemy machine-gun nest, which he destroyed with his last mortar bomb. He then advanced towards the enemy with a rifle, inflicting further casualties until he was killed[2]. This action earned him a posthumous Medal of Honor. The 26th held their position.

The Americans made five separate assaults during the week-long battle, each bigger than the last, and each with increasing artillery and air support. Eventually all three regimental combat teams from 9th (US) Division were committed, together with the 1st Division and the *Goumiers*, but each attack's gains were measured in yards rather than miles. On the evening of 5 August the Americans were less than a mile from the town, and threatening to take the heights commanding it. Regalbuto had been taken by the Canadians on 2 August, Centuripe the next day, and Adrano was threatened by the loss of these two positions. Should it fall the defenders of Troina would have difficulty in withdrawing towards Messina, and they had already suffered at least 1,600 casualties. General Hube recognised that the time had come to leave. He ordered a withdrawal to avoid his troops being cut off, and they slipped away in the hours of darkness. The next morning a 1st (US) Division patrol entered Troina. They found the town reduced to rubble, with 150 dead – German and Italian soldiers, and civilians – in the streets. A 500-pound bomb lay unexploded in the ruins of the church, and in the mayor's office were a number of wounded, including children[3].

Once the battle was over the 1st was withdrawn from the fighting and Allen and the Deputy Commander, Brigadier Roosevelt, were relieved of their posts. The reasons for their replacement remain a subject of controversy, those given ranging from a more or less routine rotation of commanders who had been in action for a considerable time, to dissatisfaction with their performance. Major General Heubner assumed command and immediately started re-instilling a sense of discipline amongst the troops.

Along the coastal highway 3rd (US) Division pressed on towards Messina.

By now the weather had become even hotter. Temperatures rose to between 100 -110 degrees Fahrenheit by about eleven in the morning, and water – always a problem – became even more precious, and the enemy added to the difficulties by lacing water points with booby-traps and mines. Soldiers carried as many as four canteens each, supplementing their own with German or Italian ones taken from the enemy. A recurrent problem for all those unwise to seek refreshment from the citrus fruit and grapes which grew in abundance – but which were often green – was the effect on their gastric systems, and many neglected to use the disinfectant tablets in their canteens, which tainted the taste of the water but made it safe to drink. Where possible, water was brought forward by mule-train and man-pack, but this was a difficult and time-consuming procedure, which failed to produce enough for the thirsty men. Knowing that the enemy ahead controlled the water supplies was a factor which drove men on, thirst outstripping caution. With regard to the use of mules, 3rd (US) Division, at least, was better prepared than the Eighth Army, for mule trains had been brought from North Africa, and more formed from locally conscripted animals, despite a lack of experienced handlers and suitable equipment.

Along Highway 113 lay a series of towns and villages. The road wound its way around headlands and over bridges which crossed the rivers which ran into the sea, and although many of the riverbeds were dry at this time of year, they often ran through deep gorges overlooked by tall hills. Each of these towns and bridges offered a position better suited to the needs of the defender than to those of the attacking troops. At 0500 hours on 2 August 30th Infantry attacked across steep cliffs to capture the bridge west of Caronia, the town itself, and to cut the road leaving it to the east. The regiment's three battalions worked in coordination to outflank the town from the northeast, from the south, and to advance across the bridge and into Caronia from the west. The response from the enemy included long-range machine-gun, artillery and mortar fire, to support the minefields and wire entanglements. For the first time since leaving the United States, 30th Infantry encountered German resistance. It cost 3/30th some forty casualties[4].

By mid-afternoon 2/15th led the rest of the 15th RCT through the 30th and took the lead in the advance eastwards. The infantry was able to by-pass the destroyed bridges but vehicles had to wait while engineers cleared mines and constructed by-passes. That evening 3rd (US) Division was in front of the next series of obstacles at Monte San Fratello, a 2,200-foot high escarpment, the western slopes of which were strewn with gullies and hummocks, above the dry bed of the Furiano River. The Germans had sown the riverbed with 'S' and Teller mines and blown the bridge, and were dug in on the hillsides. At 0830 hours on 3 August the Americans opened their attack with a two-and-a-half hour artillery bombardment, before 2/15th moved down Highway 113. Its advance was brought to a halt by heavy enemy fire. That evening the regiment's other two battalions moved south of 2/15th, across country through deep gorges, along mountain trails and around two minefields to a position on Hill 673. The two battalions attacked at 0600 hours, again without success, and made further attempts to cross the river later in the day.

Truscott now ordered a coordinated attack on San Fratello, to take place the following morning. Patrols worked throughout the night to feel out the enemy positions and to identify ways forward, and at 0600 hours the 15th and 30th RCTs attacked. 1/30th came under concentrated fire as it advanced along the ridge from Di Nicoletta to Santa Maria which caused heavy losses and forced them to retire; the entire attack was destined to meet the same fate. After an all-day battle on ground that was so rough that units only a thousand yards apart lost contact with each other, and which slowed movement so that it took five hours for 3/30th to reach 3/15th, the GIs had only climbed half-way up the ridge when a halt was called and they were ordered to wait until nightfall and then to withdraw under cover of darkness.

The night was spent in reorganisation, and the following day, 6 August, the assault was resumed. 3/30th and 3/15th fought their way close to the crest of Hill 673 by daybreak, but were exposed to enemy fire from a ridge lying to the south. One company remained isolated through the day while the remainder changed their positions, waiting until nightfall before trying again. Hill 673 finally fell half an hour before midnight, despite a German counterattack which involved a 45-minute artillery barrage after which their infantry assaulted in waves. At 0800 hours the GIs entered San Fratello town and 3/30th captured about 500 prisoners on Monte San Fratello.

7th Infantry, which had been near Caronia, passed through the 15th at daybreak on 8 August, crossed the Furiano and pushed along Highway 113 towards the sea. It by-passed the San Fratello fighting and reached Acquedolci at 0735 hours; by 1115 it was in Sant' Agata, and an hour later it was in contact with 2/30th, which had made an amphibious landing three miles further east of the latter town.

The move of Lieutenant Colonel Lyle Bernard's 2/30th by sea, together with tanks and artillery and other supporting elements, was a successful example of a manoeuvre known to the Americans as an 'end run'. The term comes from American football, where players from the attacking team run around the end of their opposition's line, as indeed was the intention here. With firm defences and difficult county facing them, Truscott's division loaded the aforementioned units into ten landing craft of various types, sailed eastwards along the coast to a point seven miles behind enemy lines, and disembarked with the mission of fighting inland to cut the highway and isolate the defenders. Five hours after coming ashore early on the morning of 8 August, they blocked the road and by noon Sant' Agata was in American hands. 250 of the enemy were killed, another hundred captured, and four *panzers* were destroyed. Disorganised by this move and under pressure at San Fratello, the Germans fell back from their advanced positions. As they withdrew an American destroyer scored a lucky hit when one of its shells detonated the explosives that they had laid under a road bridge. As the Germans had laid mines around the river bed to prevent the bridge being by-passed, they were now faced with the problem of clearing them so that they could make good their escape. The traffic jam that built up while this was being done was hit by the pursuing Americans, contributing to their 'bag'.

'Task Force Bernard' was called upon to repeat its amphibious outflanking operation on 11 August, this time to cut the highway at Brolo, halfway between Cape Orlando and Cape Calva, fifteen miles behind the German lines. Truscott's division had continued its march with the other two battalions of 30th Infantry on the coast road while 7th had swung inland. As with the previous landing, Bernard's men landed without opposition at 0243 hours, the entire force being safely ashore by 0400. The place selected for the landing, however, had been picked from aerial photographs and proved to be without beach exits. The only way inland for vehicles was to drive through a lemon grove which had several ditches running across it, then under bridges at either end of the beach, and up a steep embankment. The infantrymen reached the highway by 0345 hours and allowed an enemy vehicle to pass by unhindered to maintain secrecy. Five minutes later a motorcyclist came down the road and was shot dead, and then a car was destroyed with a bazooka. The Germans were now thoroughly alerted by the racket and commenced firing at the invaders with machine guns. Their tracer gave their positions away, and four were silenced by riflemen who hauled themselves up the slopes by clinging to bushes.

By 0530 hours GIs were atop Monte Creole which dominated the town, and within an hour all units were in their assigned positions. From now on, however, anyone attempting to get to the mountain crest came under fire from enemy machine guns and 20mm guns. About fifteen men were killed trying to take messages or equipment to those on the summit.

Down in the lemon grove, a battery of armoured field artillery fired on Brolo, while a second battery engaged opportunity targets to the west. The gun positions were dominated by high ground to their west, and the enemy were nearby in the east; the gunners were also hampered by a dearth of observation posts from which to direct fire on close-in targets. Nevertheless, they were able to give effective supporting fire until they were destroyed during the afternoon. The tanks, too, were severely hampered by the ditches in the grove and by a stone wall bordering the road, which reduced their manoeuvrability and reduced their function to being no more than static gun positions.

By seven in the morning the enemy were beginning to reconnoitre the American positions. A motorised patrol came down the road from Naso, on the inland road to the southwest of Brolo, suffering their first two vehicles being set alight by rocket and machinegun fire. A dismounted group of about thirty Germans then began working its way down a riverbed. It was allowed to get to within 700 yards before it was decimated by machine-gun fire from the summit of Monte Creole. The last incursion was made by a company-sized group which marched down the Naso River, only to be pinned down by machine gun and 60mm mortar rounds. The situation fell quiet for the night.

The next morning the enemy preparations to remove the Task Force were well in hand. A number of German vehicles which had attempted to move down the coast from the west had been stopped by naval gunfire, and an attack was in the offing from the direction of Brolo, where at least two companies of infantry had arrived in personnel carriers, and several tanks had been seen entering the town. In the woods east of Brolo, groups of the enemy could also be seen. For the Americans, a lack of mortar bombs was beginning to cause concern. Of the sixteen mules which had come ashore to transport ammunition, only two had survived when they had come under machine-gun fire as they were led up the hill. These two reached the top late in the afternoon, and attempts to bring ammunition up by manpack on the exposed slopes were of little success because of the distance and the losses inflicted by the enemy.

Shortly after midday the American artillery and mortars were brought to bear on Brolo, and heavy naval gunfire to the west of the town came from the cruiser USS *Philadelphia* with two escorting destroyers. An hour later air strikes bombed the roads and assembly areas east of Brolo. While this onslaught appeared to have halted any attempt to mount an attack from that direction, three Mark IV *panzers* remained in the town, and at 1500 hours they moved across the bridge over the Brolo River. The artillery was unable to engage them because of the high wall at this point, and the tanks managed to get into the American gun positions and to destroy two guns and two ammunition half-tracks. One of the *panzers* was put out of action during this attack, but the other two escaped.

On top of Monte Creole, the Germans brought down a heavy artillery barrage which caused several casualties. Tracer had set the undergrowth alight on the northern slopes, which burned through telephone lines that had been laid by the Americans, a loss which was difficult to replace, again because of the casualties inflicted on those who attempted repairs. The broken lines and poor radio links made it impossible to request gunfire support from the navy, which was urgently needed to forestall an enemy attack; indeed, the US Navy reported receiving few requests for support – it is easy to understand why, when communications were cut. An attempt to move the artillery to a better position to fire onto the enemy resulted in the gun positions being revealed, and the Germans were quick to bring up tanks which destroyed three guns. Machine gun and mortar ammunition was now being conserved to be used only in an emergency, and a requested air strike had failed to materialise.

The American artillery was now reduced to a single gun from one battery and four from the other. These were of use for only a little longer, however, for when the air strike eventually arrived at around 1630 hours, it succeeded in destroying four guns and bombing the battalion's command post rather than bombing the enemy. The infantry that were not on the mountainside were now under fire from their rear, being attacked by the enemy in front, and disoriented by two ammunition half-tracks which were afire and with ammunition exploding. They were ordered into the hills to establish a defensive position, the remaining mortar bombs being fired to give them cover as they moved. Now the navy returned to the battle, summonsed by a short, urgent message which somehow got through. The ships were unable to give their full attention to their task of supporting the ground forces, however: USS *Philadelphia* and her escort were firing onto the enemy positions when eight Focke-Wulf 190's arrived and attacked them. After a half-hour fight between ships and aircraft, seven of the enemy planes were downed[5].

Now came a message of hope. An unknown source radioed through to say that the 7th Infantry was on its way, and was just beyond Naso. It was a question of holding out until they arrived – the first sight of friendly forces was at 0600 hours the next morning; 1/30th made contact at 0830, passed through and resumed the advance eastwards. The encounter had cost the Germans an estimated 100 dead and twelve captured; the Americans lost four officers and thirty-seven men killed, three officers and seventy-five wounded, and three and fifty-five missing. Seven 105mm self-propelled guns were destroyed, one disabled; two half-tracks destroyed and fourteen mules killed. The Germans, once again, were not going easily – the net effect of the operation had been make them abandon Cape Orlando a day earlier than they had planned, and none of their troops were trapped by the landing.

While 2/30th was engaged in its end-run, the 7th Infantry had progressed alongside Highway 113 with the remaining two battalions of the 30th following. 15th Infantry had moved across country further south. On arriving at the Di Zappula River, 7th ran into heavy resistance, including generously laid mines in the riverbed which inflicted several casualties as the unit crossed. On the far bank 1/7th was counterattacked and forced to fall back after a five-hour battle; 2/7th resumed the advance that night (11 August) and established itself on a hill on the eastern side of the river. To the south 15th Infantry was experiencing similar problems: a determined enemy making full use of the natural advantages of the ground. The two regiments inched their way forward, taking the village of Naso and moving into the area around Castel Umberto; enemy resistance now became weaker and progress became steadier.

The 1/ and 3/30th took Cape Orlando, and on hearing of the difficulties 2/30th was in ahead of them started a speed march, reaching their sister battalion at Monte Creole. The units fighting towards Brolo also took losses. An approximate casualty return for the 7th Infantry gave fifteen officers and 400 men killed, wounded and missing for the period 7-12 August. The 15th was believed to have similar casualty numbers.

Throughout the Allied movements across Sicily, the engineers of both Eighth and Seventh Armies had been kept busy repairing and constructing roads, bridges and other facilities, such as the ports. On Highway 113 and the routes eastwards to Messina they were constantly employed: as 15th Infantry advanced along the highway on 4 August, the 10th Engineer Battalion was sent to build a road into the mountains to the right so that artillery could be moved to support the operation.

Two platoons of engineers had landed with Bernard's force on both of the landings, providing repair, clearing and construction facilities. But perhaps the most spectacular feat the engineers achieved was a few miles east of Brolo, near Cape Calava. Here the Germans had demolished a 150-foot length of Highway 113 where it ran along the cliffs 300 feet above the sea. Truscott gave the 10th Engineers until noon on 14 August to bridge the gap, a period of twenty-four hours. Two-thirds of the breach was closed by grading, but the remaining length had to be bridged, and without the use of Bailey Bridges, which were unavailable. With only one platoon able to work at a time because of the lack of space, the engineers built a bridge by daybreak, eighteen hours after starting work, and Truscott led the way across it in his jeep. By midday trucks were crossing in safety.

The advance towards Messina, although slowed, was not halted by the blown road. A considerable amount of heavy equipment, including tanks and guns, was ferried around Cape Calava in landing craft while the engineers constructed the bridge.

A third 'end run' was ordered by Patton for 15 August. This time the 157th Infantry (from 45th [US] Division), with a field artillery battalion were loaded into ships at Termini Imerese with Bivio Salica as the designated landing site, some twenty-five miles west of Messina. Either Patton did not know or did not care that Truscott's men had already passed this point, and the landing craft were met by friendly faces. The incident was not without tragedy, however, for sixteen men – all heavily laden with arms and equipment – drowned when their LCVP threw them into the sea when a davit broke on the mother-ship[6].

The drive of 3rd (US) Division continued. Patti fell, then Cape Tindari and Oliveri. Enemy resistance was light, and by 15 August 7th Infantry was in Barcellona. By that evening they were in Spadafora, only ten miles or so from Messina. The enemy had abandoned strong defensive positions at Milazzo, leaving coastal batteries, ammunition dumps and large numbers of vehicles, but at Spadafora they had engaged the Americans in street fighting before withdrawing. The next day, 16 August, found the division on high ground overlooking Messina. It was the last day of enemy resistance in Sicily.

As the Germans retreated eastwards towards Messina, their front became narrower and fewer troops were required to hold it, an ideal situation in which General Hube was able to withdraw units to their embarkation points while still maintaining a strong defence to cover the evacuation. On 8 August 9th (US) Division entered Cesarò on Highway 120, and the following day it pushed on towards Randazzo. The route was more heavily mined than any other in Sicily, and there was sufficient metallic content in the soil to make the engineers' mine-detectors all but useless. The only safe way through the obstacles was by probing, a dangerous and time-consuming activity, which played on the nerves of those undertaking the task.

The fighting in Sicily was almost over. On 9 August Guzzoni was ordered by the *Comando Supremo* to start evacuating Italian forces to the mainland; Hube ordered Operation *LEHRGANG* – the German evacuation plan – to commence with effect from 10 August.

The *Hermann Göring Division* defenders of Catania withdrew on 5 August. The leading troops from 5th and 50th Divisions who entered the city found it subject to a riot of looting as the inhabitants sacked shops and buildings. Bronte fell on 8 August, Maletto four days later. Randazzo fell to 9th (US) Division on 13 August, as 78th Division attacked it from the south.

Progress for the British forces to the east of Etna was slow; the narrow coastal strip was blocked by every means the enemy could conceive of. There was little in the way of set-piece battles, and the Allied advance was slowed as much by the destruction of roads as it was by the enemy, whose aim was to buy time for the evacuation. By 14 August the Axis forces had broken contact all along the front and had pulled back to a delay line which stretched from the west of Barcellona to the south of Santa Teresa.

50th Division occupied Taormina, thirty-five miles north of Catania, on the following day. It was apparent that the enemy were evacuating their forces to mainland Italy in stages. This came as no surprise, for details of the plan had been found on the body of a German officer on 31 July. Warnings were sent to Tedder and Cunningham, but little was done to halt the escape of the enemy forces.

Unlike Patton to the north, Montgomery had failed to use the navy to assist his advance. This was despite Cunningham suggesting the value of doing so, and the admiral was later to regret that he had not pushed his case more firmly, saying that it was not really his place, but the land force commander's, to decide how best to employ the assets at his disposal to pursue the land battle.

On 15 August, however, Monty changed his mind and requested that a commando unit with armoured support be dispatched by sea to land at Cap d'Ali the following morning, to cut off whatever German troops were south of that point and to push on into Messina. The venture was commanded by Brigadier Curry, commander of 4th Armoured Brigade, and the force comprised No 2 Commando (recently arrived on the island); a squadron of tanks; a troop of Priest self-propelled guns, a second of howitzers and a third of 6-pounder antitank guns; and a section of Sappers[7]. When they landed the commandos were too late to achieve the first part of the mission, for Conrath's troops had withdrawn to the next of Hube's phase lines, three miles further north. The commandos only managed to run into the rearguard just north of Scaletta, but by then the enemy were set on Messina. No 2 Commando passed through Tremestieri, two miles south of Messina as dawn broke on 17 August; their further advance was halted by a blown bridge over a deep ravine.

At this stage the Axis evacuation was almost complete. Hube had left Sicily at 1730 hours on 16 August, followed later that night by the German rearguard, 200 men from *29th Panzer Grenadier Division* which had been holding the Casazza crossroads west of Messina. The last senior officer to leave Messina was *Generale di Brigata* Ettore Monacci, who set demolition charges to damage the port facilities before he departed[8].

At 0635 hours on 17 August Captain Paul, the commanding officer of *Engineer Battalion 771*, reported 'LEHRGANG completed'. Among the last German troops to leave were a party from *29th Panzer Grenadier Division's* engineers, who cracked a bottle of wine which they had been towing in the sea to cool, as they approached the mainland[9].

Half an hour after Paul's report a civilian deputation from Messina visited Truscott on the ridge overlooking the port, followed an hour later by Colonel Tomasello who offered a formal military surrender. Truscott, under orders from Keyes to wait until Patton arrived, declined to accept the surrender himself but sent Brigadier General Eagles, his assistant divisional commander, into the city to arrange the surrender ceremony and to ensure that the Americans – rather than the British – were seen to be the captors of Messina.

At 0815 hours Lieutenant Colonel 'Mad Jack' Churchill, Commanding Officer of No 2 Commando, bypassed the destroyed bridge at Tremestieri in a jeep and drove into Messina. He arrived too late to claim the race, for the Americans were already there. Patton had arrived at 1000 hours and drove straight into the city to accept its surrender. British tanks arrived shortly after the ceremony had been completed. The senior British officer approached Patton, shook his hand and said, 'It was a jolly good race. I congratulate you.'[10]

The success of the Axis evacuation was considerable. Nearly 40,000 Germans were carried across the Straits, of which almost 4,500 were wounded. In addition, 9,600 vehicles of all types, forty-seven *panzers* and ninety-four guns, 1,000 tons of ammunition and 970 of fuel, and 15,700 tons of equipment were brought away for future use against the Allies. The Italians evacuated between 70,000 and 75,000 troops, some 500 vehicles, seventy-five to a hundred guns – and twelve mules.

Although they were aware of the Axis' evacuation plans the Allied commanders did little to prevent them being carried out. Tedder tasked the air forces to target the crossing points in the Straits, but they were already heavily involved in attacking airfields and other sites on mainland Italy in preparation for future operations there. RAF Wellingtons bombed the beaches north of Messina every night between 5-9 August, and USAAF B-17s struck Messina itself in three daylight missions, but the opinion expressed by the air commanders was that bombing alone would not effectively halt the evacuation. The flak concentrations along both sides of the Straits were sufficient to make the Allies give night operations priority, but the enemy response was to switch the emphasis of the evacuation to daylight hours when the bombers were less active. A sea blockade was needed.

From the naval perspective, the narrowness of the Straits and the heavy concentration of coastal batteries made this possibility unattractive, if not impossible. Cunningham felt that the best solution was for the land forces to cut off the enemy forces from their embarkation points before they could leave Sicily. But on the date that Hube was given permission to implement *LEHRGANG* Montgomery's men were fifty-two miles from Messina, Patton's seventy-five. Between them and their objective lay the rugged terrain described earlier. The possibility of arriving in Messina before the enemy were ready to leave was out of the question.

Although British Motor Torpedo Boats based in Augusta did their best to interfere with the evacuation, the searchlights and coastal batteries in the Straits drove them away. On the night of 11 August three MTBs chased six small enemy craft into Messina and knocked out one Italian motor raft, the only occasion when the enemy suffered a loss at the hands of the Allied fleet. During the night of 15 August MTB *665* was hit by coastal gunfire and sunk with all hands, and another two boats were damaged and forced to withdraw the following night. Little else was done by naval forces, for although they were ordered up the Straits as far as possible they failed to go far enough to achieve anything. On the northern coast of Sicily Task Force 88 appears not to have been informed of the evacuation, and American PT Boats were ordered not to go south of Cape Rasocolmo, which lies well away from the escape routes[11].

The entire Allied effort directed towards halting *LEHRGANG* therefore came down to what the air forces could do. The Wellingtons which operated by night were bombing the wrong beaches in Sicily, and the wrong ports on the mainland, during the period 8-13 August. Daytime sorties ran into a flak barrage which pilots considered to be even worse than that on the Ruhr. High level bombing was ineffectual against the nimble small craft, and dive-bombing was almost a suicidal venture in the teeth of the anti-aircraft fire. Although Allied aircrews claimed the destruction of twenty-three boats and hits on a further forty-three, Axis figures gave the details as six German and one Italian boats sunk or damaged beyond repair, and seven or eight others damaged[12]. This was not going to make a major impact on the evacuation.

The success of the Axis evacuation was not long in being turned into propaganda. As early as 14 August Hube had signalled Kesselring with the suggestion that the Sicilian battles be described as a great success. This message would, he felt, raise morale and confidence in Germany and would create pride in the formations that had fought in Sicily. He went on to draw a parallel with the 'miracle' of Dunkirk which had been presented to the British public as a success; should the evacuation of Sicily go as planned, then the campaign should be seen as a full success. After the initial fiasco in the opening days of the campaign, the fighting, the preparation and the evacuation, which brought back all serviceable material and men (including the wounded), went according to plan. Despite having a tremendous superiority in men and materiel, the Allies needed six weeks to capture the island, and had high losses, estimated at being one-third (sic) of their fighting strength.

Hube went on to recommend that the three German divisions and the elements of *1st Parachute Division* that had participated in the fighting be mentioned by name. He would object to any implied praise for the *Luftwaffe*, however, for the ground forces had been compelled to operate almost entirely without their support – and praise for the Italians was only justified in the case of the artillery[13].

The attitude of the Germans towards their ally was not confined to Hube's signal to Kesselring. The report on the campaign submitted by the *Hermann Göring Panzer Division* stated that 'Ninety per cent of the Italian Army are cowards and do not want to fight.[14]'

1 Whitlock.
2 Citation, Congressional Medal of Honor.
3 D'Este – Bitter Victory.
4 3 (US) Division History.
5 Morison.
6 Whitlock.
7 Saunders – Green Beret.
8 Blumenson.
9 Malony.
10 Blumenson.
11 Morison.
12 Ibid.
13 Canadian Headquarters Historical Section Report No 14.
14 Ibid

POSTSCRIPT

The campaign for Sicily was over. It had started as a compromise between the British, who saw it as a natural progression of the war, and the Americans who were only persuaded by the argument that the western Allies could not sit idly by for more than a year until sufficient forces were assembled for a cross-Channel invasion. The lack of whole-hearted American commitment to the operation and to the wider implications of a Mediterranean strategy appeared to affect the way in which the campaign was managed – or mismanaged, for it cannot be said to have gone as well as it might have done had the Allies been fully in accord.

That the Allies had not managed the campaign well boded ill for the future. Having conquered Sicily, the question was what to do next, and the inter-Allied difference of opinion about the Mediterranean had not gone away. There was still a strong body of opinion in Washington that said that further operations in that theatre were wasted, and as time progressed and OVERLORD came closer, resources were increasingly diverted to Britain. This limited the options for those who continued to plan and fight in the Mediterranean. One example of this is the steadily diminishing possibility of using the 'end run' tactics to outflank the German defence lines running across Italy, as Admiral King insisted that landing craft should be removed to the United Kingdom.

Churchill, as we have seen, was for invading and knocking Italy out of the war. Sicily, he observed, could be 'a sofa or a springboard', and he was certain in his own mind which option it should be. With the cross-Channel landing scheduled for May 1944, there was time to be filled constructively. Italy should be used to support, not replace, OVERLORD. Churchill argued his case persuasively during the TRIDENT Conference and managed to obtain agreement that Eisenhower would be instructed to plan for Mediterranean operations after HUSKY. His options would be limited, however, for his plans could only make use of the forces available to him once four American and three British divisions, and numbers of landing craft, had been redeployed to the United Kingdom. When criticizing Eisenhower's 'hands-off' style of generalship during the Sicilian campaign, it is perhaps wise to bear in mind that he was simultaneously tasked with finalizing plans for future operations and secretly negotiating with the Italian government.

The optimistic view of the way the Sicilian campaign was going, at least during its first week, led the Combined Chiefs of Staff to order Eisenhower to consider striking Italy near Naples rather than going for the toe of Italy. Salerno – Operation AVALANCHE – was on the agenda. It was approved on 26 July. On the same day the Eighth Army was tasked with drawing up plans to cross the Straits of Messina on 30-31 August, with the intention of drawing enemy forces away from Salerno.

Montgomery could have made a crossing within a week or so after Messina had fallen – indeed, Eisenhower urged him to do so. But Monty acted with his customary caution, ensuring that he had assembled massed artillery to support the operation. His plan for the crossing was not completed until 23 August, which meant that the event had to be postponed. It finally took place on 3 September, giving Kesselring much needed time for his preparations to fight the Italian campaign. When the crossing took place it was lightly opposed, the defenders withdrawing quickly. The artillery barrage which Montgomery had carefully laid on was not required.

On 5 September the Fifth (US) Army landed at Salerno, the day after the Italian surrender was announced. It had been signed at Cassibile, near Syracuse, on 3 September. On the same day as AVALANCHE the British 1st Airborne Division landed by sea in Taranto harbour. The land war had come to Italy, but its planning and execution were to carry the same problems as the Sicilian campaign, with inter-Ally suspicions being maintained by some of the commanders in this fresh stage of the war, such as General Mark Clark, who was to allow retreating German forces to escape while he went for the prestige of capturing Rome before the British – a wholly spurious fear, for Alexander had already made it clear that the city was a Fifth Army objective.

It is impossible to ignore the performances of the principal senior officers involved in HUSKY. From the top down, it is easy to find fault with the decisions and leadership of practically all of those involved in its planning and execution. Some of this criticism stems from the lack of confidence that American and British policy-makers and top-ranking officers had in their opposite numbers. The background to HUSKY illustrates the difficulties that the Joint Chiefs of Staff had in working together, but the problems did not end there. Even within national boundaries, the individual service heads often found it difficult to work together – the Americans, British and even the Germans were at one in finding fault with their respective air forces in this regard. And, of course, the criticism of partners was not confined to the Allied camp, for the Germans and Italians were also dismissive of each other.

What did Sicily achieve? It certainly kept the Axis fighting the Western Allies while the latter continued making preparations for Normandy, and the campaign obliged the Germans to keep forces committed to the Mediterranean, which were therefore unable to be redeployed to the Eastern Front. At that level, at least, it was a success and may be considered to have had a part in ensuring eventual victory for the Allies.

The campaign itself was not a shining achievement for the Allies. It highlighted differences between the Americans and British in strategic thinking, and it can be argued that in doing so it placed a degree of strain on the alliance. Some of these tensions were undoubtedly brought about by the rawness of the American forces in North Africa which engendered suspicions about their capabilities amongst some British commanders, although they themselves cannot be seen as being blameless because they failed to recognize, at least for much of the time considered by this volume, that the Americans learned quickly and were much more professional by the date HUSKY was implemented. The Sicilian campaign might well have been shorter and may have inflicted greater losses on the enemy had these differences been resolved earlier. Had Patton's Seventh Army been given a more positive role and allowed to drive straight for Sicily's north coast instead of being made to surrender Highway 124 to Montgomery, the Axis forces in the west of the island could have been isolated and dealt with at leisure, Messina could have been captured at an earlier date, and more enemy troops cut off from Italy.

The failure to cut the Straits of Messina was criticized both by Allied commentators and by the Germans. Kesselring observed that because the Allies did not attempt a large-scale encirclement of Sicily, nor try to push rapidly up the coastline of Calabria, his forces were given ample time to organize their defences. A landing on the toe of mainland Italy would have cut the escape route as effectively as taking Messina, but the Allies did not exhibit boldness. While this may in part be because of the almost half-hearted way HUSKY came about, it nevertheless represents a lost opportunity, and leads one back to the thought that the operation was seen as being a time-filler, at least by the Americans.

But this criticism of the reluctance to seize the Straits is to ignore the importance that was given to air power at the time. It is unlikely that Tedder and Cunningham would have given their blessing to a plan that would have stretched Allied aircraft to their operational limits. Von Senger recognized that the Allied objectives in Sicily were dictated by the range of fighter cover, which would also be a factor at Salerno[1].

Admiral Morison was not so sure. He argued that the Messina bottleneck should have been the target from the beginning. Seventh (US) Army landing on the north coast near Milazzo and an Eighth Army landing on both sides of the Straits, which were considerably less well protected at the date of the landing, 10 July, as they were a month later, would have surprised the enemy. Their escape route would have been severed, and they could have been driven into western Sicily and destroyed at leisure. However, as a sailor, he also saw the dangers of such an operation, and drew comparisons between the Straits of Messina and the Dardenelles in 1915, when the British and French fleets suffered serious losses when trying to force a passage through a narrow waterway well defended by coastal batteries. As is generally the case, the apparently straightforward solution was fraught with hazards, and one has to respect the decisions of those who were in command at the time, even if one does not agree with them. Morison was not the only naval officer who drew comparisons with the Dardenelles, and its lessons not to encourage adventurous schemes.

The lack of boldness was seen at operational levels as well. The *Hermann Göring Division's* report after the evacuation commented that 'neither Allied command nor manner of fighting were distinguished by bold decisions or special bravery; the method of fighting was one of pronounced caution with massed employment of superior material.[2'] This was certainly true of Montgomery's plans to cross the Straits.

Many of the Allied formations and generals that had participated in the campaign would leave for the United Kingdom and for the liberation of North West Europe. From the Eighth Army, 50th and 51st (Highland) Divisions took part in the Normandy landings, as did 1st (US) Division and 82nd (US) Airborne. The British 1st Airborne Division had to wait until September 1944, for the Arnhem landings, where 1 Parachute Brigade was again to fight for a bridge. The Divisional commander was Major General Roy Urquart, who had commanded 231 (Malta) Brigade in Sicily. Other formations continued in the Italian campaign, such as 3rd (US) Infantry Division, the British 5th and 78th Infantry Divisions and 1st Canadian Infantry Division, or took part in the landings in Southern France, such as 9th (US) Division.

During the months after Sicily Generals Eisenhower, Montgomery and Bradley departed for England and commands there. Patton, too, left the Mediterranean, but he was not destined for an early appointment. After news broke publicly of what was to become known as the 'slapping incidents', Patton's career was very much in question. On 3 August Patton had visited wounded soldiers in hospital, when he came across one whose reason for not being with his unit was that he was 'nervous', or in more modern terminology, was suffering from post-traumatic stress. Emotional after talking to badly wounded soldiers, Patton became incensed by what he saw as cowardice. He slapped the man across the face with his glove and then booted him out of the hospital tent. A week later the incident was repeated at a second hospital, with Patton again losing his temper, abusing a patient with the same problem, and threatening him with a pistol before hitting him. A report on the second incident written by the II (US) Corps Surgeon was restrained by Bradley, but it nevertheless found its way to Eisenhower through Medical Corps channels. The news was not long in breaking anyway, and soon came to the attention of four war correspondents, who also brought it to Eisenhower's attention. Eisenhower had to take action, but did not feel that the Americans could afford to lose an officer of Patton's calibre. He wrote the general a strongly-worded letter of censure, but this was not enough for the correspondents, who wanted Patton sacked in return for not publishing the story. It was only a personal appeal from Eisenhower that made the newsmen back down. Patton embarked on a series of fence-building visits and speeches, apologizing for his behaviour, a performance which received varying responses from the units he met, ranging from coolness to applause and support. It was to no avail, however, for eventually the news got to an American radio broadcaster who wasted no time in putting an exaggerated version on air. The ensuing furore was nearly enough to ensure that Patton never commanded anyone or anything again, but there were sufficient people in high places who recognized his worth to avoid this[3]. Patton would go to England, and he would take part in the battles for the liberation of Europe, but it would not be as commander of all American land forces, an appointment which might well have been his but for these events. Bradley was to get this job, and Patton would have to wait to command an army again. In August 1944 he took the US Third Army to France[4].

Patton's disgrace puzzled the Germans, for his actions with the shell-shocked patients did not seem to them to be out of line; indeed, by the standards of the German Army at the time, they were not. The orders issued by the *Hermann Göring Division* for the evacuation, for example, warned that anyone not cooperating would be shot[5]. The Germans regarded Patton as the most outstanding of the Allied generals and thought that the story was a cover for his employment in some greater plan. The Allies turned this to good purpose by having Patton visit Corsica, in an attempt to make the enemy believe that he was to lead an invasion of Northern Italy. He also 'commanded' the First United States Army Group (FUSAG), a fictitious formation that was supposedly preparing to invade France by way of Calais, again a deception designed to throw the enemy off identifying the real objective of Normandy. In all, Patton was to wait ten months before getting a real command again. It is a pity that, for many people, the slapping incident is the thing that Patton is best remembered for.

The Germans, of course, also went on to continue their participation in the war. Kesselring was critically injured in a vehicle accident in October 1943, but recovered by the following January and resumed his post of Commander in Chief South, when forces under his command fought the Allies along the Gustav Line and at Anzio. In March 1945 he replaced von Rundstedt as C-in-C West. Hube passed command of *XIV Panzer Corps* to von Senger und Etterlin in October 1943, and returned to the Eastern Front to command *First Panzer Army*. He was to die in a flying accident in April 1945.

With his appointment to *XIV Panzer Corps*, von Senger considered himself to have been finally given a proper job. Responsible for the Cassino sector of the Gustav Line, he commanded three of the German divisions which had fought in Sicily: *15th* and *29th Panzer Grenadiers* and *1st Parachute Division*; each of these formations kept the same commanders from Sicily. The fourth division under von Senger's command, *90th Panzer Grenadier*, was commanded by Baade, who had controlled the evacuation of Sicily. He was to die on the last day of the war. The *Hermann Göring Division* was also to take its place in the Italian campaign, being involved in the battles for Salerno and Anzio. The experiences of all of these formations during the Sicilian campaign, particularly in defence and delaying tactics, were to be employed in Italy.

At a practical level, lessons were learnt in Sicily that were implemented elsewhere, particularly in amphibious operations. Both Allied and Axis headquarters studied the campaign, searching for ways in which they might improve their performances in the future. Numerous recommendations were made, from which a few examples will suffice to make the point that Sicily provided an education for some individuals and organizations. The disastrous attempts to drop airborne forces near to shipping led to measures being taken to ensure that mistakes were not made in aircraft recognition: for OVERLORD, over 700 volunteers from the Royal Observer Corps served on Allied ships to prevent nervous anti-aircraft gunners from firing on friendly aircraft. Other findings led to more assertive individuals being appointed to Beachmaster posts, for some of those who had held these positions during HUSKY had not been able to stand up to more senior officers who appeared on the landing beaches demanding equipment be given to them that was not rightfully theirs.

The Germans, too, learnt from Sicily. Their post-operation reports made recommendations on coastal defence and observations on Allied tactics and competence: *15th Panzer Grenadier Division's* report considered the 'English and Canadians harder in the attack than the Americans'[6]. These observations were to be incorporated in German doctrine for the fighting that was to come in Italy and in North West Europe; it was not only the Allies that benefitted from the Sicilian experience.

Today Sicily still bears the scars of 1943. The barrack building at the *Lamba Doria Battery* still has fascist slogans painted on the walls; there are still numbers of the distinctive Italian pillboxes – often with domed roofs – dotted around the island, for example at the three bridges highlighted in this story, at Ponte Grande, Ponte Malati and Ponte Primosole; and there are buildings still scarred by shrapnel in Syracuse, Centuripe, and other places. Several Allied memorials have been erected; at the time of writing two of them, to the Durham Brigade at Primosole and to the Devonshire Regiment at Regalbuto, were the subject of proposals to relocate them to ease access or to allow for development of the land on which they stand. In Catania a very well designed and imaginative museum is dedicated to telling the story of the campaign.

And there are the cemeteries, one German, three Commonwealth. The American dead were later repatriated or taken to Nettuno, in Italy; the Italians lie in their town cemeteries or at Cristo Re, near Messina. The Allied casualties for the campaign were 5,532 killed, 2,869 missing and 14,410 wounded[7]. Statistics for the German and Italian armed forces are less precise, but the Germans are believed to have suffered some 4,325 killed, and the Italians 4,700. Figures for Italian civilian fatalities differ, but are thought to be less than originally believed, about 8,000.

HUSKY and the Sicilian campaign were but a page in the long and sometimes bloody history of Sicily.

1 Von Senger.
2 Canadian Army Headquarters Historical Section Report No 14.
3 D'Este – Bitter Victory.
4 D'Este – Patton.
5 Hermann Göering Division Order No. 31/43, 2 Aug 43.
6 Canadian Army Headquarters Historical Section Report No 14.

BIBLIOGRAPHY

The following titles are the principal sources for the information contained
in this book. The chronology of principal events does not differ, of course,
although different works tend to give differing prominence to aspects of
the campaign. For example, two of the most comprehensive studies –
Carlo d'Este's *'Bitter Victory'* and, Malony et al's *'The Mediterranean and the
Middle East* Vol V' (the British Official History), tend to be more
informative about American and British operations respectively.
Formation and regimental histories focus more closely on the activities of
their subjects than on grand strategy, and so on. I have attempted to gain
a balance by giving a taste of the whole spectrum, and can only suggest
that if more information is required on a particular aspect of the campaign
then the reader explores some of the volumes listed below. If I have
succeeded in sparking an interest that is worth following up, so much the
better!

I have chosen to give sources and references in chapter endnotes only
where it has appeared to me that there is some point of detail which
requires authentication, rather than to slavishly list every work which I
have read on the Sicilian campaign.

ALANBROOKE, Field Marshal Lord
    War Diaries 1939-1945, edited by Danchev, A & Todman, D.
    Phoenix 2002
BARNES, BS
    The Sign of the Double 'T' (The 50th Northumbrian Division – July
    1943 to December 1944). Sentinel Press 1999
BLUMENSON, Martin
    Sicily: Whose victory? Ballantine, 1969
CANADIAN ARMY HEADQUARTERS HISTORICAL SECTION
    REPORT NO 14 *The Sicilian Campaign (July – August 1943)*
    Information from German Sources 1986
CANADIAN OPERATIONS IN ITALY
    REPORTS 103, 126, 127, 129, 132, 135, 136
CENTRE FOR MILITARY HISTORY
    Tunisia. CMH 2003
COLE, David
    Rough road to Rome, a foot-soldier in Sicily and Italy 1943-44.
    William Kimber & Co 1983
COMBINED OPERATIONS HEADQUARTERS
    BULLETIN NO Y/1 *Notes on the Planning and Assault Phases
    of the Sicilian Campaign October* 1943

D'ESTE, Carlo
  Patton – A Genius for War. Harper Collins 1995
DELAFORCE, Patrick
  Monty's Highlanders - 51st Highland Division in World War Two.
  Tom Donovan, Brighton 1998
D'ESTE, Carlo
  Bitter victory: The battle for Sicily. Dutton, 1988
DILLON, Martin & BRADFORD, Roy
  Rogue warrior of the SAS: The Blair Mayne Legend. Mainstream
  Publishing 2003
DOCHERTY, Richard
  Clear the way! A history of the 38th (Irish) Brigade 1941-47. Irish
  Academic Press Ltd 1993
DURNFORD-SLATER, Brigadier John
  Commando. William Kimber 1953
FORD, Ken
  *Battle-axe Division: from Africa to Italy with the 78th Division
  1942-45.* Sutton Publishing 2003
HENRIQUES, Colonel RDQ
  Planning. War Office 1954
HERMANN GÖERING DIVISION
  Order No. 31/43, 2 Aug 43 Enclosure - Directive for Future
  Moves and Battle Actions in Sicily
HONNIBALL, FE
  *A History of 44th Royal Tank Regiment in the War of 1939-45. Part
  II Sicily and Italy 1943-1944.* Ditchling Press, Sussex 1965
HOWARD, Michael
  The Mediterranean Strategy in the Second World War.
  Greenhill Books 1993
KESSELRING, Field Marshal Albert
  Memoirs of Field Marshal Kesselring. Greenhill 2007
KING, MJ
  Porto Empedocle. Leavenworth Papers No 11. 1985
KIRKMAN, Maj Gen S C
  The Operations of 50th (Northumbrian) Division in Sicily
KIRKPATRICK, CE
  Bradley, Centre for Military History 1992
LEIGHTON, RM
  *OVERLORD versus the Mediterranean at the Cairo-Tehran
  Conferences, in Command Decisions,* Centre for Military History
  1960
LEONARDI, Lt Col Dante Ugo:
  *3rd Battalion, 34th Regiment Livorno Infantry Division in the Gela
  Beachhead counterattack: Sicily July 11-12 1943*

LEWIS, PJ & ENGLISH, IR
   Into Battle with the Durhams – 8 DLI in World War II. London
   Stamp Exchange Ltd 1990
MAHNKE, Jochen
   Assault on Sicily 1943. South African Military History Society
   Journal Vol 7 No 2
MALONY, Brig CJC, et al
   The Mediterranean and the Middle East Vol V   HMSO 1973
MATLOFF, M
   Strategic Planning for Coalition Warfare 1943-1944. Centre for
   Military History, US Army 1990
MAVROGORDATO, Ralph S
   Hitler's decision on the defence of Italy, in *Command Decisions,*
   Centre for Military History 1960
McGREGOR, J
   *The Spirit of Angus - The War History of the County's Battalion of
   The Black Watch.* Phillimore 1988
MONTAGU, Ewen
   The Man Who Never Was. J.B. Lippincott Company 1954
MONTGOMERY, Field Marshal Bernard Law:
   El Alamein to the River Sangro Hutchinson 1952
MONTGOMERY, Field Marshal Bernard Law:
   Memoirs of Field Marshal the Viscount Montgomery of Alamein
   Leo Cooper Ltd 2005
MORISON, Vice Admiral SE
   History of United States Naval Operations in World War II, Vol IX.
Oxford University Press 1954
MOSES, H
   *The Faithful Sixth - A History of the Sixth Battalion, The Durham
   Light Infantry.* County Durham Books 1995
MOSES, H
   *The Gateshead Gurkhas - A History Of The 9th Battalion The
   Durham Light Infantry 1859-1967.* County Durham Books 2001
MURCHIE, Lt Gen JC (foreword)
   *From Pachino to Ortona – The Canadian Campaign in Sicily and
   Italy, 1943.* Govt of Canada 1946
NEILLANDS, Robin
   Eighth Army: from the Western Desert to the Alps, 1939-1945. John
   Murray 2004
OFFICE OF THE CHIEF OF MILITARY HISTORY, US ARMY
   World War II: The Defensive Phase Ch 20, Army Historical Series
PACK, SWC
   Operation Husky, the allied invasion of Sicily. Hippocrene, 1977

PATTON, George S
   War as I knew it. Houghton Mifflin 1995
RHODES-WOOD, E. H.
   A War History of the Royal Pioneer Corps 1939-1945. Gale &
Polden Ltd, 1960
ROYAL MARINE BUSINESS No 1, BR 1006
   7 RM in the Sicilian Campaign. January 1944
SAUNDERS, H St G
   The Green Beret. London Michael Joseph 1949
SAUNDERS, H St G
   The Red Beret. London White Lion 1972
STOLER, MA
   George C Marshall: Soldier-Statesman of the American Century.
   Simon & Schuster Macmillan 1989
TAGGERT, Donald G
   History of the Third Infantry Division in World War II. Battery
   Press Nashville 1987

US ARMY   Joss Operation Plans 1-3
US ARMY CENTRE FOR MILITARY HISTORY Pub 72-12 Tunisia
US ARMY   2nd Armored Division Report
US ARMY   3rd Infantry Division Report
US ARMY   45th Infantry Division Reports 1&2
US ARMY   82nd Airborne Division Report
US ARMY   9th Infantry Division Reports 3&4
US ARMY   A History of the Second United States Armored
                 Division 1940 to 1946. Albert Love Enterprises, Atlanta
                 1946
US NAVY   Action Report – Western Naval Task Force,
                 Sicilian Campaign Operation 'HUSKY'

VON SENGER UND ETTERLIN, FM
   Neither Fear nor Hope, Greenhill 1989
WHITLOCK, F
   *The Rock of Anzio: from Sicily to Dachau, a history of the US 45th
   Infantry Division.* Westview Press 1998

INDEX